Hamlet's Enemy

Hamlet's Enemy

MADNESS AND MYTH IN *Hamlet*

<><><><><><><><><><><><><><><><><><><><><><><><><><><><><><>

THEODORE LIDZ

———————

Basic Books, Inc., Publishers

NEW YORK

Library of Congress Cataloging in Publication Data

Lidz, Theodore.
   Hamlet's enemy.

   Bibliography: p.
   Includes index.
     1.   Shakespeare, William, 1564–1616.   Hamlet.
2.   Mental illness in literature.   3.   Shakespeare,
William, 1564–1616.   Hamlet—Sources.   4.   Psychoanalysis
and literature.   I.   Title.   [DNLM: 1.   Psychoanalytic
interpretation.   2.   Medicine in literature.   WM49 L715h]
PR2807.L5 1975   822.3′3   74-25906
ISBN 0–465–02817–9

To the memory
of those who shaped my early years:
my parents, Israel and Esther Lidz,
my sister, Helen Herrnstadt,
and my brother, Maury.

What I have done,
That might your nature, honour, and exception
Roughly awake, I here proclaim was madness.
Was't Hamlet wrong'd Laertes? Never Hamlet;
If Hamlet from himself be ta'en away,
And, when he's not himself, does wrong Laertes,
Then Hamlet does it not; Hamlet denies it.
Who does it then? His madness, if't be so,
Hamlet is of the faction that is wrong'd;
His madness is poor Hamlet's enemy.

(V, ii, 217–226)

CONTENTS

Contents

PART TWO
Saga and Myth in *Hamlet*

Contents

PART THREE

Hamlet's Implications for Psychoanalytic Psychology

Contents

ACKNOWLEDGMENTS

I WISH to thank my friend and colleague Dr. Albert Rothenberg for his careful readings of the first and the final versions of this book and for his helpful suggestions; Professor John Stade of Columbia University for his helpful criticisms of the first version; and my friends Professor Marie Borroff and Professor L. Bartlett Giamatti of the English Department of Yale University for their suggestions after reading the final version. I deeply appreciate the help of Harriette Borsuch, who typed many revisions, checked all quotations and references, and prepared the manuscript for publication.

My studies of *Hamlet*, a hobby for over twenty-five years, have been supported in part by a Career Investigator grant from the National Institute of Mental Health.

All quotations from *Hamlet* are from *A New Variorium Edition of Shakespeare*, edited by Horace Howard Furness.

Hamlet's Enemy

INTRODUCTION

*H*AMLET again! I return to *Hamlet* as one participates in
a Mystery—to regain vitality after descending into its depths, to
skirt madness with its hero, to find release from anguish with
its heroine in her hebephrenia, to slough disillusion with the
treacherous world onto a scapegoat who carries the burden to
his destruction. I also return to sun in lines that light the world
in beauty, to absorb nurture from genius beyond envy, and to
delight in discovery with each rereading. I return to *Hamlet*
because, like the poet and the playwright, as a psychiatrist I
recognize a master in Shakespeare, a master from whom Freud
gained insights and assurance. I listen in awe because here, so
much that psychoanalysts have laboriously learned from patients flows in measured profusion—as if the Muses had whis-
pered in the poet's ear all that Apollo's Pythoness had learned
from her countless suppliants. I also return to *Hamlet* because
of an apprehension that within its elusive ambiguities lies a key
that could lead to the secret wellsprings of the human dilemma.

It is an illusion that another reading, another analysis will
lead to a clear understanding of *Hamlet* and Hamlet. There is no
end to the explication of the play. Jan Kott aptly wrote, "Hamlet
is like a sponge. If he is not played in stylized or antiquated
manner, he immediately soaks up the entire contemporary scene
into himself. It is the most unique of all plays that have ever
been written, just because of its porosity."[1] The porosity, or

3

ambiguity, that permits *Hamlet*'s constant renewal is, as I shall examine, carefully crafted by Shakespeare. But behind the play's adaptability to the changing scene and to the changing minds and moods of men, lies a more profound reason for its agelessness. It intertwines with the life of Everyman—and of Everywoman, too. *Hamlet* weighs the importance of cardinal human relationships to a person's integrity and integration, and it conveys the frailty of one's emotional equilibrium and the emptiness of one's life, no matter when and where he lives, whenever trust in these relationships is destroyed.

Finally, I return to write about *Hamlet* again because I believe that through examining the theme of madness in the play, I have gained some new insights that not only clarify the structure and action of the play but also deepen my understanding of human nature.

In Part One of this book, I shall offer a reading of *Hamlet* that focuses on the theme of madness. I believe that through pursuing the reasons why Hamlet borders on madness throughout the play and why Ophelia loses her sanity, we can clarify those time-honored issues of Hamlet's procrastination and the nature of his antic disposition, as well as the neglected question of why Hamlet, who does nothing heroic, is a hero—the most renowned hero of the Western theater. Concomitantly, we can achieve new insights into the power of the play, into the play's structure and balance, and even into the workings of Shakespeare's creative processes.

In Part Two, I shall move beyond the text of *Hamlet* to examine the sources of the play and its themes. Although *Hamlet* exists only in the lines Shakespeare wrote that construct the plot, portray character, create beauty, and set off resonances within the audience, it is difficult to convey the significance of what lies within its five acts without moving beyond the play itself, for it embodies a distillation of sagas and myths that have been central to the emergence of Western man, to the taming of his passions, and to his efforts to control nature, including his own human nature. I shall first examine some of the sources available to Shakespeare when he created *Hamlet*. Through scrutiny of these source materials, and by noting what he em-

ployed, what he omitted, what he altered, and what he com-
pacted and unified, we can gain some fascinating glimpses of
that elusive essence, the creative processes of a genius. Specifically, I shall consider Shakespeare's use in writing *Hamlet* of
plays and sagas about five mad heroes. Four of them are related
figures. Amleth, Lucius Junius Brutus, Nero, and Orestes. The
fifth, Kyd's Hieronymo, fluctuates between true and feigned
madness and uses a play-within-a-play to gain his vengeance.
After studying the immediate sources of *Hamlet*, I shall turn to
the Norse legends and myths and then move back in time, and
across Europe to the myths of Greece and Asia Minor to examine the confluence of the mythic streams that flow into *Hamlet*.
These sources arise in the heartland of the human spirit, drain
its timeless unconscious, portray what is eternally recurrent in
human affairs, and hark back beyond myth to rituals that man
once considered essential to his survival. Because its base is set
in the mythic, *Hamlet* conveys the wisdom about the essentials
in human behavior that these myths carry.

The seventh volume of Bullough's *Narrative and Dramatic
Sources of Shakespeare*, which includes sources for *Hamlet*, appeared after my manuscript was completed. I have included
pertinent material from his work in several footnotes. Some
reader may be interested in the differences between his citation
and use of sources and my study of sources in Part Two.

In Part Three, I shall consider some of the implications of
Hamlet, and of the myths that it encompasses, to psychoanalytic
psychiatry—which only means to our grasp of human behavior
and what leads to those inner conflicts that distort a person's
perceptions and understanding of the world and of those who
people it, even to the point of insanity. In so doing, I shall
contemplate how the study of phenomena that recur cyclically
—from year to year, life to life, culture to culture—can provide
us with critical guidance in this world of contingency.

In the remainder of this Introduction, I shall discuss how a
psychoanalyst's training and experience can contribute to the
understanding and appreciation of *Hamlet*, its subtleties of language as well as its characters. I shall also consider various
psychiatric and literary studies of the play, reevaluate some

aspects of psychoanalytic psychology that have pertinence to the study of *Hamlet*, and comment on other matters as a prelude to the reading of the play that follows.

Myth, Drama, and Psychoanalysis

The psychoanalyst's interest in the theater is natural enough. The myth-maker, playwright, and psychoanalyst "are of imagination all compact." Myths grew out of the rituals by which man, in his helplessness, sought to control or keep nature in its course. Everywhere people sought to make natural events understandable and controllable by anthropomorphizing nature; and the vicissitudes of anthropomorphized nature could be understood only in terms of what people knew of themselves and of their motivations to commit passionate and unpredictable acts. Myths, in seeking to explain or understand natural phenomena, often dealt with the conflicts that primal passions cause in man, and with the dread consequences that can follow when people give way to them; though often as tales of demigod heroes who dared what cannot be permitted humans, or of human beings who became godlike through their suffering.

The drama is a direct derivative of the ritual and its accompanying myth.[2] The playwright carries on, to varying degrees, the process of dramatizing tales of the impact of unrestrained impulsions upon human lives and upon society and the turmoil brought about by breaches in the bonds of kinship that form the warp and woof of society and lay the foundations for dependable relationships everywhere. In so doing, the classic dramatist exerts a superego influence, so to speak; he holds up to the audience the penalties for infractions of basic taboos and helps the spectator accept a prosaic, even troubled life in preference to the fate of the tragic heroes, who are too much in the eyes of the gods.

The psychoanalytic psychiatrist also works with the conflicts between passionate drives and the controls required by social living, and he studies basic configurations of human relationships to unravel what has gone awry in them and undermined a person's emotional balance. In a sense, he, too, is interested in a drama—usually picking up the play someplace after the first act—and seeks to enable his patient to avert a frustrating, if not a tragic, outcome and, instead, find a more gratifying and harmonious course for his life. Through his absorption with the dynamics of mental disorders, the psychoanalyst attains an ability to grasp the essentials in myths and the salient transactions in the drama. The psychoanalyst, then, is particularly well prepared to appreciate Shakespeare's grasp of human nature, even if his apprehension of meter, metaphor, imagery, style, and craft may be untutored.

The Psychiatrist's Attraction to *Hamlet*

Hamlet, in particular, attracts the psychiatrist because it is a play that directly challenges his professional acumen. He can join the characters in the play in seeking the cause of Hamlet's antic behavior. Many of Shakespeare's plays include characters who are mad or feign madness, but the entire action and structure of *Hamlet* revolve around the hero's distraction and the heroine's lunacy. In writing a play that considers the insidious spread of corruption by primal sin, the devastation wrought by talion vengeance, the relativity of the heroic, the worth of life and the attractiveness of suicide, as well as other basic existential issues, Shakespeare recognized their pertinence to the vulnerability of man's reason. In weighing the value of existence and the importance of morality, Shakespeare plunged into the depths of the unconscious, where the irrational holds sway; to do so, he chose to reshape a saga of a hero who feigned imbecility, a tale that had its roots in myths of mad heroes enmeshed in matricidal and incestuous impulsions.

Psychiatrists have been offering their opinions about *Hamlet* for almost two hundred years, about as long as there have been specialists in mental disorders to express opinions. They have participated primarily in the arguments about two issues:

whether Hamlet's madness is feigned or real, and why Hamlet procrastinates in gaining vengeance. As the older opinions have been assembled in the second volume of Furness's *New Variorium Edition* and most of the psychoanalytic commentaries have been abstracted in Holland's *Psychoanalysis and Shakespeare*, I shall not review the literature here. Rather, I shall confine myself to a consideration of those views that are relevant to my own analysis of the play and its characters.

Opinions have always varied concerning the state of Hamlet's mental health, but psychiatric concepts have also changed. Few contemporary psychiatrists would consider hereditary taint or brain disease particularly pertinent to Hamlet's condition; many would find Shakespeare's portrayal of the vacillations in Hamlet's mood and self-control more realistic than did their colleagues of past generations. Literary scholars cannot be expected to grasp how psychiatric concepts have changed. For example, in *The Question of Hamlet*, Harry Levin argued that "Hamlet is clearly thought sick rather than brain sick—neurotic rather than psychotic, to state the matter in more clinical terms." He then went on to describe behavior of Hamlet's that most psychiatrists would consider psychotic. Although a psychosis can result from sickness or damage that disturbs the brain, no such causes have been found for the vast majority of psychoses. The precipitate onset of Ophelia's psychosis is clearly to be attributed not to some sudden affection of her brain but to her inability to absorb the circumstances of her father's death. If one considers Hamlet to be mad, it would not be because of a disturbance or an inadequacy of his brain, but rather because mood swings to depression and elation impair his judgment or because he paranoidally breaks with reality in his anguish and disillusionment.

Is Hamlet's madness real or feigned? "Either/or" is a simplification desired by man but shunned by nature. Hamlet can—and I believe does—balance on the border. He can be somewhat psychotic or very much in control of himself, depending on the circumstances, as Hamlet intimates when he tells Rosencrantz and Guildenstern, "I am but mad north-north-west; when the wind is southerly, I know a hawk from a handsaw" (II, ii, 360–

361). Many contemporary psychiatrists would be satisfied with the nonprofessional judgment of Robert Bridges:

> Hamlet himself would never have been aught to us, or we
> To Hamlet, wer't not for the artful balance whereby
> Shakespeare so gingerly put his sanity in doubt
> Without the while confounding his Reason.*

and, perhaps, even more with Coleridge's apposite, "Hamlet's wildness is but *half false*; O that subtle trick to pretend the acting *only* when we are very near *being* what we act."[3]

THE FREUD–JONES INTERPRETATION

A footnote in Freud's *The Interpretation of Dreams* that was elaborated by Ernest Jones into the essay "The Problem of Hamlet and the Oedipus Complex," opened a new phase in the interpretation of *Hamlet* and, indeed, of all literature by considering the unconscious motivations stemming from Hamlet's repressed oedipal fantasies. In brief, the Freud–Jones interpretation holds that Hamlet cannot follow his vow to his father's ghost and slay his uncle because, as a child, he had fantasies of killing his father and marrying his mother and thus identifies with his uncle Claudius, who has but done what Hamlet once wished to do himself. "His moral fate is bound up with his uncle's for good or ill. In reality his uncle incorporates the deepest and most buried part of his own personality, so that he cannot kill him without killing himself," Jones later wrote.[4] The theory that Hamlet identifies with Claudius is sound enough and offers a reason for Hamlet's paralysis of will, but it is not the way the play reads. The proposition implies a priori that Hamlet's specific reaction to his situation is a necessary, rather than a potential, consequence of Hamlet's life situation as depicted in the play. If such motivations are not apparent in the play, to accept the theory we must then postulate that Shakespeare makes Hamlet delay because of the playwright's own

*From Robert Bridges, *The Testament of Beauty: A Poem in Four Books* (Oxford: Clarendon Press, 1930). Reprinted by permission of the Clarendon Press.

9

unconscious or conscious knowledge of such necessary unconscious motivation.

As Freud believed that a boy's sexualized love for his mother and desire to be rid of his father were "instinctual"—that is, built into his psyche as part of his biological makeup—he felt he could take it for granted that Hamlet had wished to kill his father and possess his mother. There are, however, alternate ways in which Hamlet could react to learning that his uncle had seduced his mother and killed his father. As Otto Rank pointed out, Hamlet could have used his obligation to avenge his father as an excuse to get rid of that man in his mother's bed, thereby acting out his oedipal wish to eliminate a father figure.[5]

WERTHAM'S INTERPRETATION

Another major psychoanalytic interpretation of *Hamlet* was propounded by Frederic Wertham who recognized the similarity of a youthful matricide he studied to both Hamlet and Orestes.[6] Much earlier Gilbert Murray in his classic essay "Hamlet and Orestes," had drawn attention to many parallels between Shakespeare's play and the Greek tragedies about Orestes;[7] and Shakespeare's contemporary Thomas Heywood had consciously used the similarity in writing his play *The Iron Age.*

As numerous commentators have observed, neither Hamlet's behavior nor the movement of the play can be grasped without recognizing the intensity of Hamlet's matricidal feelings. For example, Furnivall wrote, "Her [Gertrude's] disgraceful adultery and incest, and treason to his noble father's memory, Hamlet has felt in his inmost soul. Compared to their ingrain dye, Claudius' murder of his father—notwithstanding all his protestations—is only a skin-deep stain."[8] Wertham emphasized that Hamlet was more preoccupied with his mother's adultery than with his father's murder and that her infidelity turned his excessive attachment to his mother into bitter hostility.[9] Wertham went on to posit an "Orestes complex"—that many men develop a hatred toward their mothers that can reach a matricidal intensity because of the frustration they experience when their mothers, as they must, cease to provide them with all-embracing maternal care. I do not wish to evaluate this useful contribution here, but rather to note that although the Freud–Jones and Wertham interpretations lead to very different readings of *Hamlet* (and Jones later in his *Hamlet and Oedipus* modified his interpretations of the play to include Wertham's), both concern the triangular "oedipal" situation between a son and his mother and father. Freud focused upon Hamlet's hostility to his father for preempting his mother, and Wertham stressed Hamlet's disillusion with his mother and his hostility toward her because of her attachment to his stepfather, which he experiences as a betrayal of himself as well as of his father. The difference between the two interpretations is important both for psychoanalysis in general and for the understanding of the play.

Freud's Oedipus Complex and Its Modifications

Freud's recognition of Hamlet's intense attachment to his mother was, apparently, important to his discovery of the Oedipus complex, or, at least, to his conviction of its central position in a person's development. Freud, in essence, postulated a universal situation in the lives of children based upon the virtually omnipresent triangular relationship between parents and child. Stated simply, every child passes through a phase in which he or she wishes to possess the parent of the opposite sex and be rid of the parent of the same sex. The child comes to fear retaliation from the parent of the same sex largely because of the hostility the child projects onto that parent; that is, the child attributes to the parent feelings that are reciprocal to his own. How the conflict is repressed or resolved is critical to the child's development and forms something of a template for all later significant relationships. Psychiatry, as a study of personality maldevelopment and maladaptation, could now focus attention on a universal critical situation and could observe and compare its variations from individual to individual. Rather than simply noting similarities and differences between persons, psychoanalysis could examine how differences in the oedipal situation and its resolution related to various personality characteristics or disturbances. The recognition of other critical developmental tasks that all persons must surmount followed.

Although the discovery of the Oedipus complex marked a decisive turn in man's understanding of himself—and was a crucial step in the emergence of psychoanalytic psychology as a science of human behavior—Freud's assumption that it was inherent in the human makeup that a boy's desire to be rid of his father aroused castration fears which forced him to repress the erotic components of his attachment to his mother placed psychoanalysis in something of a straitjacket. Thus, to take some pertinent examples, he neglected the impact of the parents' relationship with each other upon the child,[10] and he paid little attention to the importance of a father's jealousy of a son in fostering the son's fear of him; furthermore until relatively late in life, Freud sought to understand the girl's oedipal transition essentially as a mirror image of the boy's. These are matters that I shall consider more fully in Part Three.

Every boy may well feel some jealousy and hostility toward his father, as well as some animosity toward his mother for withdrawing her nurturant care, but these need not be pervasive matters that dominate a man's life. What exists everywhere is the relationship between a mothering person and the child, and a basic triangular relationship between both parents and the child is almost as ubiquitous. The child, born helpless, requires total nurturant care, but in order for the child to grow into an autonomous individual, the mothering person must progressively frustrate the child's attachment to her; specifically, she must withhold the erotized aspects of her nurturant care. The mother and child never exist in isolation, and their relationship will be affected by the mother's relationship with others—particularly with her husband and her other children (if she has a husband and other children)—and by the mother's personality and the child's innate ways of reacting. Just how the configuration of relationships between parents and child will turn out and just how the relationship between any two in the triangle will be charged, so to speak, depend upon the circumstances and the personalities of those involved. Indeed, this is the bread and butter of psychiatry—the differing configurations that arise within this basic triangle and change as the child matures and his relationships with his parents and the relationship between his parents change. The triangle is always complicated by these three persons' involvements with others—siblings, grandparents, uncles, aunts, lovers—whether these figures are present in actuality or in memory.

The Role of the Family in Intrapsychic Conflicts

Although the inherent conditions of human existence virtually prescribe that the way in which the oedipal situation is lived out will color and profoundly influence all subsequent relationships, it is not the only basic relationship. The nuclear family forms a true small group in that the actions of any member affect all and produce reactions and counterreactions, and thus all of the intrafamilial relationships are significant to the way in which a child develops. The manner in which parents relate to each other influences the worth of a parent both as an object of identification for a child and as a basic love object for a child of the opposite sex. Children are jealous of the attention others receive from a parent; a girl is often rivalrous with her mother for a brother's attention as well as for the father's. Then, the human condition leads children to seek affection, sexual gratification, and security outside of their families of origin as they grow up. A girl can be torn between her love for her father and her desire for fulfillment through a husband; fathers may resent the intrusion of a girl's lover, and a mother may be jealous of her son's wife. Here again, which relationship produces intrafamilial or intrapsychic conflicts depends upon the circumstances.

The psychoanalyst utilizes his knowledge of the conflicts that can arise from these basic human relationships and lead to the intrapsychic dilemmas of his patients. He trains himself to hear how the tangled tales of frustrations that evolved from a familiar repertoire of situations which, though different in each patient, are variations upon a limited number of cardinal human themes. In the theater, as in life, in contrast to the novel, the action is not explained by the author. The psychoanalyst's training and practice in discerning such conflicts and their origins constitute major skills he can bring to the study of the drama. Hamlet is not simply related to Orestes and to Oedipus—to Orestes because of his matricidal impulsions, and to Oedipus because of his patricidal impulsions and his incestuous attraction to the mother—he is, rather, the central figure in an array of triangular intrafamilial attachments and conflicts, basic configurations which reverberate through the myths of many cultures and have, singly or in combination, provided plots for countless plays, but which are here welded into a single tragedy. The intertwining of these configurations in *Hamlet* leads to crucial insights into the human condition and its frailties.

Interpersonal Triangles in *Hamlet*

Let us consider briefly the interpersonal triangles in which Hamlet is involved to prepare for the discussion of the complex interplay between them in subsequent chapters.

First, Hamlet, as has been noted, stands in rivalry for his mother with a father figure, his stepfather, whom he seeks to kill and fears will kill him; simultaneously, Hamlet has become disillusioned with and hostile to his mother because she has married his uncle, thereby displacing his father in her affections. The substitution of a stepfather for a father in the triangle permits the direct expression of patricidal and filicidal feelings and acts and enables Hamlet to castigate his mother for her sexual activity with her husband. Moreover, the substitution allows the accentuation of the importance of a son's identification with his father and, as I shall emphasize, of how a son's self-esteem and sense of identity rest upon his mother's fidelity to his father—even though the son may earlier have resented his mother's attachment to his father.

Second, the triangular situation between two brothers and a woman that leads to the "primal" sin of fratricide sets the conditions at the opening of the play. This triangle involves a younger brother's envy of his older brother's prerogatives—here, of his crown and his wife. The situation has, as we shall examine, its roots in rituals and myths concerned with the fertility of the priestess-queen. Although not expressed in the play, we may posit that Claudius' wish to possess his brother's wife arose from jealousies over their mother's attention and affection during their childhoods—another basic human triangle.

When we leave Hamlet's relationships with his parents and turn to his prospects for love, sexual fulfillment, and marriage, we find him caught up in a third triangle, with Ophelia and Polonius. Here he is the intruder into an established parent-child relationship. The triangular relationship between a father, his daughter, and her suitor can create a critical conflict for a girl. She may be caught between her love for her father and her longings to find fulfillment and fruition through a lover who will take her from her father. In the play, the relationship between Polonius and Ophelia is heightened because Polonius' wife is dead. In the triangular relationship that exists between husband, wife, and daughter, Ophelia could, because of her mother's absence, seek to fill the gap left in her father's life. Similarly, Polonius may have found something of a substitute for his wife in his daughter, though this, too, is only conjecture based on theory and experience rather than on the text of the play. Stories of rivalries between fathers and suitors are common in fairy tales as well as myths.

Ophelia's love for Hamlet also involves Hamlet in a rivalry with Laertes; this fourth triangle involves a girl, her brother, and her suitor. Laertes' admonition to his sister not to trust Hamlet in the second scene of the play introduces a theme that reaches its climax with the fight in Ophelia's grave. The rivalry over Ophelia overlaps with the relationship between Polonius, Laertes, and Hamlet, in which Laertes identifies with his father and is obligated to avenge his death, a situation which mirrors and balances Hamlet's obligations to his own father concerning Claudius. As Hamlet tells Horatio, "by the image of my cause, I see / The portraiture of his" (V, ii, 77–78).

A diagram of the interrelationship between the triangles can be drawn as follows:

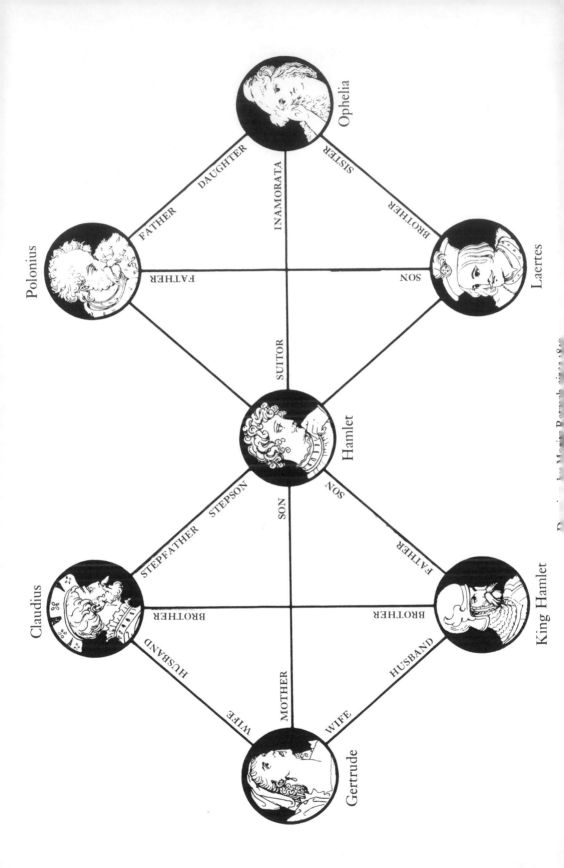

Drawing by Marjan Pejoski, circa 1890

Two basic relationships that do not enter into *Hamlet* require comment. The first is the jealousy and rivalry between a mother and daughter over the girl's father and brother. In contrast to Hamlet, Orestes had a sister, Electra, whose strong attachment to her father led her to incite Orestes to kill their mother. I shall explain later why I believe that Shakespeare specifically sought to write a play in which the hero, though in much the same situation as Orestes, does not kill his mother. Ophelia no longer has a mother, a circumstance which tends to balance Hamlet's fatherless state and also eliminates mother-daughter rivalry in the play. A second basic relationship that does not appear is the rivalry between a mother and a daughter-in-law. Gertrude seems to regard the motherless Ophelia somewhat as she would a daughter and as an acceptable potential daughter-in-law; a rivalry between Ophelia and Gertrude would not further either the theme or countertheme. However, an important relationship exists between Hamlet, Gertrude, and Ophelia that does affect the structure and action of the play: Hamlet's attitude toward Ophelia is influenced profoundly by Gertrude's infidelity. His love for Ophelia is deformed, though not obliterated, by his distrust of all women because of his disillusionment with his mother.

The relationship between Hamlet and the two women in the play is one of several other triangular relationships that cut across those I have been discussing and provide further balance and structure to the play. Another triangle exists between Hamlet, Claudius, and Polonius. Hamlet's relationship to Polonius, which is colored by their rivalry over Ophelia, is also influenced by Hamlet's and Polonius' relationships to Claudius. Hamlet kills Polonius more or less in the belief that he is killing Claudius: "I took thee for thy better" (III, iv, 32). Finally, there is the complex relationship between the three sons who feel obligated to avenge their fathers—Hamlet, Laertes, and Fortinbras. In a sense, a fourth avenging son also enters the action of the play, for it is the First Player's narration of the slaughter of Priam that incites Hamlet to action. Pyrrhus, in killing Priam, was avenging the death of his father, Achilles.

Theme and Countertheme: Hamlet's and Ophelia's Dilemmas

An understanding of why Hamlet verges on madness and why Ophelia becomes insane clarifies the action and structure of the play. The emotional stability of both characters is undermined for essentially the same reason. The major theme of the play concerns Hamlet's dilemma. He is obligated to kill Claudius to avenge his father's murder, but he is paralyzed by his discovery of his mother's infidelity and his suspicion or feeling that she may have connived in the murder. The lines of force, so to speak, in his basic relationships with his parents are suddenly reversed. He is deprived not only of his father but also of his mother when his love for her turns into bitterness because of her actions; he now is overwhelmed by hostility toward the person he had once loved most. The countertheme concerns Ophelia's plight and her inability to absorb her father's murder. She is deprived not only of a father but also of Hamlet when he kills her father. Thus, in one moment, she loses the two most significant persons in her life. She, too, must now turn away from the person she once loved most.

Hamlet was speaking for his creator when he said, " 'tis most sweet / When in one line two crafts directly meet" (III, iv, 209–210). The structure of *Hamlet* balances on the fulcrum of the death of Polonius. The relationship between hero and heroine alters. Hamlet and Ophelia can never wed. Laertes is turned into an ally of Claudius. Hamlet is no longer just a hero and avenger; he becomes a villain to Ophelia and Laertes and an object of vengeance—the pursued as much as the pursuer.

In a "reading" of *Hamlet* that pursues the topic of madness in the play, I shall emphasize the apposition of the theme and countertheme and then trace their fugue-like intertwinings as well as the shifts in the lines of force in the various triangles of interpersonal relationships in the lives of the major characters. Here, a number of interpersonal themes are integrated into one play as a group of interpenetrating and interrelated triangles of relationships. The universality of *Hamlet*'s fascination depends greatly upon the interrelationships of these basic themes that recur in lives everywhere, and perhaps to some degree, in the unconscious of everyone.

Some critics of my reading of *Hamlet* may argue that I read too much into the play, particularly in focusing on the inter-relating triangles of basic relationships and the complexity of the play's structure or "design." Was Shakespeare less of an artist than Bach, whose ability to handle musical themes in compositions such as *A Musical Offering* challenges belief? Was he less of an artist than Titian? Of course, Titian's use of a dynamic symmetry of interrelated triangles of line while simultaneously carrying the eye by his dynamic use of color may have become unconscious through practice by the time he painted *The Entombment*, but the complexity of the balance of mass, line, and color is undeniable. The ease of mastery contributes to the painting's greatness—but earlier artists measured the size and placement of each triangle that entered into their compositions.

Comments on the Design of *Hamlet*

Aside from the structure achieved by the apposition of theme and countertheme with the switch in emphasis from one to the other with the slaying of Polonius, I wish to note several other significant aspects of *Hamlet*'s design. The play is framed, so to speak, between the warlike preparations for an invasion by Fortinbras in the first scene and the arrival of Fortinbras at the court in the last scene to claim the throne, and to bear Hamlet martially from the stage with "soldier's music and the rites of war" (V, ii, 386). Each act, as we shall see, has a unifying motif or mood. In the first act the older generation gives directions to and sets limitations upon the younger generation; in the second, the older generation spies on the younger; in the third, a series of confrontations occurs; in the fourth, much as in the sonata form that developed in music, Shakespeare creates a change of pace before the final act through composing a *danse macabre;* and in the final act, which starts in the graveyard, death permeates the entire action. The play is further balanced by the repetition and reversal in the second half of actions of the first half of the play, again with the death of Polonius serving as a fulcrum.[11] Although these aspects of the play's design complement the theme and countertheme, they are not directly relevant to this study.

The Psychoanalyst and the Study of Style

In addition to his knowledge of essential themes in human lives and his understanding of the sources of conflicts between people and within them, the psychoanalyst acquires other skills useful in the study of the theater. Modern criticism, through the study of style and metaphor, has provided new sources of appreciation of *Hamlet*. Style in literature connotes that which is uniquely personal to the author and sometimes, to a specific work of the author or even to a character he seeks to portray. Herein lies the special province of the contemporary literary scholar, but here, too, the psychoanalyst has acquired some useful skills. After all, psychoanalysis is carried out primarily through the medium of the spoken word, and years of alert listening make the analyst aware of what a patient's linguistic style conveys about his personality, what a speech conceals as well as communicates.

The perceptive reader or listener can learn much from a few words in *Hamlet*. We need not move beyond Hamlet's first few speeches to see how Shakespeare conveys the essence of Hamlet in the words he utters. When Claudius, after giving Laertes permission to return to Paris, turns to Hamlet, saying, "But now, my cousin Hamlet, and my son," Hamlet's first speech comes as an aside: "A little more than kin, and less than kind." In this play with words we hear Hamlet's evaluation of his changed relationship to Claudius, as well as a touch of Hamlet's irony, cynicism, and bitterness. We are also being introduced to a character whose ancestor in myth was a hero known for his riddles and for his ability to use words in a way that concealed the truth while telling the truth. In retrospect, the reader realizes that the one letter difference between "kin" and "kind" (which may also remind Claudius that Hamlet is also still less than "king") introduces a character who may well make the most subtle use of language in our literature, and who will later trap Claudius "tropically" by the use of a trope. Then, when the king next asks, "How is it that the clouds still hang on you?" we note how Hamlet can convey a great deal without actually exposing himself when he responds, "Not so, my lord; I am too much i' the sun" (I, ii, 67)—too much the subject of your attention, too much in the glamour of the court, but also too much still a son rather than a king.

When his mother joins in urging Hamlet to cast his "nighted colour" off, saying, "Thou know'st 'tis common; all that lives must die, / Passing through nature to eternity" (I, ii, 72–73), we observe Hamlet's intellectual condescension to his mother in his reply, "Ay, madam, it is common." The queen's next, "Why seems it so particular with thee?" leads Hamlet to disclose another major characteristic. "I know not *seems*," he says, and adds that of all outward shows of grief "these indeed *seem*, / For they are actions that a man might play; / But I have that within which passeth show" (I, ii, 76, 83–85). He is concerned with the inner man—who a person is and what motivates him —rather than with appearance and prestige. He despises insincerity and pretense, a characteristic that grows into intolerance as he becomes disillusioned. Even his love for Ophelia will turn to venom when he doubts her sincerity; and his lifelong friendship with Rosencrantz and Guildenstern will not keep him from murdering them when he suspects their loyalty and sincerity. The first soliloquy which follows hard upon these remarks reveals much through its choice of words and images about Hamlet's personality as well as about his feelings about the situation at the start of the play.

LINGUISTIC STYLE AND CHARACTER

Even though many contemporary critics have turned away from the study of "character" to focus upon language, style, and imagery, these can also serve to illuminate character, and if we neglect this aspect of Shakespeare's language, we lose much. The psychotherapist strives to become attuned to what his patient conveys through the words and style he or she unconsciously selects, as well as through the various parapraxes that Freud discussed in his *Psychopathology of Everyday Life*, a work that opened a new era in the study of language usage.

In brief, we soon recognize in *Hamlet* that we are watching and listening to a Renaissance man who, though still attracted by Renaissance concepts of heroism and still bound to earlier concepts of vengeance, is more a late Renaissance figure who is concerned with reason, the inner man, and the introspective exploration of the self. Though he admires heroism, he does not, like Fortinbras, seem motivated to emulate his father. While admiring Fortinbras' singleness of purpose, he finds waging war and sacrificing lives for honor and vengeance rather absurd, as did Montaigne and Raymond Sebond. He admires Laertes and strives to perfect his own swordsmanship, but his real admiration goes elsewhere. His basic ambitions for himself, which are blocked by his obligation to his murdered father and by the emotions aroused by his mother's behavior, are reflected in his appreciation of Horatio:

> A man that fortune's buffets and rewards
> Hath ta'en with equal thanks; and blest are those
> Whose blood and judgement are so well commingled
> That they are not a pipe for Fortune's finger
> To sound what stop she please. Give me that man
> That is not passion's slave, and I will wear him
> In my heart's core, ay, in my heart of heart,
> As I do thee.   (III, ii, 62–69)

Hamlet, then, like Goethe's Faust, has two souls dwelling within his breast; or, I might say, he is the child of a transitional period who is still tied to the concept of the Renaissance hero and the Renaissance prince's obligation to seek vengeance but who has a more profound desire to lead the philosophic life, a measured life of self-sufficiency in which he "could be bounded in a nut-shell, and count myself a king of infinite space" (II, ii,

249–250). Like two predecessors at Wittenberg, Martin Luther and Doctor Faustus, he is caught up in conflicting motivations and in a struggle to preserve his immortal soul. He may be obligated to vengeance and murder, but such deeds require him to become someone other than the person he seeks to be. Herein lies one aspect of his tragedy and a basic reason for his inaction, aside from his disillusionment with his mother. Hamlet is a hero to us because he must come to terms with himself; he is not a single-minded hero who battles only against external foes. Because of his discrepant and contradictory ego ideals, he cannot be faithful to himself. As Erik Erikson commented, "Hamlet succeeds in actualizing only what he would call his negative identity and in becoming exactly what his own ethical sense could not tolerate: a mad revenger."[12]

HAMLET'S WORDPLAYS

Although of a philosophic bent, Hamlet is capable of camaraderie and will even banter salaciously, as he does when welcoming Rosencrantz and Guildenstern to the court and when, in his misery, he seeks to wound Ophelia just before the start of the "dumb-show." Though his humor often has a razor edge, his tendency to jest through plays on words appears whenever he has a lighthearted moment (or pretends to be lighthearted) and is one of his most ingrained and developed characteristics. He readily turns this trait to use in his pretense of insanity, but it is also a trait that is grotesquely exaggerated when his emotions are out of control.

As a psychiatrist, I was long ago taken with Hamlet's, "I am but mad north-north-west; when the wind is southerly, I know a hawk from a handsaw" (II, ii, 360–361). Clearly Shakespeare understood that a disturbed person's mental state reflects his emotional surroundings: enmity fosters hatred and madness, love brings security and calm. But what captured my attention was "I know a hawk from a handsaw." Does this not indicate that in Elizabethan times, just as today, one test of mental competence, of judgment, was the ability to answer such questions as: "What is the difference between a child and a dwarf?" Shakespeare clearly seems to be satirizing such queries with the ridiculous "hawk from a handsaw." Perhaps this was his intent, just as he satirizes the coroner's law about suicide in the grave-yard scene. But his wit is keen, and the closer we look, the keener it seems. "Handsaw" was a common Elizabethan corruption of "harnshaw," the word for "heron"; "hawk," on the other hand, was the name for a plasterer's implement as well as a bird. Is Shakespeare having Hamlet say, "Don't worry, I'm not so mad that I do not know one tool from another, as well as one bird from another, and I'm bright enough to confuse you by this remark," and at the same time warning his interrogators, "I know who the hawks hunting me are—I know who is the hunter (the hawk) and who the hunted (the heron)!" The sally is rounded out when we learn from Plutarch, whose writings Shakespeare knew well, that in ancient Egypt the hawk was the symbol of the north wind and the heron the symbol of the south wind.

Or let us consider the very simple sally in which Hamlet, after calling Polonius "Jephthah," tells him, "the first row of the pious chanson will show you more; for look, where my abridgements come.—" (II, ii, 400–401). Various authorities[13] have suggested that the word "pious" is an error and should read "pons" because in France such songs were called *pons chansons* or *chansons du Pont Neuf*, after the locale where they were sung. The commentators fail to see that Shakespeare was setting up a cryptic trilingual pun by using the French "chanson" and then saying "look, where my *abridge*ments come."

Another play on words, a gruesome passage, provides us with a glimpse of how Shakespeare creatively shapes source material to his purposes. When Claudius demands that Hamlet reveal where he has bestowed the body of Polonius, Hamlet tells him, "At supper . . . / Not where he eats, but where he is eaten; a certain convocation of politic worms are e'en at him. Your worm is your only emperor for diet. We fat all creatures else to fat us, and we fat ourselves for maggots. Your fat king, and your lean beggar, is but variable service, two dishes, but to one table; that's the end" (IV, iii, 18, 20–25).

The passage takes its origins from Saxo's tale of Amleth.[14] After Amleth killed the king's counselor, who had hidden in

Gerutha's bedchamber to spy on Amleth and the queen, Amleth chopped up the body, boiled it, and cast the residue into an open privy, where the hogs ate it. Later, when King Feng asked Amleth if he knew what had become of his friend, Amleth replied that the counselor had fallen into the privy and had been eaten by the hogs—a version of the truth that was, of course, not believed.

The crude episode in Saxo is refined by Shakespeare, but at the same time made more gruesome because it symbolizes everyone's ultimate fate. Further, the worms are "politic" because they eat a counselor, and because they are "politic worms," Shakespeare cannot resist the pun on the Diet of Worms.

For whom did Shakespeare insert these allusions? For the groundlings? For himself? Out of delight in fine workmanship and pride in his craft? Did anyone in the audience pick up these demonstrations of his genius? Was he thinking of Ben Jonson and saying, "Let's see you match this one, Ben." He was not doing it for us, but we can appreciate and wonder.

We empathize with Hamlet not so much because of what he does as much as because of what he says and how he says it. Few characters of the stage have a style of speech as characteristic as Hamlet's or one that so thoroughly captures our interest and admiration.

The Study of Metaphor in *Hamlet*

Caroline Spurgeon's examination of the metaphors in *Hamlet* drew attention to the pervasive imagery of disease and bodily blemish through which Shakespeare conveys both the unwholesome, morally sick state of Denmark ("the outward condition which causes Hamlet's spiritual illness") and Hamlet's own sense of contamination.[15] In *The Wheel of Fire*, G. Wilson Knight fruitfully considered the expanded metaphor of the play, its pervasive atmosphere, and its preoccupation with the theme of death. According to Knight, Hamlet is the "Embassy of Death," and Ophelia, the "Rose of May," whose bloom is frozen by the cold blasts of Hamlet's death impulsion before it can unfold and reach fruition. We are indebted to Knight for helping to dissolve the coating of romantic heroics under which Hamlet had long been hidden. He understood what troubles Hamlet, that he is preoccupied by his mother's infidelity far more than by father's murder; and he also understood the extent of Hamlet's disillusion, which fills Hamlet with a "detestation of life, a sense of uncleanliness and evil in the things of nature; a disgust at the physical body of man; bitterness, cynicism, hate. It tends toward insanity." He comes to grips not only with Hamlet's cruelty but also with his devilish joy in cruelty toward the end of the play. Still, Knight's attempt to interpret the play as an expanded metaphor on the theme of death does not quite come off. It provides a static conceptualization with minimal concern for development and change in the characters. Knight's disparagement of studies of "character" led him into an impasse in which little admirable remains in Hamlet, who is more villain than hero, closer to death than to life. Although Knight had a fine understanding of Hamlet's melancholia, he lost sight of why Hamlet is depressed to the verge of distraction.

The play deals with what happens to the characters—what they become and why, rather than simply what they are. Hamlet, we have many reasons to assume, was not permeated by the chill of death before his father's death and his mother's remarriage. Hamlet cannot be taken simply as an embassy of death who chills and kills the symbol of spring and fruition. Hamlet is potentially, at least, a highly admirable character, and indeed, contains many elements of an ideal that the men in the audience would wish to resemble, and the women to possess as a lover or son. The play holds its audience because in it we witness how the youth is kept from realizing his potential by the bitter and disillusioning ways of the world and from becoming the man we know he could become. Hamlet's world and his own self-esteem are torn apart by his mother's infidelity—and only then does he become the purveyor of death. The tragedy, therefore, is not basically his death or Ophelia's but, rather, the tragedy of the blasted hopes of youths with whom we identify. We participate in a heightened and dramatized version of the regrets we feel for the integrity, innocence, and pure loves of our own youth which were blown away by the chill winds of a self-seeking and calloused, if not corrupt, world.[16]

"Mad" and "Madness"

A strange and interesting omission in the studies by Spurgeon, Muir, and Charney of *Hamlet*'s style and imagery suggests the strength of the emotional block people have in facing problems of insanity.[17] It is, of course, interesting to note the extensive imagery of war, weapons, and explosives to which Muir and Charney direct our attention; but their neglect of the theme of madness is especially striking to a psychiatrist. For example, I have difficulty in following Charney when he says that because *Hamlet* is a vigorous and active play, "and at times a vicious struggle for survival between Hamlet and Claudius . . . then, we must logically begin our discussion not with disease but with war, weapons, and explosives."[18] No matter what the imagery may suggest, *Hamlet* is certainly not a play about war. At the start Denmark prepares for war, and the play ends with a martial flourish, but in between the regime dies of inner corruption. The play is concerned with combat through intrigue and with an internalized conflict that makes a battleground of the "soul" or "psyche." Secrecy, poison, corruption in its various forms—these are clearly significant themes reflected in the play's action as well as through its imagery. However, in considering disease as a form of corruption, Spurgeon barely noted mental illness, although she did consider the many images of corruption that reflect "not only the outward condition which causes Hamlet's spiritual illness but also his own state."[19] She properly noted how the discovery of his father's murder and his mother's conduct has so struck Hamlet that when the play opens he has already begun "to die, to die internally, because all the springs of life—love, laughter, joy, hope, belief in others—are becoming frozen at their source, are being gradually infected by the disease of the spirit which is . . . killing him."[20] She reached an interpretation akin to G. Wilson Knight's, but paid almost no attention to words and imagery referring to madness, and the same shortcoming is true of Muir and Charney. Charney asks, "What ails Hamlet?" On the basis of his study of the language, he answers that Hamlet's most grievous difficulties are melancholy, heartache, and shortness of breath. He does not seem to consider that heartache and "thought sickness" are part of the melancholy; and it is certainly strange to consider "a sigh so pitious and profound" as a symptom of shortness of breath.

It is also of interest that Levin found that the word "question," appears at least seventeen times in *Hamlet*, more than in any other play by Shakespeare; this frequency count helped Levin feel secure in emphasizing the importance of interrogation in the play.[21] Yet, if we wish to consider the frequency of the use of words, metaphors, and images as a key to the relative importance of various themes in the play, we should remark that the words "mad" and "madness" are used at least forty times; in addition, "ecstasy" (meaning madness), appears four times; "lunacy" and "distemper" three times each; "distracted" twice, and "antic-disposition," "wit-diseased," and "confusion," once each. These fifteen additional terms make a total of fifty-five direct expressions of insanity, not including the term "melancholy." In addition, there are some fifty indirect expressions concerned with loss of reason, loss of self-control, doubt of the senses, suicide, melancholy, and insanity. (Of course, categorizing such expressions is often a matter of judgment.) In any event, I believe that the frequency of "mad," "madness," and other words and expressions related to that concept underlines the need to pay specific attention to the theme of madness in *Hamlet*.

Hamnet and Hamlet

My previous remarks about Hamlet's style, his interest in the theater, his masterful use of language and wordplay, and his youthful promise lead me to break my resolve not to make conjectures about Shakespeare on the basis of interpretations of the play. But, as the conjecture is not based on psychoanalytic interpretation or theory, I do not feel bound by my former resolutions. Shakespeare had just turned thirty when his only son, Hamnet, died at the age of eleven.[22] We may imagine the bereaved playwright re-creating his son in the insubstantial state of imagination that knows no death and that held the potential for the immortality it has achieved. He could re-create his son in his own image or, at least, in the image of an ideal he had held for himself, and then, go on to relive his own disillusionment as he grew older by portraying the fate of Hamlet. One of the greatest creative minds of modern literature had a similar fantasy. In *Ulysses*, James Joyce had Stephen Dedalus say: "Is it possible that the player Shakespeare, a ghost by absence, and in the vesture of buried Denmark, a ghost by death, speaking his own words to his own son's name (had Hamnet Shakespeare lived he would have been Prince Hamlet's twin) is it possible, I want to know, or probable that he did not foresee the logical conclusion of those premises: You are the dispossessed son, I am the murdered father; your mother is the guilty queen, Ann Shakespeare, born Hathaway?" In writing *Hamlet* the poet may have also finally achieved a maturity and creativity free from malice and bitterness despite the deceitful ways of the world, and possibly even despite betrayal by his wife, and perhaps by a brother, through living in the fantasy of his creative mind and through the magic of artistry that purges the soul— much as Prospero did on his island, alone with his daughter and the creatures of imagination, after his brother betrayed him.

I shall keep myself from wandering into paragraphs that are not essential to this Introduction. It is difficult, because the play and its creator stir up so much that will have no proper place within the body of these essays, and I wish to convey to the reader some of my enthusiasm and wonderment, so that the psychiatrist will be awed by the play's beauty and craftsmanship as well as by its insights; and the Shakespearean scholar may (again) be dazzled by the development of the characters and the understanding of their motivations. We have much to gain from following the theme of madness, for even in madness we find a searching after humanity and a yearning for love; and even in Ophelia's suicide, a poignant, lingering beauty.

PART ONE

Madness in *Hamlet*

I

INSANITY IN SHAKESPEARE'S PLAYS

The Theme of Madness in *Hamlet*

IF we can approach the theme of madness in *Hamlet* and examine it rather than avoid it, lest it hurdle the footlights and infect us along with the hero and heroine, we can achieve a more meaningful grasp of the play. Is *Hamlet* a play about insanity? It is concerned with many fundamental issues of existence. It conveys how primal sin corrupts, corruption disillusions, disillusionment breeds a preoccupation with death, and a preoccupation with death destroys Eros. It is a play about vengeance and how avengers lose their souls, sin, and corrupt in turn. It is a play about many things that cannot be conveyed in brief statements but which the play transmits beyond our reason to our unconscious apprehension by its metaphor and symbolism. Yet, *Hamlet* is about insanity. Madness is the means Shakespeare used to convey the disillusion and despair that pervades the characters, and leads them to rash and self-destructive acts, and to express the dissolution of their world. Madness is, moreover, essential to the structure of the play as well as to the development of its themes.

Madness in *Hamlet*

Of course, everyone rides his own hobbyhorse in interpreting *Hamlet*, and it is natural for a psychiatrist to make insanity a basic issue. Whether Hamlet's madness is true or feigned is central to the abiding mystery of his character and motivation, and the topic of more essays than even a professional Shakespearean scholar might care to count. If we do not wish to go along with Polonius when he says, "Your noble son is mad" (II, ii, 92), let us, for the moment, grant that the play depicts a hero living in the shadow of insanity. It is more certain that Hamlet lives in the shadow of insanity than that he is a hero.

Arguments rage concerning Hamlet's sanity, but Ophelia— Ophelia has been the very paradigm of madness. For over 350 years persons have been adjudged to be "as mad as Ophelia," and the play attains a special poignancy just because in it we witness how "a young maid's wits / Should be as mortal as an old man's life" (IV, v, 155–156). Indeed, Ophelia's madness seems so appropriate to her disposition and situation that relatively little attention has been given to its cause; and yet, herein lies a key to the mystery of what ails Hamlet.

Scrutiny of the theme of insanity helps clarify not only the play but also Shakespeare's understanding of insanity, upon which, even after these many years, we can still sharpen our own. There is ample evidence that when writing *Hamlet* Shakespeare was specifically concerned with melancholia—a diagnosis that encompassed a wider range of disorders in his day than at present—and that he used the play to convey some of his own insights into the nature and etiology of madness. There are three major reasons for my assertion, each of which will be examined in turn.

First, the search for the cause of Hamlet's madness. Each major character has a theory about the cause of Hamlet's madness and although each theory has pertinence, each is insufficient and misses the essence of the problem. The mystery is carefully shrouded in a veil of ambiguity, as if Shakespeare meant to perplex—and also as if he were aware of the overdetermination of mental disorders.[1] However, in contrast to the theories of insanity that prevailed in Shakespeare's day, none of the characters blames witchcraft, the humors, or even sin; but rather each assumes that Hamlet's indisposition is due to something in his life circumstances.

Second, the careful apposition and opposition of Ophelia's insanity to Hamlet's antic disposition. Although the heroine's madness has no counterpart in the sagas upon which the play is based, it is essential to the greatness and unity of the play. Lack of appreciation of its importance to the movement and purpose of the play has led to strange criticisms of the second half of *Hamlet*: Some of these, such as the notion that Shakespeare kept Hamlet procrastinating to fill out the necessary five acts, are too foolish to consider; but even a critic as distinguished as Dover Wilson could assert "that Hamlet's procrastination is the predominant interest of the last two and a half acts" and that the various exciting incidents "form for the most part a series of detached episodes; and, though they are exciting in themselves, none except the fencing match and what leads up to it is felt to be central."[2] Such misapprehension of the play by a leading scholar provokes dismay. The play gains both balance and resolution through Ophelia's madness.

Third, Hamlet, the character about whom Shakespeare's greatest play revolves, is the literary descendant of a series of mad heroes of myth and saga. Shakespeare drew heavily not only upon Saxo's saga of Amleth,[3] who feigned imbecility to protect himself from a stepfather-uncle who had murdered his father and married his mother, but also upon the Roman story of Lucius Junius Brutus, who also acted the imbecile when in a similar predicament. Further, when Shakespeare wrote the play he had in mind not only Nero, the incest-haunted matricide who became mad, but also, we have reason to believe, Orestes, who was pursued by the Furies after he reluctantly killed his mother.

Madness in *Hamlet*

Insanity in Shakespeare's Other Plays

The thesis that Shakespeare specifically focused upon the theme of insanity in *Hamlet* may seem less strange to the reader who pauses to recall the frequency with which Shakespeare portrays madness, from the brutal usages of Titus Andromicus to the embittered misanthropy of Timon of Athens. I shall, therefore, digress to consider other plays of Shakespeare, and also to comment on the literary interest in madness during his lifetime.

Insanity is a recurrent theme in Shakespeare's comedies as well as in his tragedies. He not only depicted various types of mental disorders with uncanny accuracy and expressed deep insights into their etiologies, but he also provided some excellent ideas about therapy. His knowledge led Isaac Ray, one of the founding fathers of the American Psychiatric Association, to write some 120 years ago, "Few . . . are so familiar with those diversities of mental character that . . . result from disease, as not to find the sphere of his ideas on this subject somewhat enlarged by the study of Shakespeare."[4] Ray's equally renowned contemporary Amariah Brigham ventured, "The more we read Shakespeare, the more we are astonished . . . on no one subject . . . has he shown more of his remarkable ability and accuracy than on insanity. . . . His views were far, very far, in advance of the age in which he lived."[5] We do not have the temporal perspective required to compare Shakespeare's understanding with our own, but since Freud opened the way to the study of unconscious processes, we have been able to appreciate Shakespeare's character studies and learn from them more fully than could his earlier psychiatric admirers. I shall discuss only a few examples of his considerations of mental illness.

In *The Comedy of Errors*, one of his early plays, Shakespeare treats insanity lightly but with a humanistic approach to therapy that stands in marked contrast to the beliefs of his time. Antipholus of Ephesus, considered insane when people mistake him for his twin, is taken to a charlatan who seeks to exorcise a demon. Shakespeare pillories Dr. Pinch, satirizes his rituals and his confinement of the patient, and contrasts him with the Abbess, who offers Adriana a delightful diagnosis of the origins of her husband's illness:

> And thereof came it that the man was mad;
> The venom clamours of a jealous woman
> Poison more deadly than a mad dog's tooth
> It seems his sleeps were hindered by thy railing,
> And thereof comes it that his head is light.
> Thou say'st his meat was sauced with thy upbraidings:
> Unquiet meals make ill digestions;
> Thereof the raging fire of fever bred;
> And what's a fever but a fit of madness?
> Thou say'st his sports were hindered by thy brawls:
> Sweet recreation barr'd, what doth ensue
> But moody moping, and dull melancholy, . . .
> The consequence is then, thy jealous fits
> Have scar'd thy husband from the use of wits.
>
> (V, i, 67 86)

In his psychoanalytic study of Shakespeare's early plays, Robert Ravich suggests that Shakespeare gained his concepts of mental disorder from the great physician Johann Weyer, who combated belief in witchcraft and demoniacal possession, rather than from Timothie Bright.[6] However, neither Weyer nor his English disciple Reginald Scott attained Shakespeare's understanding of mental disorders and the subtleties of human motivation. I would tend to agree with Isaac Ray who surmised that Shakespeare gained his knowledge through careful observation of the insane rather than through reading or instruction. However, in *A Midsummer Night's Dream*, we find one source of Shakespeare's empathy for the mentally ill and evidence of his appreciation of their capacities for unusual insights:

> Lovers and madmen have such seething brains,
> Such shaping fantasies, that apprehend
> More than cool reason ever comprehends.
> The lunatic, the lover and the poet

Are of imagination all compact.
One sees more devils than vast hell can hold,
That is the madman. The lover, all as frantic,
Sees Helen's beauty in a brow of Egypt.
The poet's eye, in a fine frenzy rolling,
Doth glance from heaven to earth, from earth to
      heaven;
And as imagination bodies forth
The forms of things unknown, the poet's pen
Turns them to shapes, and gives to airy nothing
A local habitation and a name.   (V. i, 4–17)

As insanity, for Shakespeare, signified an extremity of misfortune, it naturally plays a central role in his great tragedies. In *King Lear, Macbeth, Timon of Athens,* and *Othello*—as well as in *Hamlet*—he portrays different types of mental disorders with uncanny knowledge and startling insights. Shakespeare may not have consciously understood the origins of these disorders, but he was singularly attuned to unconscious desires and motives in himself and others.

Although medicine and psychiatry remained puzzled over the causes of somnambulism and compulsions until the last years of the nineteenth century, Shakespeare's audiences have always understood why Lady Macbeth walks in her sleep and compulsively washes her hands, and even why she finally dies of despair. *Macbeth* links the act of regicide, a repetitive theme in Shakespeare's tragedies, to patricide. After she prepares the setting for Duncan's murder, Lady Macbeth says, "Had he not resembled / My father as he slept I had done 't" (II, ii, 13–14). After her husband commits the murder, she warns, "These deeds must not be thought / After these ways; so, it will make us mad" (II, ii, 33–34). She and the audience accept the power of conscience to punish a person who yields to forbidden impulsions. Macbeth is not only aware of the cause of his insomnia; but foresees that in murdering the king he "does murder sleep" and will be deprived of

Sleep that knits up the ravell'd sleeve of care,
The death of each day's life, sore labour's bath,

Balm of hurt minds, great nature's second course,
Chief nourisher in life's feast,—   (II, ii, 37–41)

Then, as the play nears its end and Birnam Wood is about to
march on Dunsinane, Macbeth asks the physician how his ill
wife fares:

Doctor: Not so sick, my lord,
As she is troubled with thick-coming fancies,
That keep her from her rest.
Macbeth: Cure her of that;
Canst thou not minister to a mind diseas'd,
Pluck from the memory a rooted sorrow,
Raze out the written troubles of the brain,
And with some sweet oblivious antidote
Cleanse the stuff'd bosom of that perilous stuff
Which weighs upon the heart?
Doctor: Therein the patient
Must minister to himself.
Macbeth: Throw physic to the dogs; I'll none of it.
                                            (V, iii, 37–47)

So things stood for 300 years until Freud, in a sense, accepted
Macbeth's challenge and initiated mental catharsis as a treatment for hysteria—in essence, to "pluck from the memory a
rooted sorrow." Shakespeare somehow grasped that dissociated
states such as somnambulism indicate inadequate repression of
unacceptable memories, that compulsive acts such as hand-
washing are unconscious efforts to "undo" a guilt-laden act, and
that self-punishment can kill.

King Lear, the play that rivals *Hamlet* in its symbolic treatment of man's frailties, also centers upon insanity. Indeed, we
may consider that the proud Lear only achieves salvation as a
man by passing through a period of insanity before he dies,
during which his misfortunes teach the rigid and self-centered
monarch his dependence upon loved ones and his vulnerability
to the inhumanity of those he once trusted.

In *King Lear* as in *Hamlet*, Shakespeare presents two mad
characters: one feigning, the other clearly insane. In contrast to

Hamlet, Edgar never leaves the audience in doubt that he is feigning madness to save his life, even though in writing the part Shakespeare displays consummate knowledge of how inmates of Bedlam behaved. Perhaps only psychiatrists can fully appreciate Shakespeare's insightful portrayal of the mad Lear. Lear's rigidity and pride are accentuated by his advanced age, and the setting in which his psychosis occurs is noted with perspicacity. When deprived of all sources of security, when expelled from his customary surroundings, and when consumed with rage because of his daughters' inhumanity, Lear becomes a broken and disoriented old man. When order is restored, when Cordelia's devotion warms his life, and when he again feels hope, Lear recovers his wits. Even today it is often difficult to persuade physicians that the aged do not become psychotic from loss of brain cells, which only diminishes their adaptability, but that they are prone to psychoses when, like Lear, they are deprived of the care and support they need or they find themselves in strange surroundings or infuriating circumstances. In the play Shakespeare uses his knowledge of such matters to convey the dangers of pride, the chastening power of misfortune, and the healing capacities of love.

We do not know where Shakespeare gained his insights into mental illnesses, a knowledge that still astonishes and perplexes psychiatrists. Like many other great playwrights, he probably suffered sufficiently himself to permit him to recognize that insoluble conflicts and unbridled passions can lead to insanity. He was not, however, unique among his colleagues in his interest in mental and emotional disorders. The new humanism of the late Renaissance had collided with the religious tradition, and the explorations of the sixteenth century had opened new vistas. Established value systems had been upset in the struggle between Roman and Anglican Catholicism and the rising Puritan tide. The political crisis of the last years of Elizabeth's reign intensified the spirit of restlessness. Poets and playwrights, concerned with conflicting emotions and motivations, looked inward to explore the self as others were charting the New World. The new spirit was expressed by John Davies, in *Nosce Teipsum:*

We that acquaint ourselves with every zone
And pass both tropics, and behold the poles,
When we come home, are to ourselves unknown
And unacquainted still with our own souls.[7]

The intellectuals were interested in the uniqueness of man and with his place in nature. Interest in the humors and in that Elizabethan malady, melancholia, became widespread. Jonson's *Every Man in His Humor,* and *Every Man out of His Humor* and Timothie Bright's medical work, *A Treatise of Melancholie,* and other such works were precursors of Burton's *Anatomy of Melancholy.*

Shakespeare's interest in inner motivation and in melancholia were in keeping with his times; it is the depth and precision of his insights and observations that amaze us. Jonson sought to create plays in which each character was influenced by a particular humor, and he may have succeeded in *Volpone;* but to Shakespeare, people were far more complex, torn by opposing motivations and prey to changing moods as they developed under the impact of the events in the play. As Herman Grimm noted a century ago, Shakespeare did not pattern his plays as did the Greek and classic French dramatists who sought to teach a clear-cut lesson by creating characters who were abstractions caught up in ideal conflicts.[8] Shakespeare conveyed the complexity of life and expressed a concept through the unfolding of characters fashioned in the semblance of real persons. Shakespeare was aware that his friend Jonson and other university-educated playwrights were following the classic model, but he did not, or fortunately, could not, adhere to their teachings.

I trust that these brief remarks concerning Shakespeare's use of insanity indicate that to focus on the theme of madness in *Hamlet* would not be "to consider too curiously, to consider so."

II

THE SEARCH FOR
THE CAUSE OF
HAMLET'S MADNESS

LET US now turn to the search for the cause of Hamlet's strange behavior. Hamlet was not, of course, the first mad hero of a play: Orestes and Ajax antedated him by some 2,000 years, and Kyd's Hieronymo was one of Hamlet's most popular Elizabethan predecessors. The causes of their sufferings are clear-cut. *Hamlet* may well have been unique in being concerned with the causes of insanity. All of the characters on stage with Hamlet are perplexed save Horatio. Hamlet, Horatio, and the audience know what ails Hamlet. They know he has put on an antic disposition after his encounter with his father's ghost. But has Hamlet deceived Horatio? Has he deceived himself? What purpose does the antic disposition serve? It does not, as in the Amleth saga, protect him from the king but instead makes Claudius wary. Some of Hamlet's disturbed behavior does not seem feigned. Moreover, while he still considers Rosencrantz and Guildenstern to be his close friends, he admits to them that he is melancholic; and at the end of the play, in his penultimate speech that we must take seriously, he seeks Laertes' pardon:

> What I have done,
> That might your nature, honour, and exception
> Roughly awake, I here proclaim was madness.
> Was't Hamlet wrong'd Laertes? Never Hamlet;
> If Hamlet from himself be ta'en away,
> And, when he's not himself, does wrong Laertes,
> Then Hamlet does it not; Hamlet denies it.
> Who does it then? His madness; if't be so,
> Hamlet is of the faction that is wrong'd;
> His madness is poor Hamlet's enemy.   (V, ii, 217–226)

Three theories are proposed by three major characters. Each theory reflects the guilt of its proponent; each has some validity but is, by itself, insufficient.

Claudius, Hamlet's uncle-father, muses: ". . . What it should be, / More than his father's death, / . . . I cannot dream of" (II, ii, 7–10), expressing his guilt over murdering Hamlet's father and displacing Hamlet in the election to the throne. Later we shall hear Hamlet confirm that herein lies one matter that has upset him greatly. He tells Horatio:

> He that hath kill'd my king, and whored my mother;
> Popp'd in between the election and my hopes;
>
> (V, ii, 64–65)

Gertrude, Hamlet's mother-aunt, has her own theory:

> I doubt it is no other but the main,—
> His father's death, and our o'erhasty marriage.
>
> (II, ii, 56–57)

Her conjecture reflects her guilt and shame over her inability to contain her sensuality through a decent period of mourning. Hamlet has already told Horatio in bitter jest:

> Thrift, thrift, Horatio! the funeral baked-meats
> Did coldly furnish forth the marriage tables.
> Would I had met my dearest foe in heaven
> Or ever I had seen that day, Horatio!   (I, ii, 180–183)

Madness in *Hamlet*

Polonius shrewdly attributes Hamlet's condition to his rejection by Ophelia, for he has forbidden his daughter to "so slander any moment's leisure, / As to give words or talk with the Lord Hamlet" (I, iii, 133–134), lest she be seduced and tender Polonius a fool. He recognizes that his restriction of his daughter was also motivated by his suspicion of Hamlet's intentions:

> I fear'd he did but trifle
> And meant to wreck thee; but beshrew my jealousy![1]
> (II, i, 112–113).

Despite Hamlet's callous behavior toward Ophelia during the confrontation scene and his degradation of her while witnessing the play-within-the-play, Hamlet gives ample evidence that Ophelia's withdrawal from him, or his withdrawal from her, has greatly upset him. He pens to her:

> *I have not*
> *art to reckon my groans; but that I love thee best, O most*
> *best, believe it. Adieu.*   (II, ii, 119–121)

Moreover, at her grave—or rather, in her grave—he proclaims to all:

> forty thousand brothers
> Could not, with all their quantity of love,
> Make up my sum.   (V, i, 257–259)

The king and queen become deeply concerned about Hamlet's melancholic and distracted state and send for Hamlet's old and good friends, Rosencrantz and Guildenstern. They are Hamlet's friends, not henchmen of Claudius. The queen is sure, "two men there are not living / To whom he more adheres" (II, ii, 20–21). They are asked by Claudius to gather:

> So much as from occasion you may glean,
> Whether aught to us unknown afflicts him thus,
> That, open'd, lies within our remedy.   (II, ii, 16–18)

The king also asks them "to draw him on to pleasures" (II, ii, 15).

The position and integrity of both Rosencrantz and Guildenstern have frequently been misunderstood. There is no evidence in the play that they spy on Hamlet for Claudius. In Shakespeare's time, just as today, when a person was depressed, his family and friends tried to keep him from his morbid preoccupations by providing diversions, and to find out if there was anything that was troubling him that could be remedied. As we shall note, Rosencrantz and Guildenstern let Hamlet know why they are at the court, and they attempt to keep Hamlet from harming himself and others. They are open in their efforts to learn from Hamlet what is upsetting him.

All of these relatives and friends of Hamlet are in agreement with Polonius when he says:

> Mad let us grant him then; and now remains
> That we find out the cause of this effect,
> Or rather say, the cause of this defect,
> For this effect defective comes by cause.
>
> (II, ii, 100–104)

They have, then, what psychiatrists term a psychodynamic orientation. They assume that he is upset by something in his life situation or in some significant relationship. They hope that by correcting whatever has gone awry they can restore Hamlet's mental equilibrium. They do not worry that his brain or his humors are affected or that he is bewitched or possessed by the devil. Why stress the obvious? Because it was in no way obvious to Shakespeare's contemporaries, nor is it obvious even to many present-day psychiatrists who believe that a depressed or insane person must have some biochemical disorder of the brain.

However, all the characters assume that Hamlet knows what is causing his distraction, not recognizing that if he knew, he might no longer be so afflicted. It is as if a psychiatrist were to ask a psychotic patient what was causing his insanity and expect a direct answer. Since Freud, we know that the crucial conflicts are usually unconscious and must be uncovered. Shakespeare has Hamlet properly tell Rosencrantz and Guildenstern "I have of late,—but wherefore I know not,—lost all my mirth" (II, ii, 288–289), and the ambiguity with which the playwright shrouds the mystery, presenting different potential causes and then partly confirming and negating each, in a sense reflects the unconscious nature of Hamlet's problems. Hamlet knows something of what is causing him to feel depressed and embittered, but not why he is so firmly in the grip of the inky blackness that possesses him. If we wish to learn the cause of his indisposition, we cannot ask Hamlet directly but must seek it in the play, for Shakespeare knew.

Let us then, as so many before us, start our search.

III

HAMLET AT THE START OF THE PLAY

THE PERVASIVE MOOD of the play and its hero is fore-shadowed in the opening exchange between the sentries, when Francisco tells us, " 'tis bitter cold, / And I am sick at heart" (I, i, 8). The first scene, a prologue, informs us that deeds of those now dead threaten the peace. The slaying of King Fortinbras by King Hamlet some thirty years earlier, even though in fair combat with terms "ratified by law and heraldry," will now involve the next generation. Elsinore and the audience prepare for an invasion, but the parapets are haunted and old Hamlet's reemergence from his grave conveys the danger from *internal* evil and corruption. We move from the first scene into an act in which the young characters of the play are instructed, constrained, and bound by the parental generation.

Hamlet in Deep Mourning

Let us consider Hamlet's emotional state when we first make his acquaintance. We learn from the king and queen that they

47

are perturbed because even though two months have elapsed since his father's death, Hamlet still has not cast off his "nighted colour" and remains in deep mourning. Hamlet takes offense when his mother asks why a father's death "seems so particular" with him. He tries to convey that his behavior is neither pretense nor even a true reflection of his emotional state:

> For they are actions that a man might play;
> But I have that within which passeth show;
>
> (I, ii, 84–85)

After commending his fidelity to his father's memory, Claudius chides him:

> but to persever
> In obstinate condolement is a course
> Of impious stubbornness; 'tis unmanly grief;
> It shows a will most incorrect to heaven,
> A heart unfortified, a mind impatient,
> An understanding simple and unschool'd;
>
> (I, ii, 92–97)

Hamlet, then, is in deep mourning. He has not yet encountered his father's ghost, and he has not yet assumed an "antic disposition," but his emotional distress seems excessive to his parents.

Mourning is a complicated psychological process. One aspect concerns the mourner's heightened identification with the deceased; in a sense, the mourner unconsciously attempts to keep the deceased alive by becoming like him, by incorporating the deceased into his own self. Insofar as the mourner fails to live up to the idealized model of the mourned person, he punishes himself by self-derogation. The mourner also unconsciously blames and punishes himself for any hatred that may have been mixed with his love for the deceased; and as most, if not all, children have sometimes had death wishes toward a parent, guilt over such wishes can become intense when the parent dies. Not only do sons commonly have such feelings toward their fathers during their oedipal periods, when they wish to retain their imagined primacy with their mothers, but adult sons also can have conscious or unconscious death wishes when waiting to inherit a father's possessions or position. When Shakespeare has Prince Hal tell his moribund father "I never thought to hear you speak again," he has Henry IV reply, "The wish was father, Harry to that thought" (*Henry IV, Part Two*, IV, v, 90–91). As the wish can be felt to be equivalent to the deed, the mourner can feel the need to repent as if he were his parent's murderer. The more ambivalent the feelings toward the lost person—that is, the more admixed the love and hostility—the more the mourner may suffer. Thus, the intensity of Hamlet's mourning would indicate the intensity of his death wishes toward his father as well as his adulation of him.

From Mourning to Melancholia

In his classic paper on the etiology of depressions, "Mourning and Melancholia," Freud was thinking of Hamlet's transformation when he explained how mourning turns into pathological depression. In "The Interpretation of Dreams," he suggested that Hamlet's procrastination in taking vengeance upon his uncle Claudius derives from just such unconscious influences, as I have noted in the Introduction. Because Hamlet had wished as a child to kill his father and marry his mother—an assumption based primarily on Freud's hypothesis that such oedipal wishes are universal but also on Hamlet's behavior with his mother in the "closet scene"—he cannot kill the man who has only done what he himself had wished to do. Hamlet identifies with Claudius and has to punish himself for his guilty wishes rather than take vengeance on his uncle. Herein, according to Freud, lies the basic cause of Hamlet's weariness with life and constant preoccupation with death, and why he can kill Claudius only when he himself is dying and has been punished. Nevertheless, important as such unconscious factors may have been, in viewing the play we soon learn that Hamlet is preoccupied with other hostile feelings and has other reasons for feeling guilty. It is always dangerous to assume that the causes of an emotional disturbance lie more in the past than the present.

HAMLET'S BITTERNESS TOWARD HIS MOTHER

As soon as the king and queen leave the stage with their retinue and Hamlet is alone with the audience, he tells us that he is not simply mourning for his father, and we realize that his mourning has turned into melancholia. He conveys the reason for his melancholy in as clear a statement of the cause of depression as can be found in the psychiatric literature. He starts his famous first soliloquy:

> O, that this too too solid flesh would melt,
> Thaw, and resolve itself into a dew!
> Or that the Everlasting had not fix'd
> His canon 'gainst self-slaughter!   (I, ii, 129–132)

And we hear why:

> That it should come to this!
> But two months dead! nay, not so much, not two;
> So excellent a king; that was, to this,
> Hyperion to a satyr; so loving to my mother,
> That he might not beteem the winds of heaven
> Visit her face too roughly. Heaven and earth!
> Must I remember? why, she would hang on him,
> As if increase of appetite had grown
> By what it fed on; and yet, within a month,—
> Let me not think on't,—Frailty, thy name is woman!—
> A little month! or ere those shoes were old
> With which she follow'd my poor father's body,
> Like Niobe, all tears;—why she, even she,—
> O God! a beast, that wants discourse of reason,
> Would have mourn'd longer,—married with my uncle,
> My father's brother, but no more like my father
> Than I to Hercules. Within a month?

Ere yet the salt of most unrighteous tears
Had left the flushing in her galled eyes,
She married. Oh, most wicked speed, to post
With such dexterity to incestuous sheets!
It is not, nor it cannot come to good;—
But break my heart, for I must hold my tongue!

(I, ii, 137–159)

It is, then, not primarily the loss of his father but the loss of his mother that possesses Hamlet. His mother, who had been the most important object of his love when he was a child, the person who doted on her only son, who "lives almost by his looks" (IV, vii, 12), has now turned faithless both to his father and to Hamlet, whose identification with the late king had just been heightened by the process of internalization. We must remember that after the closure of the oedipal period, a son can accept his father's priority with his mother but believes that he comes next in her affections. Now Hamlet has just returned from his studies at Wittenberg to attend his father's funeral, expecting to become his mother's major support and, probably, to assume the throne, but he finds he has deceived himself, his mother has hastened to marry his uncle. Disillusioned and enraged, to Hamlet the world has become:

an unweeded garden
That grows to seed; things rank and gross in nature
Possess it merely.   (I, ii, 135–137)

Further, he cannot express his hostility to his mother directly but must hold his tongue and suffer as his mounting aggression remains pent up. Nevertheless, he can unconsciously punish his mother by his suffering and, perhaps, by his suicide. In mourning for someone who is not dead but is lost as a love object, the punishment of the self for hostile feelings unconsciously serves a purpose in addition to assuaging guilt. The person who has deserted is pained by the depressed person's unhappiness and seeks to allay his pain by restoring the former relationship—as commonly occurs among lovers who have quarreled.

Madness in *Hamlet*

Suicidal gestures and attempts commonly have the purpose of forcing the loved one to show the person who made the attempt that he is still needed by rescuing him or by asking forgiveness for the neglect; in addition, such an attempt often serves as a threat of what will happen if the loved one does not change his ways. Thus, Hamlet suffers and is weary with the uses of the world because of his mother's behavior, and he wishes that the Almighty "had not fix'd / His canon 'gainst self-slaughter" (I, ii, 131–132). When Horatio appears and tells Hamlet he has come to Elsinore to attend his father's funeral, Hamlet can only reply bitterly, "do not mock me, fellow-student; / I think it was to see my mother's wedding" (I, ii, 177–178). He goes on to express how deeply the hasty wedding has wounded him:

> Would I had met my dearest foe in heaven[1]
> Or ever I had seen that day, Horatio!   (I, ii, 182–183)

Hamlet has now informed us why the intrapsychic work of mourning has not alleviated his dark mood. Self-punishment for his guilt over hostilities toward his dead father cannot touch his rage against his mother. Hamlet knows as well as Claudius that the death of fathers is a "common theme" of nature (I, ii, 103–104) and must be accepted, but his mother's hasty remarriage has dislodged his inner compass and brought disorientation and despair. His belief in his beloved mother, his estimation of his heroic father, and his own self-esteem are all shaken, and he must struggle to reorient his values.

Hamlet's life is changed, his standards overturned. His mother, who had been his ideal of a good wife and mother, is now a fallen idol: "she . . . even she" is lustridden and only "seeming-virtuous." Like every child, Hamlet had internalized something of his mother; now he feels sullied by her degrading behavior. He suffers the shame he feels for her, and he will feel debased unless he can force his mother to repent and change her ways. Further, insofar as Hamlet's ego identity rests upon his identification with his father and his pride in him, his mother's disloyalty to his father lessens his own self-esteem.

Hamlet at the Start of the Play

HAMLET'S IDENTIFICATION WITH HIS FATHER

As noted in the Introduction, Ernest Jones's classic psycho-analytic interpretation of the play stresses that Hamlet is unable to kill Claudius because Claudius has only done what Hamlet himself had fantasized as a child—killed his father and married his mother. However, when a boy comes to terms with his father's prerogatives with his mother—either out of castration fear, as Freud emphasized, or because he moved beyond the childish, egocentric conception of himself as the center of his mother's life—he usually identifies with his father and seeks to take on his characteristics. He seeks to retain his mother's love and, eventually, to gain the love of a woman like his mother by becoming a person like his father, the man his mother loves. A strong bond can develop between father and son because they are united by a common love for the boy's mother; the rivalry is minimized when both accept the different relationships to the mother permitted to each and denied the other because of the generational difference.

The boy's identification with his father is critical to his normal development. Paradoxically, he gains strength from his inability to displace his father with his mother, and much of his self-esteem, as well as his security in his masculine identity, derives from his pride in his father—if his mother admires his father. When a son gives up the fantasy of possessing his mother, he renounces in favor of his father. The play is replete with evidence that Hamlet sought to identify with his father and admired him greatly. Indeed, his praise of his father is so great that we might suspect that he, like the Player Queen, "protests too much," and that his praise hides residues of his early childhood jealousy. Though Hamlet could accept his father's priority with his mother, he resents the intrusion of still another into her bed, and between him and the primacy of her affection. His identification with his father is now heightened not only because of his internalization of his deceased father but also because they have both been ousted by Gertrude in favor of Claudius. Hamlet feels betrayed as his father's representative as well as in his own right. There is little difference between Gertrude's infidelity to Hamlet the father and Hamlet the son.

53

One way of managing the jealousy and hostility toward the father that remains as an unconscious, repressed residue of oedipal feelings is to split the father in two: into a bad preoedipal father, who was a rival, and a good postoedipal father, who is idealized and with whom the boy identifies.[2] Various psychoanalysts have noted that in *Hamlet* the father figure is split into an idealized King Hamlet, whom Hamlet can love, and a bad Claudius, whom Hamlet can hate and find disgusting because of his sexuality. There is also a Polonius father figure, who distrusts children and spies upon them and who also inserts himself between Hamlet and a woman he loves.

As the play progresses it becomes clear that Hamlet is troubled by the new evidence of his mother's sensuality. He tries to convince himself that she did not marry for love or sexual desire (as her prototype claimed in the Amleth saga).[3] After his father's death, a son may be troubled by a recrudescence of erotized feelings for his mother and may need the security of believing that she has no sexual needs or desires. Furthermore, as several psychoanalytically oriented critics have suggested, Hamlet may have had difficulty in disposing of the father figure he needs as a barrier between his mother and his recrudescent oedipal fantasies.

This, then, is Lord Hamlet at the opening of the play, depressed and embittered, with his self-esteem and emotional balance shaken by his mother's hasty marriage to his uncle. Before the day is over, two events will occur that will greatly exacerbate his precarious state.

Hamlet Suffers Two Serious Traumas

While Hamlet and the audience await the night and the return of his father's ghost to tell of the foul deeds that will not remain buried, the play's countertheme is set in motion as the triangular relationships between Hamlet, Ophelia, and Laertes and then between Hamlet, Ophelia, and Polonius are introduced.

POLONIUS ORDERS OPHELIA TO AVOID HAMLET

Laertes, about to leave for France, chides Ophelia for being responsive to Hamlet's wooing. The dialogue is lighthearted, and the audience may well believe that Shakespeare is simply informing us that Hamlet and Ophelia are in love. Laertes warns his sister not to take Hamlet's advances seriously, but simply as "a toy in blood, / A violet in the youth of primy nature, / Forward, not permanent, sweet, not lasting (I, iii, 6–8). For even if Hamlet really loves her, "his will is not his own; / . . . for on his choice depends / The safety and health of this whole state" (I, iii, 17, 20–21). His advice is given gently, even though he seems unduly concerned that Hamlet may entice his sister, her "chaste treasure open / To his unmaster'd importunity" (I, iii, 31–32). Polonius enters, picks up the drift of his son's remarks, and then, like Claudius in the preceding scene, he expresses some unflattering views of Hamlet's character. Even when Ophelia assures her father that Hamlet "hath importuned me with love / In honourable fashion / . . . And hath given countenance to his speech. / . . . With almost all the holy vows of heaven" (I, iii, 110–111, 113–114), Polonius considers such professions as "springes to catch woodcocks" (I, iii, 115) and tells his daughter not to believe Hamlet's vows, which are "mere implorators of unholy suits, / Breathing like sanctified and pious bawds, / The better to beguile" (I, iii, 129–131). Finally, Polonius directs his daughter:

> I would not, in plain terms, from this time forth,
> Have you so slander any moment's leisure,
> As to give words or talk with the Lord Hamlet.
>
> (I, iii, 132–134)

His young and devoted daughter assures her father that she will obey. Before long Hamlet, finding himself rejected by the only person he still loves, will become further embittered toward women and their infidelities.

THE GHOST'S REVELATIONS

More important, that night the second and more serious blow occurs. Hamlet's father returns from purgatory to the parapets of Elsinore to inform Hamlet that Claudius had murdered him. He is not telling Hamlet anything that Hamlet has not more or less consciously suspected. "O my prophetic soul! / My uncle?" (I, v, 40–41), Hamlet exclaims. But then the ghost goes on to inform his son that Claudius, "that incestuous, that adulterate beast" (I, v, 42), had "won to his shameful lust / The will of my most seeming-virtuous queen." (I, v, 45–46). The ghost then imparts to his young son some wisdom he gained only after his death.

> But virtue, as it never will be moved,
> Though lewdness court it in a shape of heaven,
> So lust, though to a radiant angel link'd,
> Will sate itself in a celestial bed,
> And prey on garbage. (I, v, 53–57)

Now Hamlet's world falls apart. The ghost does not use such language to complain that his wife was unfaithful because she remarried. He is saying, or (as will become apparent in the closet scene) Hamlet understands him to be saying, that his wife was unfaithful while he lived. Not only has Claudius murdered Hamlet's father and married the queen, thus robbing him of a father, the crown, and his mother; but far more searing to Hamlet, his mother who had been for him the epitome of virtue and who had seemed to worship his father is an adulteress and perhaps a murderess.[4] This is not, like his mother's remarriage, a grievance that can dissipate with the passage of time or be assuaged by replacing his mother with Ophelia. Nor is it, like his father's murder, an infamy that can be avenged by killing Claudius. He will now mourn for his mother, for as a mother she has died, and he is enraged by her behavior.

If no others saw the ghost and if Claudius did not later speak of the murder in soliloquy, we might consider the ghost and his message to be merely Hamlet's hallucination, for the ghost only expresses what Hamlet seems already to have been feeling about his mother and his uncle. Indeed, even though Hamlet assures his companions that what they have seen was "an honest ghost," he later has his doubts. He therefore contrives the play-within-the-play to gain assurance that his uncle is a murderer because

Hamlet at the Start of the Play

> The spirit that I have seen
> May be the devil; and the devil hath power
> To assume a pleasing shape; yea, and perhaps
> Out of my weakness and my melancholy,
> As he is very potent with such spirits,
> Abuses me to damn me.   (II, ii, 574–579)

Hamlet is now torn by two opposing motives. He can vent his pent-up fury and commit matricide. He will now live under the shadow of matricidal impulses as enraged as Electra. He thus becomes more proximate to Orestes than to Oedipus—and the Furies who pursue matricides are flapping their wings about his head. Or—is it possible, is it worth attempting? He can lead his mother to renounce her husband and her sexuality and again become a mother to him. He might at least force her to save her soul by repentance and by renouncing her carnality rid herself of the rank smell of sexuality that so befouls the air for Hamlet.

While Hamlet is still shaken and enraged by the revelations, the ghost then goes on to demand of his son that if he loved his father and be not duller than the "fat weed / That roots itself in ease on Lethe wharf" (I, v, 32–33), he must swear to right matters and not let "the royal bed of Denmark be / A couch for luxury and damned incest" (I, v, 82–83).

However, Hamlet's diaphanous but still puissant father goes on to add a rider to his command. It is a critical limitation that both saves and shatters Hamlet:

> But, howsoever thou pursuest this act,
> Taint not thy mind, nor let thy soul contrive
> Against thy mother aught; leave her to heaven,
> And to those thorns that in her bosom lodge,
> To prick and sting her.[5]   (I, v, 84–88)

These commandments will save Hamlet from the fate of Orestes, but they will place him in a "bind" that endangers his sanity. Hamlet will, with difficulty, keep from plunging his murdering sword into her who gave him birth. He does not, like Orestes, have an Electra to push him into the dreadful deed.[6] But Hamlet cannot subdue his emotions and repress his thoughts in order to obey the command to "taint not thy mind." At the very least, he must reactivate his mother's jaded conscience; he must find a way to save her soul and, perhaps even more important, he must express the disillusionment and vent the rage that is driving him to desperate and self-destructive deeds. In *Hamlet* we do not follow the consequences of matricide but the plight of a man embittered and possessed by a matricidal fury who is kept from committing the act by his father's spirit —or by his own superego, which developed in the image of a father so loving to Hamlet's mother "that he might not beteem the winds of heaven / Visit her face too roughly" (I, ii, 141–142). Nevertheless, although he swears to the ghost that he will remember him and wipe from his brain everything except his commandments, he follows the pledge with "O most pernicious woman!" (I, v, 105). To him his mother's behavior takes precedence over that of the "smiling, damned villain" he has sworn to kill.

The Problem of the "Antic Disposition"

Now Hamlet decides "to put an antic disposition on" (I, v, 172). Why he does so poses something of a problem. The antic disposition derives from the Amleth and Brutus legends, in which the hero's mental incompetence served as a shield; but in *Hamlet*, rather than provide an advantage, it alarms Claudius, causes him to suspect Hamlet's motives, and leads him to try to get rid of Hamlet. Of course, the antic disposition is an excellent theatrical device. It allows the members of the audience to feel that they are "insiders" on a secret hidden from most of the characters; it keeps them puzzled as Hamlet's behavior shifts; and it is the source of considerable humor. However, we must remember that the antic disposition is not the result of a carefully contrived plan but an instantaneous decision. Hamlet will make a series of such sudden, if not impetuous, decisions, moved by emotion or hunch rather than forethought. He is in a predicament that cannot be solved by cogitation or philosophic consideration. I would lean toward the theory, presented in the Introduction, that Hamlet says that he may pretend to be mad because he feels that he must struggle to retain a modicum of self-control. He is now burdened to the breaking point.[7]

Something is rotten in Denmark, for the king and queen, the dual heads of its body politic, are stewing in the corruption of regicide, fratricide, and perhaps uxoricide, and their sensual passions have displaced reason. The life of philosophy that Hamlet and Horatio have pursued in Wittenberg is far removed from this real world of deceit, passion, and ruthless ambition, and they must awaken from their philosophic dreams. This is not the world Hamlet was raised to live in, nor are the ghost's commands the tasks he expected to carry out in life. He is not being called upon by his father and former king to lead the nation's defense against young Fortinbras, who seeks to retake the lands Hamlet's father had won from Norway in honest combat. Hamlet is not being given the task of becoming a wise and responsive king, nor even the straightforward duty of avenging his father by killing Claudius. His public duty is to save the nation from its inner corruption, and his mother is at the center of that corruption; his personal task is to find meaning, direction, and a stable identity after the foundations of his trust in the world and those who people it have been shattered. The Hamlet who left Wittenberg two months before the play starts, the Hamlet he might have become, can no longer be.

The confusion and dismay that beset Hamlet after he hears the ghost's story and commands are conveyed by the rapid and disordered action at the end of the scene and by Hamlet's "wild and whirling words" (I, v, 133), including his macabre jests about the ghost in the cellerage. He is confronted by a perplexing assignment, and can properly feel

> The time is out of joint;—O cursed spite,
> That ever I was born to set it right!　　(I, v, 189–190)

IV

HAMLET'S
PRECARIOUS
EMOTIONAL BALANCE

THE MEMBERS of the parental generation, having given their advice and orders to Hamlet, Laertes, Ophelia, and Fortinbras, start spying on them in the second act. Two months have elapsed since Hamlet swore to avenge his father; but he has not yet moved "with wings as swift / As meditation or the thoughts of love" (I, v, 29–30). Claudius is still alive, and Hamlet's emotional balance has become precarious during the interlude. We may or may not be aware of his instability, depending on how the role is acted.[1] Indeed, we must rely upon reports from those who are closest to him to learn of the worsening of his condition. In the very first scene of the second act, Ophelia rushes to tell her father that she has just been frightened while sewing in her closet by the

> Lord Hamlet, with his doublet all unbraced;
> No hat upon his head; his stockings foul'd,
> Ungarter'd, and down-gyved to his ancle;
> Pale as his shirt; his knees knocking each other;
> And with a look so piteous in purport

As if he had been loosed out of hell
To speak of horrors,   (II, i, 78–83)

and she goes on to describe behavior strange enough to lead
Polonius to believe:

This is the very ecstasy of love;
Whose violent property fordoes itself
And leads the will to desperate undertakings,
As oft as any passion under heaven
That does afflict our natures.   (II, i, 102–106)

Even though we know that Hamlet has planned to feign insanity, it seems strange that he does so by entering Ophelia's
rooms in so disheveled a condition, or that he would befoul his
stockings to carry out the pretense. Perhaps he seeks to hide the
meaning of his embittered and melancholic behavior under the
guise of being depressed over Ophelia's withdrawal of her affection, but it seems a cruel and deceitful way to treat his beloved.
The obedient Ophelia has followed her father's injunctions and
repelled Hamlet's letters and denied him access to her. Just at
this critical juncture in Hamlet's life, she has let her father come
between Hamlet and herself. Polonius is certain that these
rebuffs have driven Hamlet mad, and he now hopes that a reconciliation between his daughter and the heir apparent may reclaim Hamlet's wits. His hopes are fortified when he reads the
note that Hamlet has sent Ophelia, a confused expression of
Hamlet's suffering and his undying love:

*O dear Ophelia, I am ill at these numbers. I have not
art to reckon my groans; but that I love thee best, O most
best, believe it. Adieu.*
        *Thine evermore, most dear lady, whilst this
        machine is to him, HAMLET*
                                            (II, ii, 119–123)

The message can be taken either as part of an exaggerated sub-
terfuge or as a threat to commit suicide unless Ophelia relents.
Meanwhile, Gertrude and Claudius have become sufficiently

concerned about Hamlet's condition to summon Rosencrantz and Guildenstern to court to distract their son and to find out what is troubling him. The king does not ask them to spy on their friend; rather, he requests them to "glean" whether anything "unknown afflicts him thus, / That, open'd, lies within our remedy" (II, ii, 17–18). Claudius, in greeting Rosencrantz and Guildenstern, tells them of Hamlet's melancholic state, terming it a "transformation," "Sith nor the exterior nor the inward man / Resembles that it was" (II, ii, 6–7).

When Polonius informs the king and queen that he has found the cause of Hamlet's indisposition, it is clear that all three are fully convinced that he is mad. Neither Claudius nor Gertrude takes exception to Polonius' direct statement, "Your noble son is mad" (II, ii, 92), though they are skeptical that it is because Ophelia has refused to see him that he fell into a sadness and finally into "the madness wherein now he raves" (II, ii, 149). Then, when Hamlet appears, Polonius "boards" him, and Hamlet seems neither mad nor even seriously melancholic. He uses the license afforded by his supposed madness to bait Polonius, to display his wit in playing with words and phrases. We have a brief "comic relief"—a relief, literally, because our hero's mind seems very sharp indeed.

Shakespeare has here turned the more customary situation around: the audience is not laughing at the madman; instead, the madman is making his sane interrogator laughable. The trend is feebly apparent in the Saxo and Belleforest versions of the saga in which Amleth, the butt of the courtiers' tricks repeatedly turns the tables on them. Hamlet, however, is more clearly related to the "trickster" of various myths and to the jester, the fool who makes others look foolish.

Hamlet seems to realize that Polonius has prevented Ophelia from seeing him. He advises Polonius that "if the sun breed maggots in a dead dog" (II, ii, 180), he should keep his daughter out of the sun lest she conceive. Polonius thinks Hamlet is "far gone" but considers "How pregnant sometimes his replies are! a happiness that often madness hits on, which reason and sanity could not so prosperously be delivered of" (II, ii, 206–209). The audience now knows that Hamlet's intellect is as keen as ever;

but then comes the parting exchange in which Shakespeare lets us know that despite his wit and his intact wits, Hamlet is in a precarious state. When Polonius bids him farewell, "My honourable lord, I will most humbly take leave of you" (II, ii, 210–211), Hamlet replies, "You cannot, sir, take from me any thing that I will more willingly part withal; except my life, except my life, except my life" (II, ii, 212–214).

When Hamlet first meets Rosencrantz and Guildenstern, he confirms his unwholesome state of mind. They admit that they are in the court because the king and queen have sent for them, and Hamlet does not need to ask why. He relieves them from betraying a secret by telling them it is because he has of late:

> . . . but wherefore I know not,—lost all my mirth, forgone all custom of exercises; and indeed it goes so heavily with my disposition that this goodly frame, the earth, seems to me a sterile promontory; this most excellent canopy, the air, . . . appears no other thing to me than a foul and pestilent congregation of vapours. What a piece of work is man! how noble in reason! how infinite in faculty! in form and moving, how express and admirable! in action, how like an angel! in apprehension, how like a god! the beauty of the world! the paragon of animals! And yet, to me, what is this quintessence of dust? man delights not me;   (II, ii, 288–300).

A little later, however, he confides to them that his uncle-father and his aunt-mother are deceived, for "I am but mad north-north-west; when the wind is southerly, I know a hawk from a handsaw" (II, ii, 360–361). He is aware that he is being affected by the deceit and hostility of those around him. Shakespeare properly has Hamlet's mood and behavior fluctuate with the feelings aroused in him by those persons who are most significant to him.

Madness in *Hamlet*

The Incitement to Action

Hamlet, then, has been suffering. He has become a tormented soul struggling to survive in a world that has lost its meaning for him, and he scarcely cares if he survives or not. After two months, he has still to carry out his father's bidding. He has difficulty in keeping his mind from being tainted and contriving against his mother; killing his stepfather seems a secondary matter to him. Then, the traveling players—old friends of Hamlet's—arrive at Elsinore. Hamlet bids the First Player give them a foretaste of his artistry with a speech from a play Hamlet admired for its honesty and modesty, even though it "pleased not the million; 'twas caviare to the general" (II, ii, 416). In the speech, Aeneas tells Dido of Priam's slaughter: of how Pyrrhus avenged his father, Achilles; and of how a faithful queen, Hecuba, mourned her husband.[2] While listening to the Player agonize about Priam and Hecuba, Hamlet is stimulated to move out of the inertia of his melancholy, his indecision, and his feelings that nothing matters to him. His misanthropic mood is apparent. When Polonius tells him that he will use the players "according to their desert," Hamlet chides him, "Use every man after his desert, and who should 'scape whipping?" (II, ii, 505–506). This remark led Freud in "Mourning and Melancholia" to write, "For there can be no doubt that if anyone holds and expresses to others an opinion of himself such as this (an opinion which Hamlet held both of himself and everyone else) he is ill, whether he is speaking the truth or whether he is being more or less unfair to himself."[3] Thus, we have Freud's opinion of Hamlet's mental state at the close of Act II.

As soon as Hamlet is alone, he tells himself:

> Oh what a rogue and peasant slave am I!
> Is it not monstrous that this player here,
> But in a fiction, in a dream of passion,
> Could force his soul so to his own conceit
> That from her working all his visage wann'd;
> Tears in his eyes, distraction in's aspect,
> A broken voice, and his whole function suiting

With forms to his conceit? And all for nothing!
For Hecuba?
What's Hecuba to him, or he to Hecuba,
That he should weep for her? What would he do,
Had he the motive and the cue for passion
That I have?   (II, ii, 523–535)

He berates himself for being a "dull and muddy-mettled ras-
cal," who is a "John-a-dreams, unpregnant of my cause" (II, ii,
541–542) and who, though

Prompted to my revenge by heaven and hell,
Must, like a whore, unpack my heart with words,
And fall a-cursing, like a very drab.   (II, ii, 560–562)

While the First Player speaks, however, Hamlet conceives a
way out of his uncertainty, a way to make certain that he has
not, because of his melancholy, simply hallucinated the ghost's
revelations or been tricked by an evil spirit. He has formulated
his stratagem for gaining proof of Claudius' guilt: "The play's
the thing / Wherein I'll catch the conscience of the king" (II, ii,
580–581).

Although Hamlet is now ready to test Claudius and take
measures to clear the corruption from the court, he remains
uncertain whether it is worth taking "arms against a sea of
troubles, / And by opposing end them?" (III, i, 59–60). One alternative is to retain his philosophic perspective and "suffer /
The slings and arrows of outrageous fortune" (III, i, 57–58).
Another is suicide.

To die,—to sleep,—
No more; and by a sleep to say we end
The heart-ache, and the thousand natural shocks
That flesh is heir to,—'tis a consummation
Devoutly to be wish'd.   (III, i, 60–64)

He ponders that uniquely human problem, the existential
dilemma of "to be, or not to be." He is not so obsessed with his
father's murder that he must hasten to revenge. He would pre-

fer to turn his back on the whole sorry mess. What does life hold for him? He can kill his uncle. If fortunate, he will assume the throne. But his mother's obliquity will remain with him. Why should he not be much possessed by death? Hamlet, as others who choose the negative answer when they weigh the worth of life and death, finds the balance weighted by his disillusionment with the person whose love was central to his well-being.

Hamlet is aware that he must leave off considering all sides of a question if he is to act heroically. He is considering more than his reasons for not ending his life when he tells himself:

> Thus conscience[4] does make cowards of us all,
> And thus the native hue of resolution
> Is sicklied o'er with the pale cast of thought,
> And enterprises of great pith and moment
> With this regard their currents turn awry
> And lose the name of action.   (III, i, 83–88)

He is not the type of Renaissance hero whose life can readily be guided by the need for vengeance or power. He has been schooled in contemplation. If he is to act, as he has sworn to the ghost he will, he must become impetuous. Later he will even praise rashness: "Our indiscretion sometimes serves us well / When our deep plots do fail" (V, ii, 8–9).

V

CONFRONTATIONS

As ACT III develops, the atmosphere of spying and uncertainty gives way to a series of confrontations—of Hamlet by
Ophelia, Claudius by Hamlet, Hamlet by Gertrude, and Gertrude by Hamlet—that move the play to its climax.

The Confrontation by Ophelia

Shortly after he describes death, with its release from life's
burdens, as "a consummation / Devoutly to be wish'd" (III, i,
63–64), Hamlet is confronted by Ophelia while Claudius and
Polonius hide behind the arras as "lawful espials." Despite Hamlet's continuing love for her, indicated by the way he ends his
musings as he sees her approach: "The fair Ophelia?—Nymph,
in thy orisons / Be all my sins remember'd" (III, i, 89–90), he is
soon carried away into a tirade against Ophelia, against all
women, against himself, and against all mankind. Both Ophelia
and Hamlet seem to feel that the other has withdrawn from their
relationship. Ophelia, of course, knows that she has repelled
Hamlet, but here she accuses him, intimating that he has abandoned her. She seeks to return his gifts because "Rich gifts wax
poor when givers prove unkind" (III, i, 101). Despite such unfair

blame, Hamlet is being given the opportunity to reclaim his love. He could become engaged in a lovers' quarrel that ends in reconciliation, but because of his aversion to pretense, his anger that Ophelia has obeyed her father rather than adhere to him, his suspicion that they are being observed, but most of all, because of his disillusionment in his mother that has led him to distrust all women, he attacks her rudely and bitterly.

He no longer can admire Ophelia's beauty, for the time gives proof that "the power of beauty will sooner transform honesty from what it is to a bawd than the force of honesty can translate beauty into his likeness" (III, i, 111–113). Hamlet has learned what his father had learned only after his death, that:

> virtue, as it never will be moved,
> Though lewdness court it in a shape of heaven,
> So lust, though to a radiant angel link'd,
> Will sate itself in a celestial bed,
> And prey on garbage. (I, v, 53–57)

He mocks Ophelia for believing he loved her, but in so doing he is really denouncing his mother's and his uncle's deceitfulness. He sees no sense in preserving his family line or mankind, for "why wouldst thou be a breeder of sinners? I am myself indifferent honest; but yet I could accuse me of such things that it were better my mother had not borne me" (III, i, 121–124). He grows more vituperative and pronounces his misogynistic curse: "If thou dost marry, I'll give thee this plague for thy dowry: be thou as chaste as ice, as pure as snow, thou shalt not escape calumny. Get thee to a nunnery, go" (III, i, 135–137). He ends his tirade with, "I say, we will have no more marriages; those that are married already, all but one, shall live; the rest shall keep as they are" (III, i, 147–149).

Ophelia is overwhelmed by his invective and his rejection of her, but she takes his rantings as a symptom of his madness and laments for his noble mind, now o'erthrown, and for his "most sovereign reason, / Like sweet bells jangled out of tune, and harsh" (III, i, 157–158).

Ophelia may seem to have overemphasized the extent of Hamlet's irrationality, but it is just such misanthropic tirades that led Freud to conclude that Hamlet was mentally ill. Claudius and Polonius, however, do not find what Hamlet said either mad or indicative of a frustrated love for Ophelia. Claudius has heard Hamlet's bitterness and his statement that all marriages "but one, shall live." He recognizes the danger and determines to get rid of Hamlet by sending him to England as quickly as possible, for "Madness in great ones must not unwatch'd go." (III, i, 189).

Although disappointed in the outcome of the confrontation, Polonius still shrewdly continues to believe that "The origin and commencement of his grief / Sprung from neglected love" (III, i, 177–178). But it is the loss not of Ophelia's love but of Gertrude's love, or, more properly, his loss of the mother he once loved but must now renounce as faithless.

Confronting the King

As Hamlet awaits the start of the play-within-the-play, his mood has changed. He talks almost too freely, clearly stimulated by having finally moved into action and by the prospect that his doctored version of *The Murder of Gonzago* will trap his uncle. Now he can tell Horatio of his admiration and affection for him:

> Give me that man
> That is not passion's slave, and I will wear him
> In my heart's core, ay, in my heart of heart,
> As I do thee.   (III, ii, 66–69)

He praises Horatio's equanimity and judgment so warmly that he checks himself, saying, "Something too much of this" (III, ii, 69). Soon his remarks become rash. When Claudius greets him, "How fares our cousin Hamlet?" he responds with a play on words: "Excellent, i' faith; of the chameleon's dish; I eat the air, promise-crammed; you cannot feed capons so" (III, ii, 88–89). His witty remark covertly indicates his feeling that Claudius has castrated him and kept him "heir" to the throne. It is a brash insult and threat that allows Hamlet to vent his anger but puts Claudius on his guard.

The bawdy banter with Ophelia before and during the play is difficult to assess. The repartee may not have been inappropriate for an Elizabethan courtier, though Victorian critics were shocked by the *double entendres*. Ophelia, raised at court, is not naïve or unworldly. Still, it is likely that he is now degrading Ophelia, treating her like a "nun"—a whore. He seeks to provoke his mother's jealousy by refusing to sit by her, finding Ophelia "metal more attractive." All in all, Hamlet seems hypomanic, slightly out of control of himself, inappropriately elated and loose in his talk. Still, as is the case with manic or hypomanic individuals, the melancholy lurks just beneath the surface. "What should a man do but be merry?" he asks Ophelia, "for, look you, how cheerfully my mother looks, and my father died within's two hours" (III, ii, 118–119).

PROVOKING GERTRUDE'S CONSCIENCE

Although Hamlet says the play is intended to catch the conscience of the king—to function as a mousetrap that catches the prey with a trope—and succeeds all too well, for it also tips Hamlet's hand, we can readily discern that Hamlet is equally interested in provoking his mother's guilt feelings.

When the Player King, who believes he will soon die, tells his Queen[1] that he hopes she will find another husband as kind as he has been, the Player Queen impatiently cuts him off:

> Oh, confound the rest!
> Such love must needs be treason in my breast;
> In second husband let me be accurst!
> None wed the second but who kill'd the first.
>
> (III, ii, 167–170)

To this, Hamlet, like a one-man chorus, croaks, "Wormwood, wormwood!" And again, the Player Queen says:

A second time I kill my husband dead,
When second husband kisses me in bed.

(III, ii, 174–175)

And still again:

Both here and hence pursue me lasting strife,
If, once a widow, ever I be wife!   (III, ii, 212–213)

This leads Hamlet to comment, "If she should break it now!" and Gertrude to venture, "The lady protests too much, methinks" (III, ii, 220). Her remark permits Hamlet, in turn, to twist the blade by countering, "O, but she'll keep her word" (III, ii, 221).

THE CHANGE IN HAMLET'S MOOD

Upon seeing his murder of Hamlet's father reenacted, the king rises to the bait; and "frighted with false fire" (III, ii, 254), he stops the play and rushes from the room. Hamlet is elated with his success and gloats to Horatio, as well he may. However, his remarks are loose and even hypomanic. The poor quality of his several rhymes suggests that Shakespeare had intended to portray hypomanic behavior,[2] even though he does not let Hamlet complete a cheap rhyme by calling his uncle an ass (III, ii, 272). Hamlet has convinced himself—and Horatio—of his uncle's guilt, but to the court his behavior can only seem mad, replete with insults to the king and queen.

When Rosencrantz and Guildenstern appear, informing Hamlet that he has angered the king and summoning him to his mother's closet, Hamlet parries their efforts to talk sensibly with him with a brilliant series of wordplays that are too bitter and upsetting to be humorous. As his friends tell him, his remarks are uncontrolled, indeed, they verge on the "flight of ideas" typical of manic behavior. After receiving a rapid flow of insults from the prince, Rosencrantz begs Hamlet to confide the cause of his distemper to them, pointedly warning him, "you do surely bar the door upon your own liberty, if you deny your griefs to your friend" (III, ii, 322–323). The advice leads to an episode that offers us a warning against making simple interpretations of Hamlet's character and behavior. Hamlet presses Guildenstern to play the recorder. When Guildenstern protests that he does not know how, Hamlet insists, " 'Tis as easy as lying" (III, ii, 341) and goes on to tell him,

> Why, look you now, how unworthy a thing you make of me! You would play upon me; you would seem to know my stops; you would pluck out the heart of my mystery, . . . 'Sblood, do you think I am easier to be played on than a pipe? Call me what instrument you will, though you can fret me, you cannot play upon me.—(III, ii, 347–355).

Hamlet is unreasonable in his attack upon Rosencrantz and Guildenstern. They were brought to the court to help him, distract him, and look after him in his madness. They have no reason to believe that they are supposed to choose sides in a mortal struggle. Now they have implored Hamlet to confide in them, but he accuses them of lying and heaps insults upon them.

Polonius interrupts Hamlet's admonishment of his friends with a more peremptory summons from his mother. Hamlet tries to bait him, but Polonius will not rise to it and simply agrees that a cloud looks like a camel, a weasel, a whale, or anything Hamlet wishes to have it resemble. Although Hamlet comments to himself, "They fool me to the top of my bent" (III, ii, 367), Polonius is simply mollifying a madman.

The tide has shifted. The act opened with Hamlet's confrontation by Ophelia, while Claudius and Polonius spied upon them. Then Hamlet used the players to confront Claudius with his crime and Gertrude with her infidelity to his father's memory, while Horatio and he spied upon or, at least, observed their reactions to the play. Now he is being summoned by his mother, who intends to confront him with his outrageous and insulting behavior, but instead, he will confront her with her misbehavior. The child takes the initiative from his parents assuming the role of moral guardian. In the process, Hamlet loosens, as he must, the superego restraints he had taken on through identifying with his parents, and in the process lacks self-control.

THE SOUL OF NERO

Hamlet starts off to see his mother in a state of high excitement:

> now could I drink hot blood.
> And do such bitter business as the day
> Would quake to look on. (III, ii, 373–375)

He is not talking of murdering Claudius, and when he says:

> Soft! now to my mother.
> O heart, lose not thy nature; let not ever
> The soul of Nero enter this firm bosom;
> Let me be cruel, not unnatural;
> I will speak daggers to her, but use none;
> My tongue and soul in this be hypocrites;
>
> (III, ii, 375–380)

He is trying to calm the violence raging within him. It is here, just before the climactic turn of the play, that Hamlet compares himself with Nero, the matricide who had an incestuous passion for his mother.[3] The reference cannot be considered casual. Nero must have been very much in Shakespeare's mind when he wrote the play, for he changed the name of Hamlet's stepfather, which was Feng in the sagas, to Claudius. The Emperor Claudius was Nero's stepfather and great-uncle who "incestuously" married his niece.

CLAUDIUS AT PRAYER

En route to his mother's chamber, Hamlet passes Claudius at prayer and decides not to kill him. His failure to seize the opportunity when Claudius is defenseless is taken by many as the climax of the play. Hamlet's delay, even after he has become convinced of his uncle's guilt, will permit Claudius—who now knows Hamlet's feelings—to send him into exile. A great deal of nonsense has been written about this episode. Some critics have even expressed the idea that Shakespeare could not end the play at this juncture because he had written only three of the necessary five acts, forgetting that as Shakespeare wrote the play, he would not have composed the scene if he did not have a reason for so doing. Shakespeare specifically shows by this incident that Hamlet was not kept from gaining vengeance through lack of opportunity. Orestes slew his stepfather Aegisthus at the altar while he was offering a sacrifice, much as Paris killed Achilles; and Laertes will tell Claudius that to gain vengeance on Hamlet he is ready "To cut his throat i' the church" (IV, vii, 127).

The scene might well be considered the moral climax of the play, even though it is not the play's dramatic climax. When Hamlet spares Claudius he does not save his own soul but loses it. He is not performing an act of mercy but one of self-damnation. In the bitterness of his soul, in his rage at his uncle, Hamlet lacks humanity. He sees an opportunity to avenge his father, but he tells himself:

> And now I'll do't; and so he goes to heaven;
> And so am I revenged. That would be scann'd:
> A villain kills my father; and for that,
> I, his sole son, do this same villain send
> To heaven.
> Oh, this is hire and salary, not revenge.
> He took my father grossly, full of bread,
> With all his crimes broad blown, as flush as May;
> > (III, iii, 74–81)

Hamlet's father's ghost had complained that he had been:

> Cut off even in the blossoms of my sin,
> Unhousel'd, disappointed, unaneled;
> No reckoning made, but sent to my account
> With all my imperfections on my head;
> Oh, horrible! oh, horrible! most horrible!
> > (I, v, 76–80)

The underhanded manner in which Claudius killed King Hamlet is contrasted with the way King Hamlet had slain "the ambitious Norway" (I, i, 61) in honorable combat. Similarly, the Greek tragedies emphasized the mutilation of Agamemnon's corpse to lay his ghost, as I shall note in Chapter XI. Hamlet decides to await a more appropriate time to take his vengeance, even if it is more dangerous.

> Up, sword, and know thou a more horrid hent;
> When he is drunk asleep, or in his rage,
> Or in the incestuous pleasure of his bed;
> At gaming, swearing; or about some act
> That has no relish of salvation in't;
> Then trip him, that his heels may kick at heaven
> And that his soul may be as damn'd and black
> As hell, whereto it goes.   (III, iii, 88–95)

While Hamlet is carried away by his black thoughts, his enemy, in praying, almost achieves repentance and a chance for eventual salvation. He admits his guilt:

> Oh, my offence is rank, it smells to heaven;
> It hath the primal eldest curse upon't,
> A brother's murder!   (III, iii, 36–38)

For a moment he is contrite and might be saved. But the hope for salvation is an illusion, for he is a "limed soul, that struggling to be free / Art more engaged" (III, iii, 68–69); and soon the net of his evildoing will envelop him once again. His villainous deeds, like Macbeth's, engender further villainies. Yet his very inability to pray holds some potential for his redemption. He has enough moral insight to wonder:

>   what form of prayer
> Can serve my turn? "Forgive me my foul murder?"
> That cannot be, since I am still possess'd
> Of those effects for which I did the murder,
> My crown, mine own ambition and my queen.
> May one be pardon'd and retain the offence?
>   (III, iii, 51–56)

Although he has broken one of the oldest and most fundamental taboos—coveting his brother's wife and killing his brother to possess her—he is, nevertheless—as G. Wilson Knight insisted —human, perhaps sinning because of an all too human weakness. Since he cannot give up his wife and throne, he has no way to "save" himself except by compounding his crime. His evil act has corrupted him, the queen, and the state, and it will corrupt Laertes even as it has been destroying Hamlet. Soon, in seeking to save his life, Claudius will resort to other infamous deeds and lose his life, his wife, and his soul.

While Claudius' fate is sealed by his inability to make the renunciation that might permit him to pray, Hamlet's principles and probity reach their nadir. In the grip of his hatred for the man who murdered his father and who has stolen his mother, he seeks the everlasting damnation of his foe. Passion threatens to overwhelm his humanity, and he must struggle to contain his matricidal impulsions. He has become incapable of love: he has turned against Ophelia and he will soon vent his hostility toward his mother. He is caught up in passions that are gaining control over his thoughts, feelings, and behavior. He has become, to use Knight's term, "an embassy of death" and will leave a swath of death in his trail. He traverses the lip of the Pit, but he will seek his mother's redemption and, in so doing, escape perdition.

Hamlet Confronts Gertrude

The time has come when Hamlet must vent his feelings about his mother, which have been growing more violent and now threaten to destroy his life or his sanity. Desperate and enraged, Hamlet enters his mother's closet, frightening her severely. It is difficult to imagine how, in the ensuing scene, Shakespeare could have been more explicit about what has been preoccupying Hamlet.

THE DEATH OF POLONIUS

After an initial heated exchange, Hamlet responds to his mother's question, "Have you forgot me?" with an embittered:

> No, by the rood, not so;
> You are the queen, your husband's brother's wife;
> And—would it were not so!—you are my mother.
>
> (III, iv, 14–16)

He insists that his mother not budge until she has seen the inmost part of herself. He is going to try to force the issue, to make Gertrude repent, change, and become his mother again— all else seems secondary to him. He acts with such intensity that Gertrude cries, "What wilt thou do? thou wilt not murder me? / Help, help, ho!" (III, iv, 21–22). Polonius, hidden behind the arras, echoes her cry for help; and Hamlet whips out his rapier. Crying, "How now! a rat? Dead, for a ducat, dead!" (III, iv, 23), he stabs through the curtain and kills unseen the father of his beloved. When Gertrude exclaims; "Oh, what a rash and bloody deed is this?" (III, iv, 27), Hamlet can reply only, "Almost as bad, good mother, / As kill a king, and marry with his brother" (III, iv, 28–29). Hamlet is so preoccupied with his need to express his feelings to his mother that when he discovers that he has slain Polonius, he tells the corpse:

> Thou wretched, rash, intruding fool, farewell!
> I took thee for thy better; take thy fortune;
> Thou find'st to be too busy is some danger.—
>
> (III, iv, 31–33)

and lets it lie there while he returns to chastising his mother. And we, too, leave Polonius forgotten on the floor, barely noting that with this act the play reaches its dramatic climax.

Until this juncture, a person viewing the play for the first time might expect, or at least hope for, a felicitous outcome; in which Hamlet gains the throne and Ophelia and Hamlet are reconciled; but now the play, just like *Romeo and Juliet* after Romeo slays Juliet's kinsman Tybalt, must move inevitably to a tragic outcome. We shall, as does Shakespeare, leave the consequences of Hamlet's rash deed until later while we follow Hamlet in his need to confront his mother and wring her heart, as he will "If it be made of penetrable stuff" (III, iv, 36).

Hamlet does not inform his mother that he has learned that Claudius poisoned his father, nor does he question her about her possible involvement in the murder. Either course would give Gertrude the opportunity to swear that she is innocent of complicity and to become Hamlet's ally, as she does in the First Quarto version of the play and in the Amleth saga. The difference in the versions indicates that Shakespeare deliberately left the question of Gertrude's knowledge of the murder ambiguous. Hamlet, however, does not seem as concerned with the murder as with her infidelity and her continuing sexual relationship with Claudius.

In reply to the queen's demand, "What have I done, that thou darest wag thy tongue / In noise so rude against me?" (III, iv, 39–40) Hamlet lashes out:

> Such an act
> That blurs the grace and blush of modesty,
> Calls virtue hypocrite, takes off the rose
> From the fair forehead of an innocent love,
> And sets a blister there; makes marriage vows
> As false as dicers' oaths.   (III, iv, 40–45)

When his mother asks what act of hers is he attacking "That roars so loud and thunders in the index?" (III, iv, 52), Hamlet compares her two husbands, with Claudius "like a mildew'd ear, / Blasting his wholesome brother" (III, iv, 64–65). He tries to insist that Gertrude could not have married Claudius for love:

> You cannot call it love, for at your age
> The hey-day in the blood is tame, it's humble,
> And waits upon the judgement; and what judgement
> Would step from this to this?   (III, iv, 68–71)

He cannot conceive what could attract her to Claudius; it cannot even be madness but must be a devil. He cannot understand her sensuality:

> O shame! where is thy blush? Rebellious hell,
> If thou canst mutine in a matron's bones,
> To flaming youth let virtue be as wax
> And melt in her own fire; proclaim no shame
> When the compulsive ardour gives the charge,
> Since frost itself as actively doth burn,
> And reason panders will.   (III, iv, 82–88)

His mother cannot stop his denunciation of her, and Hamlet becomes more specific:

> Nay, but to live
> In the rank sweat of an enseamed bed,
> Stew'd in corruption, honeying and making love
> Over the nasty sty,—   (III, iv, 91–93)

His father's ghost then reappears to remind Hamlet of his blunted purpose—to take vengeance on Claudius and not to berate his mother but rather to "step between her and her fighting soul" (III, iv, 113). Hamlet is temporarily quieted. Here, in contrast to the Ghost's first appearance, only Hamlet sees his father's spirit.

Gertrude sees her son staring at empty space, his eyes popping and hair standing on end as he discourses "with the incorporal air." We are clearly left with the impression that Hamlet is hallucinating, needing to project—or extroject—his father as a superego figure in order to bolster his failing self-control. This time he sees the martial Dane not in "the very armour he had on / When he the ambitious Norway combated" (I, i, 60–61) but, according to the First Quarto, in his nightgown or night robe, a garb more appropriate for a ghost—or for a husband in his wife's bedroom.

Madness in *Hamlet*

The queen is now convinced that her son is insane. She tells him:

> This is the very coinage of your brain;
> This bodiless creation ecstasy
> Is very cunning in.   (III, iv, 137–138)

Her admonition only leads Hamlet to protest and plead:

> Mother, for love of grace,
> Lay not that flattering unction to your soul,
> That not your trespass but my madness speaks;
> It will but skin and film the ulcerous place,
> Whilst rank corruption, mining all within,
> Infects unseen. Confess yourself to heaven;
> Repent what's past, avoid what is to come,
> And do not spread the compost o'er the weeds,
> To make them ranker. Forgive me this my virtue,
> For in the fatness of these pursy times
> Virtue itself of vice must pardon beg,
> Yea, curb and woo for leave to do him good.
>   (III, iv, 144–155)

Denmark has grown so corrupt that a son must admonish his mother to forego illicit sexuality. The world is topsy-turvy: parent and child roles are reversed, and virtue must beg vice's pardon. Having finally touched his mother's conscience, when she cries, "O Hamlet, thou hast cleft my heart in twain" (III, iv, 156), he tells her:

> O, throw away the worser part of it,
> And live the purer with the other half.
> Good night; but go not to mine uncle's bed;
> Assume a virtue, if you have it not.   (III, iv, 157–160)

And he expresses his hope that he is not irrevocably lost to her but that

when you are desirous to be blest,
I'll blessing beg of you.—   (III, iv, 171–172)

When the queen, probably referring to the dead Polonius, asks in desperation, "What shall I do?" (III, iv, 180), Hamlet returns to his obsession:

Not this. . . .
Let the bloat king tempt you again to bed;
Pinch wanton on your cheek; call you his mouse;
And let him, for a pair of reechy kisses,
Or paddling in your neck with his damn'd fingers,
Make you to ravel all this matter out,
That I essentially am not in madness,
But mad in craft.   (III, iv, 181–188)

For the first and only time since he warned his friends that he might assume an antic disposition, Hamlet insists that he is *essentially* "not in madness, but mad in craft." Here, he is clearly not pretending to be mad but is desperately seeking to convince his mother to heed him and change her ways. Yet he has, through what he has said and done, almost surely convinced his mother that he is insane. He has almost ignored the fact that he has inadvertently slain Polonius; he has bitterly condemned his mother for remarrying; he has ranted against her sexual activity with her husband; and he has, to her perception, been hallucinating. Since he has not confided in her that he has learned that Claudius murdered her first husband, or that he knows or suspects that she had been unfaithful when his father was alive, Gertrude can only believe that Hamlet is insanely jealous of her sexual relationship with Claudius.

Shakespeare deliberately chose to keep the question of Gertrude's complicity in King Hamlet's murder ambiguous. Hamlet expresses his feeling that her remarriage and her infidelity are akin to murder, but Gertrude is never given a chance to exonerate herself as in the First Quarto. In a sense, Hamlet's feelings are more important to the play than whatever Gertrude actually did. Shakespeare may have also appreciated that Hamlet could not confront his mother directly with either his knowledge of her marital infidelity or his suspicion that she plotted to kill his father. In order for Hamlet to reverse the parent and child roles and seek to act as his mother's conscience or superego, he has to wait until the pressures within him are unbearable. Then when he finally can express his feelings, he verges on losing his self-control. Nevertheless, as distraught as he is, and despite the almost uncontrollable intensity of his bitterness, Hamlet does not go the way of Orestes or Nero. In this scene, which is poignant with despair and longing, he seeks not only to save his mother from damnation but also to make her recant and again become the person he idealized, or, at least accepted as a mother.

REKINDLED OEDIPAL JEALOUSY

There is probably no other place in our literature where a son reprimands his mother so fully and explicitly for having sexual relations with her husband. Because bitter feelings like those which Hamlet expresses about his mother's sexuality are, since Freud, considered an almost universal though transient silent preoccupation of male childhood, one aspect of the appeal of *Hamlet* is just this overt and dramatic cry for a mother to renounce her sexual life with her husband that virtually all sons have had to repress. Hamlet is not a child, but his oedipal feelings had been reawakened, first, by his expectation that he would assume primacy in his mother's affections after his father's death, and then, by his jealousy of his mother's relationship with Claudius. *Hamlet* is a play that reaches its climax when the hero[4] kills a father figure in his mother's bedchamber (though, as we have seen, his beloved's father rather than his own) and denounces his mother's sexual life in his effort to regain her after she has deserted him for another. The emphasis upon Hamlet's preoccupation with his mother's sensuality and his disgust with the sexual act itself, the location of the scene in the mother's chamber, the presence of a hidden interloper, the appearance of the father's ghost to protect Gertrude from Hamlet's rage if not his passion—all indicate Shakespeare's empathy for a son's feelings, which in turn, he rearouses in the audience.

Any doubts that Shakespeare wished to stress the incestuous and matricidal aspects of this scene in which Hamlet verges on losing his sanity are dispelled, as I have noted, by Hamlet's comparison of himself to Nero as he prepares to confront his mother.

We may consider that, symbolically, Hamlet has now come to grips with his reawakened oedipal jealousies and surmounted them. He has ceased being a child in relation to his mother and even seeks to stand in his father's place by controlling his mother's sexuality. He has done what he can about his mother's behavior, and he is now ready to move against Claudius.

VI

THEME AND
COUNTERTHEME

HAMLET is ready to move against Claudius and fulfill his
obligation to his murdered father, but Polonius lies dead on the
floor. Hamlet has not lived out the childhood oedipal fantasy of
killing his father in order to possess his mother; nor, as he may
have imagined as he impulsively thrust through the arras, has
he killed his stepfather. He has, rather, murdered Ophelia's
father. With the slaying of Polonius by mischance, the play
makes the subtle transition from its emphasis of the theme to
emphasis of the countertheme. A fugue-like complication that
heightens the action ensues as a counterpursuit of Hamlet is
added to Hamlet's pursuit of Claudius.

Now, the dominant interest shifts from the triangular relationship between a son and his mother and father to focus on
the triangular relationship between the young man, his beloved,
and her father. It is a theme deeply rooted in myths and sagas
that tell of a woman torn between her old love for, and loyalty
to, her father and her love for the man who has won her by
vanquishing her father. It is a theme whose variations and divergent outcomes I shall consider in Part Two.

The balance of the play now swings over on the fulcrum of
the slaying of Polonius which, when it took place, seemed al-

most incidental, for Shakespeare was focusing the audience's attention on the confrontation between Hamlet and Gertrude. Hamlet will now be pursued as he pursues. He will no longer simply be the wronged hero. Even though he did not intend to kill Polonius, Hamlet will be a villain to Laertes and Ophelia. Laertes will be bound to avenge his father, and Ophelia can no longer let herself dream of marrying Hamlet. Because of the murder and Ophelia's ensuing insanity and death, Laertes, a potential ally of Hamlet's, will be united with Claudius. Hamlet and Laertes will come into open conflict in Ophelia's grave, and in the end both will die, in essence dueling over her.

Hamlet realizes the change in his position when he looks at Polonius' corpse and says, "This man shall set me packing" (III, iv, 211). He will be hurried off to England and his life endangered, but he is prepared to counterattack, to hoist the engineer of a plot against him "with his own petar." It is not clear to what Hamlet refers when he says, "Oh, 'tis most sweet / When in one line two crafts directly meet" (III, iv, 209–210), but the lines could describe Shakespeare's own consummate skill and economy in balancing theme and countertheme on the slaying of Polonius. Ophelia will soon lose her wits, and now, our study of the theme of madness, rather than focus primarily on Hamlet's precarious emotional state, must also examine the nature of Ophelia's madness and how it is apposed to Hamlet's plight.

A *Danse Macabre*

The fourth act opens with a *danse macabre*. A gruesome, dysphoric atmosphere permeates the theater, as the slaying of Polonius begins to dominate the play's action. The scenes convey chaos and distraction. In a reversal of Act I, Laertes returns for his father's funeral and Hamlet leaves the country. Laertes is spurred to vengeance by the "ghost" of his sister—a sister without her senses—as Hamlet had been by the ghost of his father. Claudius' plot is foiled by Hamlet's countermove; and

Laertes, carried away by his desire for vengeance, becomes corrupted by Claudius. Rosencrantz and Guildenstern, unaware
that, in serving their king, they are to lead Hamlet to his death,
are sacrificed in the deadly game. The act, with its fugue-like
characteristics, ends with a lament for the blighted promise of
hope and beauty as Ophelia drowns in her woes.

A foreboding of doom emanates from the stage as Gertrude
tells Claudius how Hamlet, "in his lawless fit" and "in this
brainish apprehension," killed "the unseen good old man."
Then, the spectator, like the king, is filled with "discord and
dismay" as Hamlet drags Polonius' body around the castle, hides
it, and dashes away from Rosencrantz and Guildenstern as if
playing hide and seek. Despite his contemptuous remarks about
Polonius, Hamlet is now feeling the impact of his rash act; but
he cannot cope with its implications. His behavior is bizarre and
highly inappropriate as he seeks to deny the tragedy and his own
misery by making grotesque witticisms and attacking others.

He is apprehended and placed under guard, for Claudius realizes,

> It had been so with us, had we been there;
> His liberty is full of threats to all,
> To you yourself, to us, to every one.   (IV, i, 13–15)

The king no longer needs to find excuses to send Hamlet to
England but rather seems lenient in sending abroad rather than
keeping "restrain'd, and out of haunt, / This mad young man"
(IV, i, 17–18). Although Hamlet tries to handle the situation by
inappropriate levity, his mother knows that underneath "He
weeps for what is done" (IV, i, 27).

As everywhere in the play, Hamlet's mental state is difficult
to evaluate, but here he clearly increases his disadvantage by
feigning insanity, if he is feigning. In these opening scenes of
the act, he seems to lack self-control and to be moderately manic
with a paranoid tendency. He cannot permit himself to give way
to his grief or let himself realize what he has done to Ophelia;
instead, he resorts to a veneer of jocularity.[1] Hamlet no longer
conceals his animosities and is even reckless in expressing them.
He openly insults Rosencrantz and Guildenstern and accuses

them of abandoning him to seek the king's favors. He informs the king that Polonius is at supper, "Not where he eats, but where he is eaten" (IV, iii, 20). He puns on the Diet of Worms, commenting that "We fat all creatures else to fat us, and we fat ourselves for maggots. Your fat king, and your lean beggar, is but variable service, two dishes, but to one table; that's the end" (IV, iii, 22–25). To which Claudius can only reply, "Alas, alas!" He insults the king, telling him that Polonius is in heaven, but "if your messenger find him not there, seek him i' the other place yourself" (IV, iii, 33–34). He does not act rashly; he does not act heroically; he speaks rashly and endangers his cause.

Claudius now sends Hamlet to England, but we learn that he is being sent not for his health, in the hope that "Haply the seas and countries different / . . . shall expel / This something-settled matter in his heart" (III, i, 171–173) but rather to his death. Now "like the hectic" in the king's blood he rages, and Claudius can only be cured of his fears by Hamlet's death. Hamlet, in parting, meaningfully but manically takes his leave of Claudius by calling him "mother" (IV, iii, 48, 50).

However, in the next scene an interlude in which he encounters Fortinbras' army, Hamlet is again eminently sane. Indeed, he is never saner than when he comments shrewdly on the senseless venture that will lead to

> The imminent death of twenty thousand men,
> That for a fantasy and trick of fame
> Go to their graves like beds, fight for a plot
> Whereon the numbers cannot try the cause,
> Which is not tomb enough and continent
> To hide the slain?   (IV, iv, 60–65)

Here, Shakespeare has Hamlet express his contempt for wars pursued for no purpose other than honor and self-advancement, and yet he is still enough of a Renaissance prince to admire a young man who does not let reason, or "conscience," stand in the way of action. Even though Fortinbras' venture has something ridiculous about it, Hamlet is again incited to action. He decides that

Madness in *Hamlet*

> Rightly to be great
> Is not to stir without great argument,
> But greatly to find quarrel in a straw
> When honour's at the stake.   (IV, iv, 53–56)

Circumstances have turned against Hamlet, and he is being sent to his death, but we know he will gain his vengeance as he now determines:

> Oh, from this time forth,
> My thoughts be bloody, or be nothing worth!
>   (IV, iv, 65–66)

Ophelia's Madness

Some weeks pass after Hamlet departs for England, but the grotesque atmosphere of impending disintegration continues to pervade the theater, as the effects of Polonius' death multiply. Now Ophelia is mad and will soon be dead; Laertes in his search for vengeance will be seduced into treachery.

Shakespeare carefully places Ophelia's madness in apposition to Hamlet's, illuminating the causes of each by making Ophelia's plight the female counterpart of Hamlet's dilemma. The action around Ophelia's insanity forms the countertheme to the action surrounding Hamlet's madness, balancing the plot and leading to Hamlet's death as well as to Ophelia's. Each dies more or less because there is nothing left for them but to desire death as an escape from an existence that has become intolerable.

Whereas Shakespeare is ambiguous about the reality of Hamlet's insanity and depicts him as on the border, fluctuating between sanity and madness, he portrays Ophelia as definitely, one might even say classically, insane. Even before she comes on stage, a gentleman gives us an excellent description of her condition. Would that psychiatric texts could describe as clearly!

She speaks much of her father; says she hears
There's tricks i' the world; and hems and beats her
    heart;
Spurns enviously at straws; speaks things in doubt,
That carry but half sense; her speech is nothing,
Yet the unshaped use of it doth move
The hearers to collection; they aim at it,
And botch the words up fit to their own thoughts;
Which, as her winks and nods and gestures yield
    them,
Indeed would make one think there might be thought,
Though nothing sure, yet much unhappily.
                        (IV, v, 4–13)

She does not storm, or "take arms against a sea of troubles"
(III, i, 59); but rather, as a passive, obedient and very feminine
person she is simply

                 poor Ophelia,
Divided from herself and her fair judgement,
Without the which we are pictures, or mere beasts.
                        (IV, v, 80–82)

She sings one ditty about her love who is dead and gone, as
if referring to her father, then another about a girl abandoned
because she let her valentine tumble her before being wed—a
bawdy bit that has led some critics to consider that the sweet
Ophelia might have been distraught because she had given in to
Hamlet's "unmaster'd importunity" (I, iii, 32) and was now pregnant, with marriage to Hamlet no longer possible. However, to
most, including those in the play, who knew her best, the cause
of Ophelia's madness seems apparent. Claudius says:

Oh, this' the poison of deep grief; it springs
All from her father's death.   (IV, v, 72–73)

And Laertes muses about his mad sister:

O heavens! is't possible a young maid's wits
Should be as mortal as an old man's life?
Nature is fine in love, and where 'tis fine
It sends some precious instance of itself
After the thing it loves.   (IV, v, 155–159)

The comment is accentuated by Ophelia's chant:

They bore him barefaced on the bier;
Hey non nonny, nonny, hey nonny;
And on his grave rains many a tear.—   (IV, v, 160–162)

The gentle Ophelia, it seems, cannot absorb her father's murder. However, it is not her father's murder that has driven her mad but, rather, his murder by Hamlet, the person she loves and upon whose love she has placed her hopes. Now, she can never marry him, and worse still, she has an obligation to hate him; indeed she must feel hatred toward him for depriving her of her beloved father, her original love.[2] Shakespeare, then, has not only placed Ophelia's insanity in apposition to Hamlet's but has emphasized the same crucial human frailty as the cause of the emotional disturbance in both the hero and heroine.

As we have seen, Hamlet mourns for his father, but his melancholy is induced by his bitterness against his mother because of her hasty marriage to his uncle; and his anguish and rage against his mother become intolerable when he learns that she has been untrue to his father. Hamlet is tormented by his desire to take vengeance against his mother, the person who had once been closest and most dear to him. He manages to control his matricidal impulses, but his mother is lost to him as a love object. He struggles to regain her by imploring her to renounce her sexual life with Claudius and return to him and become faithful to his father's memory. At the very moment when Hamlet believes he may have succeeded, he inadvertently kills Polonius bringing new woes on himself and sealing Ophelia's fate.

Ophelia, like Hamlet, mourns for her father, but his death is not a sufficient reason for her to lose her sanity. She, too, is in the intolerable predicament of having to turn away from the person she loves and idealizes because that person is responsible for her father's murder. Her father is dead, and Hamlet, as his slayer, is barred to her affections. She can no longer transfer her attachment from her father to Hamlet. Her entire orientation to the future has suddenly been destroyed.

Both Hamlet and Ophelia, then, are faced by the sudden and irretrievable loss of a love object because of that person's unforgivable behavior in killing, actually or symbolically, a beloved parent whose death requires vengeance. Shakespeare clearly saw how such situations could engender a violently confused emotional state and lead a person to feel that the world was empty and worthless and those who inhabit it perfidious and deceitful. Life becomes intolerable; the sufferer escapes the dilemma by abandoning rationality and when that fails, by abandoning life itself.

Now, the reader might not think that Polonius, a man already in his dotage, a spying busybody whom Hamlet considered a tedious old fool, could be so important to Ophelia. Indeed, one might similarly wonder why Hamlet should be so concerned about the deceitful and wanton Gertrude. Oedipal attachments do not, as we know from countless patients, involve a rational evaluation of the parent. If raised with reasonable parental care, the boy has a deep attachment to his mother, and the girl to her father. Ophelia's attachment to Polonius is accentuated by her motherless state. As a widower, Polonius may have been overly protective of his daughter and especially affectionate to her; and Ophelia, as commonly happens in such situations, may have felt free to fantasy that she could become a replacement for her mother in her father's life, and thus form a particularly intense attachment to him. Similarly, Hamlet is fatherless, but his situation differed from Ophelia's as he had lost his father much more recently. Nevertheless, as we have noted, his father's death could lead to a recrudescence of Hamlet's old attachment to his mother as well as a heightening of his identification with his father. He could then feel that his mother's infidelity to his father was also an infidelity to him.

Ophelia, we should note, is already under considerable emotional stress at the time her father is killed. The vacillations in

Hamlet's attitude and behavior toward her could not but be extremely unsettling to the very young woman who idolized and idealized him. She is, one day, his most beloved, who must never doubt his love (II, ii, 115–123); shortly thereafter, she is the object of his venom and the recipient of his malignant curse; and then, on the same day, she finds him bantering salaciously with her. She cannot know that Hamlet's attitude toward her reflects his disillusionment in his mother. To her, Hamlet's inconstancy can only mean deceitfulness or madness. Ophelia finds him mad, and, hopefully, mad because she has been forced to reject him. Hamlet slays Polonius by mistake; he had not, like Claudius, committed a premeditated murder for his own advancement. We must even consider that were Hamlet not so out of control, he might still beg Ophelia's forgiveness for his error. However, that is not the way the play was written, or could have been written.

The Rivalry Between Polonius and Hamlet

It is apparent that Hamlet slays Polonius in error, and in the heat of impassioned excitement. Even though he has just left Claudius in another room, he may have, as has often been suggested, thought that Claudius was behind the arras. On seeing Polonius fall, Hamlet exclaims, "Thou wretched, rash, intruding fool, farewell! / I took thee for thy better" (III, iv, 31–32). As psychoanalytic commentators have observed, Hamlet is, in a sense, living out the oedipal fantasy of killing that man in his mother's bedroom.[3] One might even surmise that unconsciously he is defending himself against the father who caught him in his mother's bedroom preoccupied with patricidal and incestuous fantasies. It is also clear from the text that Hamlet has been struggling to repress his matricidal impulses, and may have displaced his murderous feelings impetuously onto the spying intruder. Nevertheless, symbolically, Hamlet murders Polonius.

Hamlet is hostile to Polonius throughout the play. He never says a civil word to him, and he mocks and baits him at every encounter. Hamlet certainly does not follow his own admonition to Polonius, "Use every man after his desert, and who should 'scape whipping? Use them after your own honour and dignity; the less they deserve, the more merit is in your bounty" (II, ii, 505–508). Although Hamlet considers him a tedious old fool—and he is sometimes played clownishly—Polonius, though sententious, prating, conniving, and now a trifle senile, is not a fool. His famed speech to his son consists mostly of rather conventional advice on how to be successful, but the tawdry is almost offset by

> to thine own self be true,
> And it must follow, as the night the day,
> Thou canst not then be false to any man.
>
> (I, iii, 78 80)

and this, above all, is precisely what Laertes forgets, and thus he loses his honor and his life. Hamlet's behavior throughout the play is inappropriate not only toward an old man, but even more so toward the father of the girl he loves. However, it indicates how a young man may feel about his beloved's father and, particularly, about one who forbids his daughter to spend any time with him. Polonius is yet another father figure who comes between Hamlet and his love, even as Hamlet's father stood and Claudius now stands between Hamlet and his first love, his mother.

We know that Hamlet believes correctly that Polonius has kept Ophelia from him. He warns Polonius to keep his daughter out of the sun lest she conceive (II, ii, 183); later he calls Polonius "Jephthah, judge of Israel" and refers to his daughter as his treasure (II, ii, 384–385). He thus connects Polonius to the biblical figure who, like Agamemnon, sacrificed his virgin daughter to gain a victory. As I have previously remarked, Polonius' murder symbolically concerns the jealousy that exists between a girl's father and her suitor—a rivalry that led fathers in myth and fairy tale to set insurmountable tasks for anyone who would win their daughters, or to require the suitors to enter a contest with them that ended in the death of one of them.

Ophelia, classically, is more or less in the position of the girl who, though attached to her father, dreams of the hero who will come and win her from her father, abduct her, or even slay the tyrannical father—but who is then caught in an unbearable situation when her hero carries out her fantasy and kills her father.

Hamlet and Laertes Compared

The killing of Polonius not only brings Laertes into an alliance with Claudius but also permits Shakespeare to contrast Hamlet with Laertes. Actually, Shakespeare carefully compares the behavior of three sons of murdered fathers. In some respects, Hamlet, Laertes, and Fortinbras can be considered as three different personifications of the "hero," each of whom represents different unconscious fantasies, or different configurations of traits.

Lest the audience believe—as have numerous commentators —that Hamlet has been deterred from killing Claudius by external circumstances rather than by inner conflicts, Shakespeare does not let Laertes find the king's guard a deterrent. He moves with decisiveness and dispatch:

> The ocean, overpeering of his list,
> Eats not the flats with more impetuous haste
> Than young Laertes, in a riotous head,
> O'erbears your officers. (IV, v, 95–98)

And though, in contrast to Hamlet, he has no claim to the throne, the people follow him, shouting "Laertes shall be king!" (IV, v, 102). They break down the doors of the throne room; and in response to the queen's admonition "Calmly, good Laertes" (IV, v, 112), the young man declaims:

That drop of blood that's calm proclaims me bastard;
Cries cuckold to my father; brands the harlot
Even here, between the chaste unsmirched brows
Of my true mother.   (IV, v, 113–115)

It is not simply that Hamlet has less ardor for vengeance and
a reluctance to move against his philosophic principles; but
rather that these incitements to vengeance, which motivate Laertes, are precisely the ones Hamlet lacks. Hamlet's mother has
performed "Such an act that . . . takes off the rose / From the
fair forehead of an innocent love, / And sets a blister there" (III,
iv, 40, 42–44)—the blister resulting from the harlot's brand.
Claudius has not only killed his father but also, as Hamlet says,
"whored my mother" (V, ii, 64).

Claudius does not flinch before Laertes' attack. He is a villain
but not a coward. He does evil to gain his ends, but he behaves
like a true king and quietly calms Laertes. But then Laertes'
mad, hebephrenic sister wanders in. Unable to say what troubles her, she rambles about herbs and flowers—a metaphor that
symbolizes herself as the blighted "Rose of May"—and she in-
censes Laertes to vengeance. "Hadst thou thy wits, and didst
persuade revenge, / It could not move thus" (IV, v, 164–165). Yet,
I would hazard, that if Ophelia were asked, she would—just as
Hamlet's father defended Gertrude—beg Laertes to spare Hamlet's life.

Laertes in his fervor to avenge his father and sister is willing
to play the foul game of the king, who, when he learns that his
first plot to take Hamlet's life has failed, persuades Laertes to
seek vengeance through duplicity and poison. Laertes is the son
of Polonius, the politician and diplomat, who though preaching
honesty to his son, delights in spying and condones lying as
when he taught his emissary how:

Your bait of falsehood takes this carp of truth;
And thus do we of wisdom and of reach,
With windlasses and with assays of bias,
By indirections find directions out;   (II, i, 63–66)

95

Laertes, whom Hamlet considers "a very noble youth" (V, i, 212) now will lose his nobility, his good name, and his soul in the pursuit of vengeance.

Ophelia is soon dead. She does not her "quietus make / With a bare bodkin" (III, i, 75–76) but, in accord with her personality, passively finds refuge from her hopeless plight in quiet waters, where, garlanded with flowers, clinging to beauty even in dying, she

> Fell in the weeping brook. Her clothes spread wide,
> And, mermaid-like, a while they bore her up;
> Which time she chanted snatches of old tunes,
> As one incapable of her own distress,
> Or like a creature native and indued
> Unto that element; but long it could not be
> Till that her garments, heavy with their drink,
> Pull'd the poor wretch from her melodious lay
> To muddy death.[4]   (IV, vii, 177–184)

As her brother has said of her, "passion, hell itself; / She turns to favour and to prettiness" (IV, v, 182–183). Beauty, innocence, hope of fulfillment are gone; they cannot survive the intrigue and corruption of the Danish court, or the obligation for vengeance.

VII

THE FINAL ACT—
DEATH

Death permeates the play's final act, which properly starts in a graveyard and ends with the palace turned into a charnel house. The consequences of the two murders—the theme and countertheme, Hamlet's antic disposition and Ophelia's madness, Hamlet's and Laertes' vengeance—coalesce to lead to the inevitable end when the stage and state will be wiped clean of the opposing figures, all of whom are now contaminated. Poison will end the lives of those already poisoned. A new cast will be able to start a new play, a new cycle in history.

At Ophelia's Grave

The stage is handed over to the clowns—in the roles of gravediggers. Their words and actions directly continue the tragedy, but it is not their tragedy. Death is their business: "Custom hath made it . . . a property of easiness" (V, i, 65–66). It matters little to them that Ophelia committed suicide or that Prince Hamlet is mad. The clowns as gravediggers; humor as a thin mask for tragedy! Their low comedy heightens the impact of Hamlet's sudden realization that Ophelia is dead and that his passionate act has killed not only her father but also his hope of love.

The clowns are digging Ophelia's grave, spewing old bones and old saws out of it. Her death gives them reason to argue about the coroner's laws concerning suicide and the legal responsibility of the insane; it also permits Shakespeare to satirize matters that were just as confusing in his day as in ours. Hamlet, having been at sea since we last saw him, does not know Ophelia is dead, but he has good reason to be preoccupied with death since his father's death and his mother's remarriage, and particularly since he killed Polonius and sent Rosencrantz and Guildenstern to their doom.[1]

Now, as if viewing a painting of the Dance of Death, Hamlet sees the skeleton beneath the trappings, the pride, the pretense, the skin of Everyman. A skull he picks up might be "the pate of a politician . . . one that would circumvent God" (V, i, 75–77), which the gravedigger "now o'er-reaches" (V, i, 76); or that of a courtier now "knocked about the mazzard with a sexton's spade; here's fine revolution, and we had the trick to see't" (V, i, 85–86); or that of a lawyer—"why does he suffer this rude knave now to knock him about the sconce with a dirty shovel, and will not tell him of his action of battery?" (V, i, 95–97); or of a great buyer of land, now with "his fine pate full of fine dirt?" (V, i, 101). He has a duel of wits with the first clown over Ophelia's grave, and is outscored by the clown's down-to-earth wit, or is it by his literality? "How absolute the knave is!" Hamlet muses, "We must speak by the card, or equivocation will undo us" (V, i, 129–130). He learns that had he gone to England and remained mad it would be no great matter, for it would not "be seen in him there; / there the men are as mad as he" (V, i, 145–146). Here too, we find the one person who knows with certitude the cause of Hamlet's madness. We have traced the perplexity of Gertrude, Claudius, Polonius, Rosencrantz, Guildenstern, and Hamlet himself about the cause of Hamlet's madness. Psychiatrists and literary scholars have continued to puzzle about Hamlet's mental state these many years since Hamlet first thought it meet "to put an antic disposition on." Yet the first clown can set the matter straight for us. When Hamlet asks him, "How came he [Hamlet] mad?" he is told, "Very strangely, they say," "How 'strangely'?" "Faith, e'en with losing his wits" (V, i, 147–150).

Hamlet contemplates another wit whose wits are now gone when he picks up the skull of Yorick, that "fellow of infinite jest" (V, i, 174). He gazes at the emptiness where "hung those lips that I have kissed I know not how oft" (V, i, 177–178)—the jester, the mad source of laughter at others, to whom Hamlet is mythologically and spiritually kin. From thinking of his childhood hero Yorick, he begins—as Horatio tells him—"to consider too curiously" (V, i, 194), tracing the transformation of Alexander into a beer-barrel bung, when grim reality with personal tragedy for him displaces his detached ruminations.

With the "maimed rites" that "betoken / The corse they follow did with desperate hand, / Fordo it own life" (V, i, 207–209) the court enters, accompanying Ophelia to her grave. Here, after the rites accorded a virgin in burial instead of at her wedding, in which "she is allow'd her virgin crants, / Her maiden strewments, and the bringing home / Of bell and burial" (V, i, 220–221), Gertrude scatters flowers, grieving,

> Sweets to the sweet; farewell!
> I hoped thou shouldst have been my Hamlet's wife.
> I thought thy bride-bed to have deck'd, sweet maid,
> And not t' have strew'd thy grave.   (V, i, 231–233)

Then, when Laertes, in a display of grief, jumps into the grave and asks to be buried with his sister, Hamlet cannot contain himself. It may be, as some commentators have maintained, that Hamlet cannot tolerate sham, but his actions would seem to me to be excessive, highly inappropriate, and a defilement if carried out primarily to chide Laertes for his excesses. The latent rivalry between brother and lover flares up, and Hamlet seems unable to tolerate the realization that Ophelia has been so important to another. Hamlet challenges Laertes to show by deed which of them loved Ophelia most, unable to recognize that he has been responsible for Laertes' grief. Yet when Laertes curses "The devil take thy soul!" and grasps Hamlet's throat, Hamlet counters insightfully,

> Thou pray'st not well.
> I prithee, take thy fingers from my throat;
> For, though I am not splenitive and rash,
> Yet have I something in me dangerous,
> Which let thy wisdom fear. (V, i, 247–251)

And now, with Ophelia in her grave, Hamlet can proclaim to the world,

> I loved Ophelia; forty thousand brothers
> Could not, with all their quantity of love,
> Make up my sum— (V, i, 257–259)

Ophelia, whom he could only hurt while she lived, because of the misogyny born of his mother's infidelity.

He rants madly or outrageously in his challenges to Laertes. Oblivious to the inappropriateness of his behavior, he can pathetically ask Laertes, "What is the reason that you use me thus? / I loved you ever" (V, i, 277–278). He attacks rather than suffer the recognition of his own guilt. His jealousy overwhelms him, for, as he will later tell Horatio, "the bravery of his grief did put me / Into a towering passion" (V, ii, 79–80).

Gertrude quiets Laertes, assuring him,

> This is mere madness;
> And thus a while the fit will work on him;
> Anon, as patient as the female dove
> When that her golden couplets are disclosed,
> His silence will sit drooping. (V, i, 272–275)

As his mother predicts, when calm returns, Hamlet repents his behavior:

> I am very sorry, good Horatio,
> That to Laertes I forgot myself;

For, by the image of my cause, I see
The portraiture of his; I'll court his favours;

(V, ii, 75–78)

Rosencrantz and Guildenstern "Go to 't"

In the lull between the storm in the graveyard and the final cataclysm, Horatio and the audience learn that Hamlet has sent his former friends, Rosencrantz and Guildenstern, to their deaths. Hamlet justifies his action with "Why, man, they did make love to this employment; / They are not near my conscience" (V, ii, 57–58) and Horatio seems to admire it, exclaiming, "Why, what a king is this!" (V, ii, 62). Although the Elizabethan audience may have admired the counterthrust, Hamlet's action was, once again, impulsive. There was nothing heroic in the act that dispatched the friends who had sought to help him. Uninformed by Hamlet that Claudius had murdered his father, Rosencrantz and Guildenstern could only regard his behavior as insanely irresponsible and a very real danger to their king and queen. Yet, because they were also concerned with the welfare of Claudius, they became anathema to Hamlet. Hamlet stands on his princely prerogative and maintains:

> 'Tis dangerous when the baser nature comes
> Between the pass and fell incensed points
> Of mighty opposites.   (V, ii, 60–61)

He asks Horatio if "is't not perfect conscience / To quit him [Claudius] with this arm?" (V, ii, 67–68). He expresses a bitter, existential truth, but his sacrifice of his childhood friends was rash and unnecessary; the act is paranoid because Hamlet displaces his hostility to Claudius onto Claudius' envoys and projects his own hostility onto his companions. It indicates how dangerous Hamlet has become. He is no longer "Most generous and free from all contriving" (IV, vii, 136).

Madness in *Hamlet*

"The Readiness Is All"

Now, as the play is about to end, Hamlet "is much possessed by death" as he accepts the challenge to fence for sport with a man who is obligated to avenge Polonius and Ophelia. It may be that, as Claudius anticipated, he remains sufficiently "free from all contriving" and is so filled "with his envy" of the report of Laertes' consummate swordsmanship "That he could nothing do but wish and beg / . . . to play with him" (IV, vii, 105–106); but it is more likely that the weariness with life expressed in his first soliloquy has now become indifference about whether he lives or dies, because of the various events that have aggravated his disillusionment and hostility—because of his guilt over his three slayings and his part in Ophelia's suicide, as well as by his loss of her.

Hamlet considers refusing to fence with Laertes; "How if I answer No?" (V, ii, 163).[2] Although he seems unable to assimilate and evaluate the situation, he unconsciously realizes that something is amiss; but he no longer cares. He confides to Horatio, "But thou wouldst not think how ill all's here about my heart; but it is no matter" (V, ii, 200–201). He can no longer consider himself a righteous young man, for he has destroyed Ophelia, injured Laertes, and contrived to send his childhood friends to execution. Guilt and innocence are no longer black-and-white matters. Despite his ideals, he has been responsible for evil. He has learned

> There's a divinity that shapes our ends,
> Rough-hew them how we will   (V, ii, 10–11)

and he is willing to let it. He defies augury and goes to meet his fate. After all, the one thing he—as all men—can know with certainty is that death is inevitable. Hamlet expresses the ultimate riddle or paradox of mankind: "If it be now, 'tis not to come; if it be not to come; it will be now; if it be not now, yet it will come" (V, ii, 208–210). Hamlet, he of the riddles, can riddle no more profoundly than this. And he goes on to give his answer to it—perhaps the only answer and, therefore, the essence of wisdom: "the readiness is all. Since no man, of aught he leaves, knows, what is't to leave betimes? Let be." (V, ii, 210–211).

Death is as good an answer as any for what has happened to his world in the few months since he was summoned home from Wittenberg. He did not, we might say, waste his time there, for in his philosophic "the readiness is all" he has found the heroic answer and becomes heroic in moving beyond the fear of death —and the fear of life.

What remains? A modern drama might well drop the final curtain as Hamlet completes this speech and Osric enters carrying the foils.

The Poisoner Poisoned

The final scene of the play is, however, essential to Shakespeare's play and to a play of such mythic significance. It contains more than the dashing dramatic swordplay during which the audience knows what Hamlet does not—that he is fighting for his life, since even one "hit" from Laertes' envenomed foil will mean his death. Hamlet is now calm and rational, appreciative of his guilt in Laertes' eyes. He apologizes to Laertes: "Give me your pardon, sir; I've done you wrong" (V, ii, 213). And now, abandoning his claim "That I essentially am not in madness, / But mad in craft" (III, iv, 187–188), he tells Laertes and the court, "I am punish'd / With sore distraction" (V, ii, 216–217), and insists that it was not he who wronged Laertes but his madness:

> Hamlet is of the faction that is wrong'd;
> His madness is poor Hamlet's enemy.
> Sir, in this audience,
> Let my disclaiming from a purposed evil
> Free me so far in your most generous thoughts,

That I have shot mine arrow o'er the house,
And hurt my brother.   (V, ii, 225–231)

Hamlet finally but belatedly pleads that he did not mean to kill Polonius and that he was not in control of himself at the time. However much commentators argue about Hamlet's madness, and however psychiatrists diagnose his condition, Hamlet here lets us know, in a final plea to preserve his honor and his soul, that he has, at times, swung beyond the limits of sanity.

Hamlet's appeal moves Laertes, who may now wish to forego the treachery into which his thirst for vengeance has let Claudius entice him; but he has passed the sticking point. He falsely responds that until the matter is properly adjudicated,

I do receive your offer'd love like love,
And will not wrong it.   (V, ii, 238)

With the guilt of the poisoned foil weighing upon him, Laertes cannot now be a hero; and Hamlet cannot serve as a foil to let Laertes' skill shine "like a star i' the darkest night" (V, ii, 243). Hamlet triumphs in the fencing match, as a hero should, but perhaps only because Laertes finds the contest "almost 'gainst my conscience" (V, ii, 283) and the victory is but nominal, since both contestants are fatally poisoned in the swordplay.

The play ends, as it must, in a Gotterdämmerung brought about by treachery—Gertrude, Claudius, Laertes, and Hamlet all die, joining Polonius, Ophelia, Rosencrantz, and Guildenstern, as well as Hamlet's father. They are killed by poison, as were old Hamlet and the Player King; either by the envenomed foil or by the poisoned wine: by poison symbolic of the corruption and deceit that has poisoned each of them. The holocaust also reflects Hamlet's psychic state: his rage at those he had loved; his hatred of himself; his anger at the deceitfulness of the world, which has become for him "a sterile promontory" (II, ii, 291) surrounded by "a foul and pestilent congregation of vapours" (II, ii, 294–295). His world is empty of meaningful persons; he has withdrawn his attachment from them all. Indeed, little remains for any of the other characters caught in their own deceits—all, in Claudius' words, like limed souls "that struggling to be free / Art more engaged" (III, iii, 68–69). The devastation that wipes out the court is akin to psychotic delusions or hallucinations of the end of the world, brought on by withdrawal of "cathexis" from it.

Symbolically, the situation in which Hamlet finally avenges his father is in accord with Freud's interpretation of the reason for his prolonged delay: when Hamlet is dying and has paid for his own incestuous and parricidal fantasies, he can kill Claudius, the person who killed Hamlet's father and married his mother. We also note that he kills Claudius only after his mother is dead —when he no longer unconsciously needs a father figure to stand between himself and his incestuous desires. Hamlet finally kills Claudius by forcing his own poison down his throat; yet even though Claudius has just killed his mother and has fatally poisoned him, Hamlet is still preoccupied with Claudius' sexual life with his mother:

> Here, thou incestuous, murderous, damned Dane,
> Drink off this potion!   (V, ii, 312–313)

As that "fell sergeant, death" (V, ii, 323) grips them, Laertes and Hamlet absolve each other from guilt, each seeking to save the other's soul as he comprehends his own guilt. Both recognize how they have betrayed themselves by passions originating in Claudius' crime, which, like the "cease of majesty," draws "What's near it with it" (III, iii, 15, 17). Fundamental rules of society supported by the basic taboos against fratricide and the seduction of a brother's wife, were broken by the heads of state, and the corruption has poisoned all.

Enter Fortinbras

Now, Fortinbras, who has been a major figure in the tragedy, even though he has been on stage only momentarily, appears to close the play. Because his father had been slain by Hamlet's father, he is Hamlet's natural, hereditary adversary. His actions frame the play. At the start, he is threatening to invade Denmark to regain the lands his father had lost along with his life to Hamlet's father. At the end, he is about to gain the throne without even having sought it. Caught up in his obligations to avenge his father's honor by killing his uncle, and seeking a way to salvage his mother's honor, Hamlet never has the opportunity to defend his father's honor against the son of his foe. Claudius has prepared to defend Denmark against an external foe, but his reign collapses because of his own transgressions. Consistent with the play's focus on inner, not external, conflicts, the state, like the main characters, dies of an imposthume "That inward breaks, and shows no cause without / Why the man dies" (IV, iv, 28–29).

At the conclusion, while "soldiers' music and the rites of war / Speak loudly for him" (V, ii, 386–387), Fortinbras has four captains

> Bear Hamlet, like a soldier, to the stage;
> For he was likely, had he been put on,
> To have proved most royally.   (V, ii, 383–385)

The play ends as it begins, on a military note.

VIII

HAMLET AS HERO

HAD he been put on!" Like all else in the play, Shakespeare leaves Hamlet's status ambiguous. This most renowned hero of the Western stage is a strange sort of hero. Indeed, some have even questioned if he properly is a hero at all. G. Wilson Knight, as we have noted, saw him as the embassy of death. To Ophelia and Laertes, he becomes a villain, or, at least, an enemy. In his madness he kills needlessly and causes Ophelia's insanity and death. The role of Hamlet can be interpreted diversely, but any careful reading eliminates that of romantic hero and even that of a proper Renaissance hero. In a contemporary version, Hamlet might even be an antihero in revolt against his parents, against the older generation, against the establishment—disillusioned and anomic because the older generations have not lived up to their teachings, and "Virtue itself of vice must pardon beg" (III, iv, 154).

Hamlet is not a hero who has captivated countless hearts because of his deeds, even though he does ultimately avenge his father. Audiences empathize with him primarily because he represents a youth filled with promise and idealism, skilled with words as well as with sword, a wit as well as a philosopher, a young man first touched by love but whose hopes and promise are blighted by the deceits of the world and, particularly, by the infidelity of his mother. He symbolizes youth on the threshold of adulthood. The spectator or reader is caught up in the tragedy of adolescent hopes turned into despair and empathizes because he, as all men, mourns his own lost innocence and idealism. The audience relives with Hamlet the dissipation of high intentions, and like Brecht's Mack the Knife sighs, "To be a good person —Yes—who doesn't wish it, but the circumstances . . ."

Insofar as Hamlet is regarded as the embassy of death who destroys the blossoming Ophelia, he should not be taken as a static symbol. As the play begins, he, too, is a symbol of spring; he only becomes a chilling, destructive figure as his life is blighted by the corruption of the court, the world he reenters. We shall see in Chapter X that Amleth, in the saga that Shakespeare knew and followed in many respects, retrieved his mother from her errors, slew his treacherous uncle, and became a great hero. Shakespeare, however, did not create a conquering hero but a tragic hero of a new type—a hero whose major task is to conquer himself, not his foes. He must struggle with his passions and overcome his matricidal impulses in order to reclaim her, even though his sanity totters in the process. He is a hero who, although a prince, is caught up in personal problems with his parents and with his beloved and her family as much as, if not more than, such matters of heroic magnitude as avenging his father and protecting his country from foreign assault. He is also heroic in the way he confronts the crucial existential problem of knowing that death is man's ultimate fate; he faces the problem, and weighs his thoughts and feelings about life and death instead of disdaining death with traditional heroic bravura. When Hamlet attains the capacity to face both life and death with equanimity, he achieves a type of salvation in a way that can be imparted to and shared by any audience.

Hamlet's character and conflicts are set off by two men, Horatio and Fortinbras, who remain after death has cleared the stage. They have remained essentially uninvolved in the machinations of the court. Both are men Hamlet admired, and they represent divergent ego ideals that Hamlet could not unify within himself. Horatio is to Hamlet a man

> Whose blood and judgement are so well commingled
> That they are not a pipe for Fortune's finger
> To sound what stop she please.   (III, ii, 64–66)

"Not passion's slave," Horatio possesses a philosophic equanimity that Hamlet esteemed and sought to achieve but could not maintain. Hamlet is a tragic hero, in part, because he is forced to turn from his concept of the good life (which Horatio represents) to pursue vengeance and to become involved in a passionate jealousy of a father figure who possesses his mother. It is this rekindled childhood jealousy of, and disillusionment in, his mother because of her sexuality that warrants Freud's emphasis on the importance of Hamlet's oedipal feelings as a key to his character and behavior.

Fortinbras, on the other hand, was to Hamlet a young hero,[1]

> a delicate and tender prince,
> Whose spirit with divine ambition puff'd
> Makes mouths at the invisible event;
> Exposing what is mortal and unsure
> To all that fortune, death, and danger dare,
> Even for an egg-shell. (IV, iv, 48–53)

Determined to restore the honor lost to his name after his father's defeat by Hamlet's father, Fortinbras simply finds an excuse to attack Poland when restrained by his uncle from waging war against Denmark. Such attributes are difficult to unite with the virtues of a Horatio; but to Hamlet, they are the proper characteristics of a king—and indeed, to judge by Hamlet's praise of him, King Hamlet may have been of such mettle. It was this direct and uncomplicated hero Hamlet favored for election to the throne of Denmark, to start a new and less corrupt cycle in its history.

IX

RECAPITULATION

I HAVE presented a reading of *Hamlet* that focuses on the theme of madness. It clarifies the origins and nature of Hamlet's instability and of Ophelia's madness, as well as the essential similarity between the situations in which Hamlet and Ophelia are caught. It also sharpens our grasp of the structure of the play, for the theme and countertheme concern Hamlet's and Ophelia's dilemmas, respectively, with Hamlet's fortunes and Ophelia's sanity balanced on the slaying of Polonius. The reading also illustrates how Shakespeare's understanding of the causes of mental and emotional instability not only foreshadowed but, in some areas, continues to overshadow Freud's insights.

The Movement of the Play

At the start of the play we see the youthful Hamlet not simply mourning for his father but already melancholic and weary of life because of his mother's hasty marriage to his father's brother. He is disillusioned with her and embittered because he feels his mother has given in to her sensuality and sullied his father's memory; and he can no longer believe, as a son seeks to believe, that he was second only to his father in his mother's affection. Then, Hamlet's world collapses and his sanity totters when he is told by his father's ghost that Claudius had poisoned him and that Claudius and Gertrude had cuckolded him. Hamlet, who had come to terms with his triangular relationship to his mother and father, is now caught in a triangular relationship between his father and uncle with an obligation to avenge his father, and also in a new triangular relationship with parents—with a mother and stepfather. His self-esteem, based upon his identification with a father he once believed his mother idolized, is seriously shaken. His oedipal jealousy of his mother is rekindled, and he now feels that both he and his father have been betrayed by her. His bitterness to his mother now reaches a murderous intensity. His love for Ophelia is affected: although he now has a great need for a loving person to replace his mother, his feelings toward his mother spill over and blight his relationships to all women. His behavior toward Ophelia vacillates markedly, so that Ophelia becomes perplexed, dismayed, and particularly vulnerable to the next blow that befalls her.

Hamlet's grip on reality is loosened because he is forced to turn against the person he had once loved most. Distrusting his own senses, he convinces himself of Claudius' guilt by the superbly dramatic play-within-the-play, but he uses it to mobilize his mother's conscience as much as to "catch the conscience of the king." Struggling to contain his matricidal impulses, Hamlet castigates Gertrude for her remarriage and especially for her sexual life with Claudius. Venting his rage eases his psychological burden and finally enables him to focus upon his task of avenging his father.

At this juncture, when Hamlet has gained both solid evidence of his uncle's perfidy and the psychological ability to move against him, the play doubles back on itself, so to speak, and its countertheme becomes dominant. Hamlet kills Polonius, and the relationships between Hamlet, Ophelia, and Polonius become the focus of attention. Hamlet becomes the pursued as well as a pursuer; to Ophelia and Laertes, he becomes a villain rather than a hero. Ophelia is now caught in a predicament very similar to Hamlet's: she must now turn against the person she had loved deeply. She cannot endure the conflict in her emotions, losing her sanity and then drowning herself as she drowns in her sorrows.

The theme and countertheme now come together. The plot becomes fugue-like, as Laertes joins with Claudius in seeking Hamlet's death and Hamlet prepares to take vengeance against Claudius. Hamlet is endangered, in a sense, because he has displaced his hostility to his mother onto Ophelia and his hostility to Claudius onto Claudius' representatives, Polonius, Rosencrantz, and Guildenstern. Already disillusioned with the world because of his mother's behavior, Hamlet becomes even more weary of life when he hears of Ophelia's death and recognizes his responsibility for it. Hamlet and Laertes fight in Ophelia's grave over their possessive love for Ophelia—as, in a way, they will duel over her in the final scene. Hamlet can now face life and death with equanimity. "The readiness is all," he says and he is ready for either. In the end, the main characters all die of poison, reflecting the moral poison that flowed from the king's and queen's transgressions. A new regime, under Fortinbras, brings hope for the rebirth of the nation.

The Psychoanalytic Moment

A study of the psychodynamic configurations in the play invites reconsideration of some basic psychoanalytic concepts, as well as of the psychoanalytic meaning of the play itself. I shall only designate some of these matters here, and return to consider them more fully in Part Three. Shakespeare differentiates between the causes of mourning and melancholia very much as Freud did. He does not emphasize the hostile component of Hamlet's ambivalent feelings toward his deceased father as a cause of his depression; instead Shakespeare stresses the narcissistic blow and loss of self-esteem Hamlet suffers because of his mother's behavior, which arouses a hostility to his mother he cannot express, as well as the disillusionment with the world and those who people it because of his disillusionment with his mother. However, the play does not, in itself, consider the instinctual nature of the oedipal situation, or require that Hamlet be preoccupied with his hostility to his mother and uncle because of a fixation at the oedipal phase of development. Rather it deals with what a mother's betrayal of her husband can do to a son and with the importance of the parents' relationship with each other and to their child. We can see in the play how Hamlet's self-esteem depends upon having a mother he can cherish and respect; his emotional stability rests not only on his trust in her but also on his belief in her fidelity to the father he envied and may have wished to displace. Further, we can note that when Hamlet must assume a parental, punitive role with his mother and stepfather, he lacks self-control and his behavior takes on grandiose manic and even paranoid characteristics.

When we turn to consider Ophelia, we find that Shakespeare has created a situation that is almost the mirror image of Hamlet's. Ophelia is deprived not only of her father but also of Hamlet, because he is responsible for her father's death. Shakespeare has focused on a critical conflict in a woman's development—her ability to shift her attachment from her father to a man who can bring her fulfillment as a woman. Here, the conflict between the father and the lover, a recurrent theme in myth, leads to a tragic outcome for Ophelia. I shall later consider how and why the girl's problem in achieving release from her father and the parental family differs from the boy's oedipal transition.

The theme and countertheme of *Hamlet* focus on the importance of the family as a unit, not just on the dyadic relationships that were emphasized predominantly in early psychoanalytic theory, and which influenced the way in which the oedipal triangle was conceptualized. The play primarily stresses the importance of continuing intrafamilial relationships to a person's emotional stability rather than solely, or primarily, the influence of early childhood relationships on later life.

Madness in *Hamlet*

The Existential Movement

Beyond the psychodynamic issues, *Hamlet*, from its opening scenes, presents to us that core existential dilemma brought about by man's ability to choose between life and death. It is a conflict that Freud unfortunately sought to handle by equating fears of death with castration anxiety. The play weighs through its action, as well as through Hamlet's soliloquies, the benefits and burdens of life on the one hand and surcease through suicide on the other. Although the question of the value of life may seem more fundamental than the interpersonal and family themes, it is not weighed independently of these but as intimately related to them. The play examines how the desire to live or die depends on the worth of meaningful relationships, and how the loss of a cardinal "love object," sometimes through death but predominantly through disillusion and hostility, can swing the balance to the side of death.

Hamlet, as a classic tragedy derived from and closely related to myth, fills a cultural superego function. It is concerned with infractions of basic taboos essential for the stability and preservation of the family and thereby of society. It questions the obligation to maintain honor through the pursuit of vengeance, a belief that held sway through the Middle Ages and Renaissance, when the family had to serve as the primary protector of its members. It reinforces basic ethical principles by conveying the consequences of passionate misdeeds carried out for personal gain or through a misguided sense of obligation.

Like a dream, the play contains a multiplicity of interrelated and overlapping themes that are difficult to isolate. I have sought to select the core themes that are joined together compactly and cohesively, but these exist in a context of related matters that enrich the play by stirring up fantasies and repressed unconscious memories and longings in the spectator. To convey something of the fullness of what *Hamlet* contains and why it has so captivated different ages and cultures, I must leave off trying to examine its content and form and turn to a study of the sagas and myths that enfold it. Myth can convey through its own type of symbolic expression much that cannot be expressed in logical sequences—much that is valid and meaningful precisely because it is unconscious, paradoxical, and even contradictory in seeking to express the fundamental themes that recur from life to life and culture to culture, themes that thus have a constancy amid continual change.

Let us, then, turn to Amleth, the son of Horvendile, god of spring, and of Gertrude—once Groa, the Earth herself—and to Fortinbras the Elder, who was Koll, or Winter, in the sagas; to Lucius Junius Brutus and the overhasty marriage of Tarquinus Superbus, at which the funeral baked-meats did thriftily furnish the marriage tables; to Orestes and Electra, whose mother and stepfather had ample justification for betraying and killing Agamemnon; and let us see where into the depths of the human mystery these tales take us.

PART TWO

Saga and Myth in *Hamlet*

◇◇◇◇◇◇◇◇◇◇◇◇◇◇◇◇◇◇◇◇◇◇◇◇◇◇◇◇◇◇◇◇◇◇◇

In plays like *Hamlet* or the *Agamemnon* or the *Electra* we have certainly fine and flexible character study, a varied and well-wrought story, a full command of the poet and the dramatist; but we have also, I suspect, a strange, unanalyzed vibration below the surface, an undercurrent of desires and fears and passions, long slumbering yet eternally familiar, which have for thousands of years lain near the root of our most intimate emotions and been brought into the fabric of our most magical dreams. How far into the past ages this stream may reach back, I dare not even surmise, but it seems as if the power of stirring it or moving with it were one of the lost secrets of genius.

GILBERT MURRAY,
"Hamlet and Orestes"

THE FUNCTIONS
OF MYTH

THE SOPHISTICATED and carefully constructed *Hamlet* contains in the shadows of its ambiguities the residues of age-old myths that reflect some of man's basic impulses, desires, and fears, and transmit across the ages what man may have been like before societal taboos and institutions forced the containment and repression of primal passions. These myths tell of filicidal acts carried out to propitiate the gods, but also because of unbridled intrafamilial jealousies and hatreds; of incestuous deeds carried out to fructify the soil, but also because of unrestrained lust; and of other acts that continued to foster discord from generation to generation. Even though the cruder acts do not enter into *Hamlet* directly, they are present in the atmosphere and are suggested by the action. They stir the unconscious of the spectator and rouse from its depths primal wishes that had arisen in early childhood, and then were repressed with varying degrees of effectiveness, but which continue to flicker through dreams during the dark of sleep.

Myth and Dramatic Catharsis

The play sets off certain resonances in one person and different ones in another, and with greater or lesser intensities according to the person's makeup and experiences; but the greatness and timelessness of the play relates to its capacities to evoke a fascination with impulsions that threaten to emerge in all, to overwhelm and lead us into catastrophe despite our ego and superego controls—our efforts to guide our lives wisely and ethically. We are carried along with the impulsions and passions of the characters, feel the release and ecstasy of giving vent to the repressed in us; but then feel purged through suffering the consequences with them, and emerge more content with our more controlled and prosaic lives. The play brings that release, too, of letting each of us know that he is not alone in having such tabooed thoughts or impulsions—which unites us with the characters in the play, and through them with the remainder of mankind.

Myth and Basic Socialization

The taming of man for civilized life, through the control of acts of passion and vengeance that would disrupt society, was a lengthy process repeated in all parts of the world. Although the solutions differed from one ethnic group to another, the basic problems that required resolution were everywhere much the same: how to curb the sexual and aggressive drives that so easily disrupt any social system and, especially, how to control intrafamilial murder and incest in order to insure family stability, which everywhere forms the basis of communal living. Fathers, mothers, sons, and daughters must be able to live together despite the passions that arise among them because of the needs, loves, hatreds, desires, and jealousies they have for one another. As the family enlarges, the controls must envelop the extended family and the clan, and the leader must be protected against the envy and ambitions of others.

Every society develops taboos, customs, and laws to direct and control the behavior of individuals and regulate their relationships. The child growing up in a society acquires self-control by assimilating the society's mores and rules as well as the behavior and ethical standards of parental persons. Yet, the culture and the societal mores are not born into the individual: the child grows into and assimilates the customs, rules, and traditions that the society has slowly evolved. Still, the epochs of gradual socialization of the ethnic group—or of mankind—have not affected the newborn babe one whit, but only those who raise him, and the setting in which he grows up. To become capable of living within a social system and with his fellow man, each individual must, so to speak, recapitulate in his own life the control or repression of the same basic drive-impelled forces that beset his primitive ancestors. Of course, when the setting properly provides for a child's basic needs and directs his drives into socially useful channels, many of the primitive conflicts that augment hostile and incestuous impulsions may never arise or may stir up only moderate waves within the sheltered harbor; but the potentiality is born into everyone, and when the developmental milieu is deficient, chaotic, insecure, brutal, or seductive, these impulsions can mount and give rise to devastating storms, needs for vengeance, and misplaced sexuality. The socializing and repressive forces never extinguish the basic drives, and although they may emerge only in dreams and fantasies, each person will have at least unconscious connections with the urges and wishes that are forbidden civilized man.

The development of myths has played an important—perhaps a central—role in the taming of antisocial passions, even though, paradoxically, the myths often concern violent infractions of basic taboos. The classic drama continues to carry out some of the functions of myth for the audience. It shares with myth the capacity to make tangible what is almost inexpressible—inexpressible because it is concerned with diffuse emotions and involves much that has been kept from conscious awareness and thereby from the clarifying power of language.

Myths serve many purposes. They attempt to account for ritual as a means of controlling nature; they explain nature's regularities and inconsistencies; they create or preserve genealogies and relate man to his imagined supernatural forebears; they preserve and magnify the heroics of ancestors to provide a people with feelings of distinction and distinctness, as well as other such functions of placing a people in nature and distinguishing them as a people. One highly significant function of mythology is to control acts that would threaten the foundations of the society; and, interestingly, this function would seem to derive from efforts to help nature keep in course and to control its vicissitudes.

Characteristics of Mythic Thought

As Schlegel noted long ago in his *Lectures on Dramatic Arts and Literature*, that which ever eludes consciousness is fixed and made visible through myth. It makes the evanescent and inexpressible tangible through analogy, by evoking a multiplicity of associations, feelings, and fantasies that are related to one another through some shared symbol—or only unconsciously, because a forbidden theme has been repressed. In its condensed symbolic form myth can, like a dream, express ambivalent, contradictory feelings concerning an act or impulse: the desire and the fear, the temptation and the abhorrence, the lust and the disgust. By and large, myth seeks to make tangible the eternally recurrent. Mythic time, we might say, differs from historic time; because of this difference, myths can encapsulate some fundamental truths about human existence. Instead of being concerned with the sequence of events leading up to some unique, never-recurring episode, myth emphasizes the cyclic and recurrent in events. Myths tell tales symbolic of the return of life with spring after earth's winter death; of the cyclic phases of the moon, of the annual wheel of the constellations; but also of how each person ages and dies, and how the life cycle is repeated by his children; of how sons seek to replace fathers; of sibling rivalries; of how mothers side with sons against husbands; of daughters torn between fathers and lovers; and of other such happenings that transpire in all cultures. The individual in the myth, as the myth itself, is but another example of a universal theme, ever unrolling differently and yet ever the same. Time passes, but it will again lead to the old.

Ritual and Myth

The type of myth with which we are concerned probably had its origins in primitive ritual.[1] A major function of ritual, if not its prime purpose, is to maintain the ordered recurrence of events vital to human existence—the reappearance of spring, the essential rains, the harvest, the turn in the lengthening dark of the year—as well as to ease birth, and to promote the transitions of puberty, marriage, and death.

Ritual was man's way of attempting to keep nature in order. Ritual is usually the prerogative or function of males, who require artificial means of relating to nature to compensate for feelings that women are inherently more closely united to nature through menstruation, conception, and childbirth. Man sought to influence nature by sympathetic magic: ritual copulation in the fields would assure fertility; the Yule fires he lit would cause the days to lengthen. Man lived in awe of nature, which engulfed him and controlled his fate. Unable to control nature, he had to subject himself to it and pattern his life to its immutable regularities; but he was also aware of the aleatory in nature, which was a major source of insecurity and catastrophe. The fickleness of nature was a major preoccupation, and being human, he sought to control the uncontrollable by ritual, which even included sacrificing a king, the king's priest, or some substitute in the process. The collective willing of the people that accompanied ritual could help bring about the desired manifestation, as in Hopi rain rituals; or ancestor spirits who could control nature would be induced or obligated to do so by the ritual as in New Guinea.

Animism and the Control of Nature

Early man, in seeking to explain the consistencies and inconsistencies of natural phenomena could, like the young child of today, understand nature only in animistic terms, not because he lacked intelligence but because he had not yet developed scientific ways of thinking. Contemporary nonliterate peoples continue to rely on ritual, sorcery, and magic as instrumental techniques in the many areas for which they have no other means of coping; and, of course, even highly civilized peoples resort to ritual and belief in elaborate mythologies, particularly concerning matters in which more logical or more scientific methods do not provide security. Piaget in his *The Origins of Intelligence in Children,* has shown how the young child who thinks "preoperationally" considers that inanimate objects have wills, motives, and power to carry out their wishes: the sun rises because it is tired of sleeping; the clouds move to make a wind; and so forth. The child believes that objects in nature were created by or for man; that parents can control nature, and that his or her own wishes can influence natural phenomena. Early man and nonliterate ethnic groups—like the child who believes that the sun, moon, wind, and earth have wills of their own—went on to anthropomorphize nature; that is, to understand acts of nature in the only way he could—in terms of human motivation. (A residue of such ways of thinking can be noted in the phrase "acts of nature.") Anthropomorphization permitted man to do something about controlling natural phenomena; anthropomorphized nature could be conceived of as gods, giants, or demons who could be appeased, placated, threatened, or influenced by magic, prayer, or sacrifice. Natural events could be deemed the outcome of acts of the immortals' lovemaking, rivalries, or overt conflicts. Kings, priests, and heroes might be thought to have special relationships with such deities, much as children are apt to consider that their parents have power over nature.

In anthropomorphizing the remainder of nature, man could only endow it with the desires, emotions, drives, and conflicts he knew existed in himself and in other men and women. He did not conceive of his gods as having attributes different from his own, though he might believe that they would live out in deed what he might but dimly fantasy. He gradually elaborated his attributions of human qualities to nature into tales about the gods, and about ancestral heroes who had been close to the gods and who had protected his forebears from their enemies—of how they fought demons, dragons, and giants representative of adverse natural forces. Myth equated some characteristics of inanimate and vegetal nature with some aspect of human nature. Equating human life to plant life made it possible to deny the finality of death by holding up the expectation of rebirth and resurrection according to the pattern in vegetal life of annual death in the fall and reappearance each spring— a mental maneuver utilized by virtually every ethnic group which forms an inherent, though masked, core belief of many religions.

Mythic thinking categorizes together events that might otherwise seem disparate and unrelated. For example, marriage and the coming of spring were connected through the ritual in which a selected youth copulated with the May Queen or earth priestess to assure the fertility of the soil; the winter solstice was related to regicide through myths of the slaying of the old king, symbolic of the dying year, by his supplanter. As Lévi-Strauss in *The Savage Mind* has insisted, nonliterate or "primitive" peoples are obviously capable of categorical thinking, but the manner in which they categorize may be obscure to us. Categorizations that bestows a type of equivalence to man and nature are essential for efforts to influence nature by magic or ritual— efforts that diminish feelings of helplessness before the contingencies of nature.

Saga and Myth in *Hamlet*

Myth and the Control of Human Nature

In developing rites and myths to cope with natural phenomena, man told tales about the wellsprings of human behavior in terms of the motives, passions, and perverse inclinations that led deities and heroes representative of anthropomorphized nature to behave as they did. Thus, myths have much to say about human nature as well as the remainder of nature. Further, man had to learn to live with human nature, which is even more unpredictable than other natural phenomena. He sought to understand and control the inconsistencies in himself and others, the forces that welled up within him and disrupted his plans, the conflicts within himself and between people. Such matters also contained prime sources of catastrophe. Therefore, while myths concern the power of external nature—which he holds in awe—upon man they also concern the power of nature within him, the forces that unsettle and tantalize him and to which he wishes to give way, but at the same time he wishes to hold in check lest they overpower.

One means of keeping human behavior within the bounds required for social living was the development of myths that told not only of the awesome or dreadful deeds carried out by heroic progenitors but also of the horrors that befell them as consequences of such acts. Indeed, the awful deed may once have been proper in its ritual setting, like a king's sacrifice of his son to assure the fertility of the soil or to placate a god whose plague had decimated the populace. Tantalus' sacrifice of his son, Pelops, whom he then served as a meal to the Olympians, was assuredly once deemed an act of piety or a ritual sacrifice, similar to Abraham's aborted sacrifice of his beloved son Isaac. But as the myth became divorced from ritual and the nature of the ritual became abhorrent to the Greeks and therefore to their gods, Tantalus became abhorrent and was charged with hubris; and then with filicide, for which the gods punished him in Hades, and for which his descendants were fated to sin and suffer even unto the fourth generation.

A myth can thus reinforce the cultural superego or a basic

taboo by holding before the members of a society that which befell an ancestor who was almost a god when he carried out an "unnatural" act or gave way to a forbidden impulsion—forbidden because it endangered the harmonious development of the individual or the stability of the social system. Because the solidity of the family is fundamental to the stability of any society, many of the most telling myths concern the consequences of disruptions of intrafamilial relationships.

As firm cultural directives for human behavior were established in a society, its people increasingly believed that proper, ethical individual and group behavior could control natural phenomena. Thus, man relied less upon the performance of ritual and more on ethics; but here, too, he was directed by lessons taught from his mythology. In the myth of Oedipus, for example, at first the land was thought to have become barren and blighted because Laius was impotent or because Jocasta, who as queen represented the earth, had been befouled by incest; but in a later era, the people believed that the country had been punished because incest was a sin, abhorrent to the gods. Of course, ethics, even in the form of organized religious belief, could not displace ritual completely. Even in recent times, Christianity could not eliminate the need people, particularly peasants, had for ritual that would assure the fertility of their lands. Virtually all religions have compromised and incorporated old rituals into their rites and old myths into their belief systems.

The Myths in *Hamlet*

In the study of *Hamlet* we are, of course, interested in how the underlying mythology applies to human behavior. Drama, like myth, had its origins in ritual; and the classic drama continues to be related to myth. The great tragedies often derive from myths the means of focusing upon the eternal and essential problems man encounters in the control of his passions, as well as the consequences of his failures. *Hamlet* is of this order of drama, and it holds its central position because it brings together, blends, and holds in apposition certain of the most salient myths concerned with cardinal recurrent problems besetting and fascinating man.

Freud and Jones, as I have discussed, related Hamlet to Oedipus because of his preoccupation with his mother's sexual life and his difficulties in killing his father's murderer; whereas Frederic Wertham, as well as Gilbert Murray and many other literary critics, emphasized Hamlet's more apparent relatedness to Orestes. The synthesis of these two interpretations, the oedipal and the oresteian, leads not only to a deeper comprehension of the play's extraordinary power but also to an understanding of the relationship of the two myths and why variations of them are such common themes in mythology.

It is significant that when Freud sought to express one of his most profound insights into human behavior, he utilized a myth as transmuted into a Sophoclean tragedy. Through the analogy of a myth, Freud could approximate the complexities of unconscious motivations and conflicts, with their ambiguities, contradictions, condensations, displacements, and symbolizations. The psychoanalyst not only finds in myth ways of transmitting to others what is otherwise almost inexpressible except through lengthy and cumbersome dissertations, but he also discovers in some myths the same crucial themes and conflicts he hears in various forms from his patients.

Since such myths and classic tragedies are concerned with intrafamilial forces and their influences upon individuals, they cannot but be important to the analyst who seeks ways to make such family influences tangible: to designate the continuity between deeds of parents and the lives of their children, to grasp themes that haunt family lines, and to convey how a family curse that a person believes he has left continents and decades behind him nevertheless reappears from within the fugitive. Yes, it is often in myth—and in myth crystallized into drama—that the psychiatrist finds the parallels to his case material, which enables him to generalize from the individual case to eternally recurrent themes and conflicts, eternally recurrent because they are consequences of the human condition. Focusing on these themes and problems created by the necessities of the human condition brings existential and structuralist approaches into conjunction with the psychoanalytic.

Shakespeare's attention was drawn to several legends and myths of diverse origins—Norse sagas, Greek mythology, Roman legend and history, the Old Testament—as he consciously or unconsciously noted their common or overlapping basic themes. Eventually they coalesced in his creative mind into a new unity that expressed something particularly important to him: something he needed to say, something that may even have tormented him until he expressed and brought it to life through the characters he created—who then, as is the way with such children of genius, seemed to create the play by living out their fates. Now, even though we know little of Shakespeare's life and even less about his emotional problems, we may surmise that in writing *Hamlet* he was attempting to resolve a major intrapsychic crisis that gravely threatened his equanimity. The conjecture has validity only through analogy with other playwrights. August Strindberg sought to work through his paranoid jealousy of his first wife and find some resolution for his anguish in writing *The Father*; and later, as I have discussed elsewhere, to find some way of coping with conflicts he could not solve in his own life through creating his "dream plays."[2] Eugene O'Neill struggled to gain some surcease from the problems with his parents that haunted him and to replace his anger toward them with compassion through writing *Long Day's Journey into Night*. Tennessee Williams sought to gain perspective and rid himself of his guilt about his psychotic sister in *A Glass Menagerie*. The major work or works of these—and still other—playwrights deal with intensely personal problems. A play's capacity to promote emotional catharsis and help restore personal equilibrium appears often to start with its creator.

As the sixteenth century came to a close, Shakespeare's plays took on a new quality, including a rather pervasive emotional tone that seems to reflect the author's depressed mood and his preoccupation with disillusionments caused by broken loyalties and the fickleness of women. If Shakespeare, in writing *Hamlet*, was dealing with problems that were central to his own life, then this man who was without peer in understanding his fellow man, was also entering upon themes and conflicts that have been germane, if not central, to virtually every man.

In turning to the myths and legends that merge in *Hamlet*, I shall proceed in two stages. First, I shall examine the sources available to Shakespeare which, I believe, entered directly into his conceptualization and construction of the play. Then, I shall turn to the origins of these sources in ritual and myth and consider how vital they have been to mankind across the ages.

XI

SHAKESPEARE'S
SOURCES

IN the first section of this study, we examined the nature and origins of Hamlet's antic disposition and Ophelia's madness. We noted how an understanding of Ophelia's insanity clarifies what troubles Hamlet and how the apposition of her predicament to Hamlet's brings balance to the play. The importance of the theme of madness in the play is also evident from the fact that Shakespeare not only utilized the saga of Amleth, a "mad hero," as his vehicle, but modified it by using material derived from tales and plays about three other mad or witless heroes: Lucius Junius Brutus, who feigned stupidity to protect himself from his uncle-king; Nero, the mad incestuous matricide, whose uncle Claudius had pretended in his youth to be too stupid to be worth assassinating; and Orestes, who became mad after killing his mother. As we shall see, the playwright grasped the relationship among these figures and blended them to create a new hero, a new type of hero who continues to hold a very special place in the minds of men. Then, in creating Ophelia, and constructing the countertheme that encompasses her, Shakespeare appears to have been influenced by the plight of Amleth's first wife, an unnamed English princess; and, further, the playwright recognized her relationship to both Jephthah's daughter and Orestes' ill-fated sister, Iphigenia. Furthermore, in constructing the play he developed a dramatic device that his contemporary Kyd used in the highly successful *Spanish Tragedy*, a revenge play in which characters fluctuate between madness and sanity. Examining these sources and Shakespeare's use of them provides insights not only into his intentions but also into his creative capacities.

Tradition, backed by some scanty evidence, holds that in writing *Hamlet*, Shakespeare reshaped an earlier play, often designated as the *Ur-Hamlet*. We have no definite knowledge of that revenge play. The first reference to a *Hamlet* play, a derogatory comment, is found in a letter by Nash prefixed to Greene's *Menaphon*, which was published in 1589, a date which makes it unlikely, but not impossible, that it was a play by Shakespeare. Then, in 1594, Henslowe recorded the revival of a *Hamlet* at Newington Butts. We cannot be certain that Lodge's remarks in 1596 in his *Wit's Misery and the World's Madnesse* about a ghost which cried, "like an oesterwife, Hamlet, revenge" did not refer to an early version of Shakespeare's play.[1]

If an *Ur-Hamlet* existed, whoever wrote it based it on the Amleth saga, either as recorded in Latin by Saxo Grammaticus in his "history" of the Danes at the end of the twelfth or the beginning of the thirteenth century, or as translated by Belleforest in his slightly altered French version, published in 1564. Since we do not know how the author of the *Ur-Hamlet* may have used the saga, and since we do know that Shakespeare was thoroughly familiar with either Saxo or Belleforest (as will become apparent), I shall assume that the differences between the Amleth saga and the play are Shakespeare's doing.[2]

Although some readers are surely sufficiently familiar with the Amleth saga and others may find themselves less than intrigued by this most interesting of Saxo's tales of the Danish heroes, I must ask the reader to accompany me through a summary of the story. I wish not only to compare the play to the first part of the saga—as has been done before—but also to comment on how portions of the second half of the saga, usually neglected as irrelevant to the play, influenced the development of *Hamlet*. In the subsequent chapter, I shall comment on other Norse tales and myths that are related to the Amleth saga and have relevance to the implications of the play.

The Amleth Saga

During Rorick's reign in Denmark, the brothers Horvendile and Feng were co-governors of Jutland. After Horvendile, the elder brother, had ruled for three years, he gave Feng his turn and set off on adventures as a Viking sea rover. Horvendile soon became so famous that King Koll of Norway sought to increase his own renown by vanquishing him. They eventually met, and after each promised to provide the loser with a proper funeral, they engaged in single combat in a spring-tide wood. After Horvendile killed and buried Koll, he sacked the Norwegian coast. Then, tired of the life of a sea rover, and as Feng by this time had ruled for three years, he presented the best of his spoils to King Rorick, gained Rorick's daughter, Gerutha, as his wife, and returned to govern Jutland. Amleth was their only child. Feng, who was envious, eventually waylaid and slew Horvendile. He justified his fratricide by claiming that Horvendile had been about to kill the gentle Gerutha, who was greatly loved by her subjects. He then married his sister-in-law and ruled by himself.

Amleth, who was only a boy when his father was slain, feared that his uncle would kill him to preclude his vengeance. Amleth therefore pretended to be a harmless imbecile subject to fits, during which he would besmatter himself with filth. He imparted an impression of grotesque madness—indeed, of being "some absurd abortion due to a mad fit of destiny" (Saxo, ¶ 107). Still, he would sometimes fashion barbed hooks of wood, harden them in the fire, and say that he was making darts to avenge his father. His skill in making these hooks led Feng to fear that he was not as incompetent as he seemed. Feng decided to test Amleth's mental competence by seeing if he could be seduced into sexual relations, that is, to ascertain if he were capable of "knowing" a woman. He was taken to a remote forest for the seduction. En route, Amleth was told by his companions to look at the "meal," meaning the sand, to which he replied that it had indeed been ground fine by the ocean storms. Then, left alone in the forest, he was accosted by a young woman and was about to give way to his lust when he was deterred by a warning signal sent by a foster brother who was among his companions. Nevertheless, he did not pass up his opportunity; instead, he carried the woman off into a thicket where he could take his pleasure unobserved. Because the young woman had also been fostered with Amleth, and, even more, we may hope, because she had enjoyed the experience, she agreed to keep his competence secret. When Amleth boasted about how he had ravished her, she denied it so convincingly that the truth was disregarded.

Feng, however, was not fully convinced and followed a friend's advice in arranging another test. He pretended to go on a journey and left Amleth closeted in his mother's bedchamber, where Feng's friend was hidden. Feng felt certain that if Amleth were dissembling, he would take the opportunity to confide in his mother. Amleth, who was wary of a trap, pretended idiotically to be a cock hopping around the room. When he felt the spy hidden in the bedstraw, he impaled him with his sword, cut up his corpse, boiled the pieces, and threw them in the privy for the hogs to eat. Amleth then returned to Gerutha and revealed that he had been wearing the "mask of a fool" to save his life until he could avenge his father. He castigated his mother, saying, " 'wantoning like a harlot, thou hast entered a wicked and abominable state of wedlock, embracing with incestuous bosom thy husband's slayer, and wheedling with filthy lures of blandishment him who had slain the father of thy son.' " Saxo continues by remarking, "He rends his mother's heart with his reproaches and redeems her to walk in the ways of virtue" (Saxo, ¶ 112). Gerutha assured her son that she had only married Feng for Amleth's and her own safety. Overjoyed to learn that he was sound of mind and capable of avenging Horvendile, she warned him that no one in the court could be trusted.

When Feng could find no trace of his spy, Amleth told him that his friend had fallen in the sewage and been devoured by the swine, but Feng, of course, did not believe him. Feng, who had become more fearful of Amleth, wished to be rid of him but feared the wrath of his wife and her father, the powerful Rorick. He decided to send Amleth to England accompanied by two retainers bearing instructions, graven in wood, directing the king of England to hang Amleth. Before Amleth departed, he instructed his mother to cover the walls of the Great Hall with hangings and to hold a funeral feast for him after precisely one year—a feast he promised to attend. En route to England, Amleth altered the instructions so that they ordered the king of England to hang his two companions and wed his daughter to Amleth.

When welcomed with a banquet at the English court, Amleth refused to eat or drink. That night he told his companions—so that the spies he expected would be concealed in his room could hear—that he had refused to eat with the king because the king was the son of a slave, the queen a commoner, and the bread and water defiled. The king, who had been unaware of these allegations, investigated them and found that they were correct. Impressed by Amleth's unbelievable "wisdom," the king betrothed his daughter to him and hanged the two courtiers. Amleth pretended to be enraged because his companions had been killed but accepted weir-gold in compensation, which he then concealed in two hollow staves.

A year after Amleth left Jutland he returned alone, as filthy as formerly, and with nothing except the two staves. He amazed all by appearing in the Great Hall while his funeral banquet was in progress. When asked what had become of his two companions, Amleth simply showed his two staves. Then he cut himself with his sword as if by accident, and the courtiers nailed the sword in its scabbard. Amleth plied the funeral guests with wine until they all fell into a drunken stupor, then cut down the wall hangings, entrapped the courtiers in the cloth by fastening it with the wooden hooks he had previously fashioned, and sent them all to their deaths by setting the hall afire. Since Feng had retired from the banquet, Amleth went to Feng's bedroom and exchanged his sword with his uncle's. He then awakened Feng and told him that the hour of vengeance had come. Feng jumped out of bed and grabbed the sword that had been affixed to its scabbard. Unable to defend himself, he was slain by Amleth.

Amleth then made a speech in which he told the people that he had chosen to avenge his father single-handed rather than endanger his friends. They were not to mourn the despot Feng but remember the kindly Horvendile, whom Feng had slain, and they were to pity his mother, a weak woman who had been forced to bear the ignominy of marrying her husband's brother and murderer. Finally, Amleth claimed the throne and was acclaimed king. The first part of the saga ends with Saxo saying that Amleth "left it doubtful whether we are to think more of his wit or his bravery."

In the second part of the saga, Amleth becomes a great hero, but only a few aspects of the story have pertinence to *Hamlet*. In a way that is rather common in myth, the saga replays some episodes from the first part, with an altered perspective, for Amleth is now an established hero.

After he killed Feng and became the ruler of Jutland, Amleth returned to England lavishly equipped and bearing a shield on which his life story and exploits were exquisitely depicted. He was married to the English princess, which put the king of England in a dilemma. The king and Feng had made a pact to serve as each other's avenger, should that become necessary. Thus, the king was torn between the sanctity of his oath and his affection for his daughter and his new son-in-law; but he held his vow to be more important than his family bonds. Because the English king had recently lost his queen, he decided to dispatch Amleth as his envoy to the Scots' Queen Hermatruda, asking her to become his wife. The king knew that Hermatruda had remained unmarried because she slew all who came to woo her. When Amleth and his retinue camped for a night near the queen's residence, her spies filched his shield and the letter from the king. After contemplating the deeds depicted on Amleth's shield, Hermatruda decided that Amleth was the man she had been waiting to marry. She changed the king's letter to read that she was to marry Amleth, an act similar to Amleth's alteration of Feng's message to the king of England in the first part of the saga. When Amleth arrived at her court, she wooed him and told him that he had made an unfortunate mistake in marrying a woman whose forebears had been slaves when he could have her, a person of proper royal ancestry, as a wife. Amleth, overjoyed at her proposal, gave way to her embraces and married a second wife.

Amleth returned to England with Hermatruda, protected by

his Danes and her Scots. Although his first wife, the English princess, was unhappy, she remained loyal to her husband and even vowed to love Hermatruda, lest her son hate the woman who had supplanted her in Amleth's affections. She warned Amleth that her father would try to kill him, and "by this speech showed herself more inclined to love her husband than her father" (Saxo, ¶ 127). Forewarned, Amleth attended the king's banquet of welcome wearing a mail undershirt, which foiled the king's attempt to stab him. In the ensuing battle, Amleth lost most of his men, but on the following day he propped up his dead men to make them appear ready to attack. The king's men were so frightened by the size of Amleth's forces after the previous day's slaughter that they fled—"conquered" by those they had killed—and the king was slain in the rout.

After despoiling Britain, Amleth returned to Jutland with both of his wives. Rorick had died, and Gerutha had been stripped of her wealth by his successor, her brother Wiglek. Amleth presented his richest spoils to Wiglek but then attacked and subdued him. Wiglek then recruited allies to regain his throne from Amleth. When Amleth saw that he was so badly outnumbered that he probably would be defeated, he sought a suitable person for Hermatruda to marry should he be killed. Hermatruda, however, promised that she would not forsake him even in the field, saying that " 'the woman who dreaded to be united with her lord in death was abominable.' " Saxo continues, "But she kept this rare promise ill; for when Amleth had been slain by Wiglek in battle in Jutland, she yielded herself up unasked to be the conqueror's spoil and bride" (¶ 130). So ended Amleth, of whom we are told, "Had fortune been as kind to him as nature, he would have equalled the gods in glory, and surpassed the labours of Hercules by his deeds of prowess" (¶ 130).

A COMPARISON OF THE SAGA WITH *HAMLET*

The similarities between the Amleth saga and *Hamlet* are obvious. In both, the father of the hero is a Danish ruler who had slain the king of Norway in honorable combat but who was killed by an envious younger brother, who, in turn, married his queen and became ruler. In each case, the hero feigns witlessness as a protection while awaiting an opportunity to avenge his father. His uncle becomes wary and spies on him with the help of courtiers. The hero eludes a test in which a young woman is used as "bait." Then, a counselor hides in his mother's bedchamber to hear what the hero will say to his mother; the hero detects the spy and kills him and disposes of the body in a gruesome manner. The hero castigates his mother for forgetting his father and admonishes her to give up her sexual life with his uncle. The uncle then sends the hero to England accompanied by two companions carrying instructions for the king to have the hero slain, but the hero changes the instructions and sends his companions to their deaths. He then returns to his home unexpectedly to appear at a funeral, and he soon thereafter kills his uncle in an episode in which there is an exchange of swords.

It is of particular interest that certain characteristics that distinguish the hero in the first part of the Amleth saga were transferred to Hamlet, traits that are rather unusual for a hero but well suited to Shakespeare's highly intelligent, contemplative, and introspective Hamlet. These include the reliance on wits rather than physical bravery, the use of riddles, and the adherence to truth, but truth so told that it is disregarded.

Amleth uses his intellect to conceal his intelligence, whereas Hamlet takes pride in his intellect; and instead of pretending to be witless, he pretends to have lost his wits. Unlike imbecility, however, madness is potentially dangerous to others. However, Amleth is related to other mad heroes, and he served well for a play about a mad hero, and particularly for consideration of what the madness has to do with the hero's relationship with his mother. Both Amleth and Hamlet are embittered by their mothers' second marriages and sexual behavior, as well as by the murders of their fathers, and both seek to have their mothers redeemed through foregoing their sexual lives with their husbands. Hamlet, however, internalizes his hostilities, suffers, and becomes emotionally unstable.

THE TRANSFORMATION FROM SAGA TO PLAY

There are also many differences between Saxo's saga and *Hamlet*. Some of the differences derive from other sources, but some are subtle transformations of aspects of the saga, and others are suggested by situations in the saga. The changes in the names are of interest, even if not of real moment. For example, the change of the name of the hero's father from Horvendile to Hamlet underlines the importance of a son's identification with his father and, consequently, the idea that the queen's infidelity to her husband is also an infidelity to her son. The change of the name of Koll or Collerus to Fortinbras emphasized the Norwegian king's strength and heroic qualities rather than his mythic relationship to winter. As I have previously commented, the change of the uncle's name from Feng to Claudius was not casual but very meaningful.

Many clear-cut situations in the saga become hidden, veiled, or ambiguous in the play. Feng's public slaying of Horvendile becomes the secret poisoning of King Hamlet. Feng's open suspicion of Amleth's witlessness and his efforts to uncover the ruse are turned into a search for the cause of Hamlet's madness. Amleth's purposeful filthiness becomes an indication of Hamlet's distraction or his lovesick state. The sexual temptation of Amleth becomes Hamlet's confrontation by Ophelia when she tries to find out if he is mad because of her rejection of him. The girl, the "foster sister" in the saga, is possessed sexually by Amleth, whereas Shakespeare only permits a suspicion that Ophelia may have been seduced by Hamlet. Gerutha's specific denial of complicity in her husband's murder and her alliance with Amleth in his plans for vengeance, though preserved in the First Quarto version, are left ambiguous in the later versions of the play.

The transformation of Feng's shadowy friend killed by Amleth in his mother's bedchamber into Polonius is a major stroke of genius that is central to Shakespeare's play. It consolidates the plot by interconnecting the theme and countertheme, and by suddenly shifting Hamlet's relationship to Ophelia. Hamlet's disposal of the body is not as crude as Amleth's; instead of feeding it to the pigs, he simply taunts Claudius that Polonius is at supper, "Not where he eats, but where he is eaten"[3] (IV, iii, 20). Hamlet's comment that "We fat all creatures else to fat us, and we fat ourselves for maggots" (IV, iii, 22–23) is a departure from the saga that reminds the audience of the inconsequentiality of ambition in the face of man's inevitable fate of becoming food for the inconsequential worm.

The journey to England, an example of a widespread myth of a young hero sent on a journey carrying a letter ordering his death,[4] which takes a year in the saga, is shortened to a few weeks by the device of the fight with the pirates.[5] Amleth's first stay in England and his betrothal to the princess have no place in the play. Shakespeare does not have Hamlet return to appear and triumph at his own funeral, a type of resurrection, but makes a telling and dramatic change by having him return to Ophelia's funeral to learn how he unwittingly destroyed her, a blow that further dissipates his will to live.

Although the end of the play differs from that of either the first or the second part of the saga, it contains elements from both. The fatal exchange of foils between Hamlet and Laertes is foreshadowed by the puzzling and peculiar episode in which Amleth exchanges his useless sword with Feng's—an unnecessary detail that is surely a carry-over from an early tale of how a ritual mock king did not permit his ritual slaying, as I shall discuss in the following chapter. Amleth's oration to the people, justifying his murder of Feng, turns into Hamlet's insistence that Horatio remain alive to tell Hamlet's story lest the slain prince leave a wounded name behind him. The trapping of the courtiers and the burning of the Great Hall by Amleth suggest the final slaughter in *Hamlet*; and Saxo's closing lines of the saga, "Had fortune been as kind to him as nature, . . ." would seem to suggest Fortinbras' closing comment about Hamlet, "For he was likely, had he been put on, / To have proved most royally" (V, ii, 384–385).

THE INFLUENCE OF THE SECOND PART OF
THE SAGA ON *HAMLET*

Although none of the action in the second part of the Amleth saga enters into *Hamlet*, it had a significant influence upon the play, an influence that has been overlooked, insofar as I have been able to determine.

Clearly, Hermatruda's vehement protest that she will not survive Amleth and remarry, only to wed his vanquisher, his uncle Wiglek, immediately thereafter, directly suggests the Player Queen's protestations when the Player King speaks of his hopes that she will find a good second husband. Thus, this final aspect of the second part of the saga is incorporated into the play-within-the-play. Shakespeare used the episode not only as a way for Hamlet to express his feelings and twist his mother's conscience but also as a means of emphasizing the fickleness of women. We may also note that the name "Gertrude" is a combination of "Gerutha" and "Hermatruda."

Although Amleth's first wife has no place in *Hamlet*, I find a clear relationship between this unhappy princess and Ophelia. As has often been noted, the young woman Feng used to tempt Amleth sexually may be deemed a characterless precursor of Ophelia. In "Hamlet and Orestes," Gilbert Murray compared this "foster sister of Hamlet's" to Electra, who had a rather incestuous interest in Orestes. The "confrontation" scene clearly derives from the seduction episode, even though it ends in an outburst of misogynistic vituperation instead of a sexual conquest. However, it seems more apposite to compare Ophelia with the English princess. The princess, like Ophelia, was severely hurt by Amleth's rejection of her, and her father was killed by Amleth, as Ophelia's father is by Hamlet. The princess was caught between her loyalty to her father and Amleth, but in contrast to Ophelia, she remained true to her husband despite her displacement by Hermatruda and even helped Amleth vanquish her father. The dilemma in which a young woman is torn between deep attachments to her father and to her lover or suitor is a recurrent theme in Norse and Greek mythology, and we shall later examine its relationship to the Year Drama as well as to matrilineal succession. Shakespeare, in keeping with the mood of the play, has Ophelia remain obedient to her father but at the same time, makes Hamlet so important to her that she cannot survive her father's death at his hands.

Lucius Junius Brutus

Some of the differences between the Saxo saga and *Hamlet* find their origins in the Roman legend of Lucius Junius Brutus. We can be certain, for reasons that will become apparent, that Shakespeare was very familiar with the legend and consciously or unconsciously utilized it in writing *Hamlet*.

Lucius Junius Brutus, who became the first consul of Rome, had as a youth feigned imbecility to keep from being murdered by his uncle-king, who had murdered his father. Some scholars believe that Saxo fused the story into the Amleth legend, and Belleforest specifically states that Amleth sought to save himself by following the example of Junius Brutus. The connection to *Hamlet* is, however, more direct. Long before the play was produced, Shakespeare had developed a major episode in the Brutus legend into his early poem *The Rape of Lucrece*. While he may have read the story in Livy's *Roman History*, it is almost certain that he knew the version given by Dionysius of Halicarnassus in his *Roman Antiquities*. A summary of the story will make clear not only its similarities to the Amleth saga but also its contribution to *Hamlet*.

The story tells of how Lucius Tarquinius, called Superbus, slew Servius Tullius[6] to become king of Rome and was, in turn, overthrown and exiled by Brutus. Tullius, who became king by matrilineal succession when his father-in-law, Tarquinius Priscus, was assassinated, sought to maintain harmony within the family by marrying his two daughters to Tarquinius' sons, Lucius and Aruns, a move which would have returned the kingship to the Tarquins after his death. It so happened that his aggressive and ambitious daughter Tullia was married to the phlegmatic and loyal Aruns, whereas his older daughter was wedded to the ruthless Lucius. Eventually, Lucius and Tullia corrected the mismating by poisoning their spouses and marrying one another. Tullia, impatient to become queen, then incited her husband to show his spirit and overthrow her father. When Lucius' attempt to have the Senate depose Tullius and make him king failed, he caught his father-in-law by surprise by appearing in the Senate dressed as king. When Tullius opposed him, he threw the old man down the Senate steps, and as the injured king was returning to his home, Tullia had her aides stab him to death and then drive her over his body in her carriage.

Lucius Junius Brutus was the son of Tarquinia, sister of Lucius Tarquinius. Lucius Tarquinius had killed Brutus' older brother (according to Livy) or both his father and older brother (according to Dionysius) to gain the estate that Tarquinia had inherited. Some intimated that he was motivated by incestuous jealousy of his sister. Lucius Junius, still young and without a protector, decided to feign stupidity to make Tarquinius consider him harmless, accepting the name of Brutus, which means "dullard," as Hamlet means "doltish."[7] He was raised in the royal household—not, according to Dionysius, out of kindness but so that Tarquinius' three sons could be amused by his inanities.

When a snake emerged from a wooden pillar in the palace (Livy) or because a plague afflicted the city (Dionysius), Tarquinius sent two of his sons, Titus and Aruns, to Delphi to consult the oracle, sending Brutus along to keep them entertained on the journey. Much to their amusement, Brutus took along a cornel wood staff as an offering to the priest of Apollo. The staff, however, had a core of gold, like the two staves that Amleth brought with him from England. The offering thereby symbolized Brutus himself—a core of gold hidden beneath a worthless exterior. After receiving the message of the oracle concerning the snake or plague, whichever, a message that the historians have unfortunately failed to hand down to us,[8] the young Tarquins sought to learn from the oracle which of the king's three sons would eventually succeed to the throne. A voice from the depth of the cleft pronounced, "Whichever of you shall first kiss your mother, he shall possess the sovereign power at Rome." Titus and Aruns agreed to keep the message secret from their brother Sextus and either drew lots as to which of them would first kiss their mother (Livy) or agreed to kiss her simultaneously (Dionysius). Brutus, who apparently was better versed in mythology, understood the oracle differently. He pretended to fall and kissed the earth, the mother of us all.[9]

Soon after their return to Rome, Sextus Tarquinius raped

Lucretia, who, in Shakespeare's poem, compares her misery to that of Hecuba witnessing Priam's slaughter, as in the Player's speech in *Hamlet*. Then, after her husband and father swore to avenge her, Lucretia killed herself despite their pleas. Brutus, who was with Lucretia's father when he was summoned by her, saw his opportunity. Throwing off his cloak of stupidity, he roused Lucretia's kinsmen and the populace to put an end to the tyranny of the Tarquins. Like Amleth after he killed Feng, and like Lucius Junius' reputed descendant, Marcus Brutus, after he killed Julius Caesar, Lucius Junius Brutus addressed the people. In his speech he reviewed the various infamies committed by Tarquinius Superbus. One of these has particular importance to us: "He destroyed his own brother by poison because he would not consent to become wicked—assisted by his brother's wife, whom this enemy of the gods had even long before debauched. This is the man who in the same days and with the same poison killed his wedded wife, a virtuous woman—and before the funeral pyre which had received these miserable bodies had died away, he gave a banquet for his friends, celebrated his nuptials, and led the murderess of her husband as a bride to the bed of her sister" (Dionysius, bk. 4, p. 79).

And thus, we here find the origins of "the funeral baked-meats / Did coldly furnish forth the marriage tables" (I, ii, 180–181), and the overhasty marriage that weighs so heavily upon Hamlet at the start of the play. Further, in following Dionysius' version, as Shakespeare must have, we discover the probable source of the alteration and expansion of the Amleth story to have Claudius seduce his brother's wife, secretly poison his brother, and then marry his sister-in-law with indecent haste. We also find that although Brutus was sent abroad with two companions and outwitted them, he did not, like Amleth, return to his own funeral, but virtually to attend Lucretia's funeral after her suicide as Hamlet returned to witness Ophelia's funeral after she had killed herself. Lucretia's suicide served to mobilize her avengers, which led to the end of the Tarquin rule of Rome; Ophelia's suicide mobilizes Laertes, and led indirectly to the start of a new royal line in Denmark. I should also note that after Brutus became consul of Rome, he met his end very much as did

Hamlet. In defending Rome against an attempt by the Tarquins to regain their power, he fought Aruns Tarquinius in single combat, and like Hamlet and Laertes they simultaneously slew one another.[10]

Now, although the Amleth and Brutus legends supplied many of the ideas that the poet rewove into a new fabric when writing *Hamlet*, neither suggests Hamlet's father's ghostly return from purgatory with his stern mandate to Hamlet not to let his "soul contrive / Against thy mother aught" that set the bind that so frustrates Hamlet. We must now turn to the plays about Hamlet's Greek predecessor, Orestes, to find a likely source for this and for several other aspects of *Hamlet*.

Euripides' *Orestes*

There are excellent reasons to believe that Shakespeare was influenced in writing *Hamlet* not simply by the Orestes myth but specifically by Euripides' *Orestes* and *Electra*. The question of the influence of Euripides is important for two reasons. First, Euripides' psychological interests make him a playwright who was, in some respects, a more relevant precursor of Shakespeare than any of his English predecessors and contemporaries. Second, the connection, if established, would shed new light on Shakespeare's conceptualization of the play. However, as many scholars, including Gilbert Murray, whose opinion requires respect and consideration, do not believe that Shakespeare was familiar with the Greek tragedies, the matter must be examined carefully.

The similarity between Hamlet and Orestes has been appreciated by literary critics at least since Herder referred to Hamlet as "Shakespeare's Orestes" in his *Literatur und Kunst* (1800). Gilbert Murray carefully enumerated and discussed the similarities between *Hamlet* and the Orestes plays of Aeschylus, Sophocles, and Euripides. However, Murray believed that the "only point of contact lies at their common origin many thousand years ago."[11] He found no reason to believe that Shakespeare knew the Greek tragedies, although he thought it possible that some of his university friends could have told him the stories or even described specific scenes to him. In writing the essay, Murray was emphasizing the durability of the mythic across the ages and attempting to show how dramatists of genius tap these tales that stirred the interest of primitive man and continue to hold a salient position in the unconscious processes of all men.

Florence Anderson states in her study of mad heroes that Euripides was not only popular in Elizabethan England, but that Latin translations of his plays were produced in the universities.[12] Although we cannot be positive that Shakespeare saw or read Euripides' *Orestes* and *Electra*, it is almost inconceivable that he did not know the story of Orestes. He was very much at home with tales concerned with the Trojan War. John Pickering's *Interlude*, or poetic allegory, about Orestes was published in London in 1567; in it Pickering compared Orestes to Nero and provided a general presentation of the story. A lost play by Dekker, *Orestes Furens*, was produced in London prior to *Hamlet*.

Ben Jonson's familiarity with the Greek playwrights is attested to by the lines in his homage to Shakespeare in the First Folio edition of the Bard's plays:

> From thence to honour thee, I would not seeke
> For names; but call forth thund'ring Aeschelus,
> Euripides, and Sophocles to us.

It is improbable that Jonson would here have referred to dramatists with whom Shakespeare's readers were unfamiliar.

Any doubt that the dramatists of the period were familiar with Euripides' *Orestes*—and recognized its similarity to Shakespeare's *Hamlet*—is dispelled by Thomas Heywood's *The Second Part of the Iron Age*. Although published in 1632, it was written much earlier, though after *Hamlet*. The play contains a "closet" scene between Orestes and Clytemnestra that fuses Euripides' version of Orestes' murder of his mother with the closet scene in *Hamlet*. In the scene, Agamemnon's ghost appears to Orestes but remains invisible to his mother, who believes that her son has become mad. The ghost indicates that Clytemnestra and Aegisthus had murdered him and incites Orestes to kill his mother.

Aside from the analogies between the stories of Orestes and Hamlet, there are also a number of actual similarities in the situations and lines of Euripides' *Electra* and *Orestes* and Shakespeare's *Hamlet*. As Murray carefully noted these similarities, I shall only comment upon several that have particular pertinence to the development of *Hamlet*.

Let us first review the general context of Orestes' plight.

When Agamemnon returned from Troy, he was murdered by Aegisthus (a half-cousin-half-uncle who had erroneously been reared as his half-brother[13]) in collaboration with Agamemnon's wife, Clytemnestra. Both had justifications for the murder and did not seek to conceal it. Lest Aegisthus kill Orestes to prevent him from avenging his father, Electra gave Orestes who was then a child to their father's friend, Strophius, to raise in Phocis. There he became inseparable friends with Pylades, Strophius' son. When he became a young man, Orestes was ordered by Apollo through his Delphic Oracle to avenge his father even though it meant killing his mother. He returned to Mycenae and with the help of Pylades slew Aegisthus; then, incited by Electra, he reluctantly killed his mother. He was then pursued by the Erinnys, or Furies, the chthonic protectors of maternal rights—that is, he was driven mad by the memory of his awful deed.

Amleth, like Orestes, had been young and defenseless when his father was slain, but he was not sent to an alien country; instead, he protected himself, so to speak, by *alienation*. Orestes, like Hamlet, was reluctant to kill his mother; but in contrast to Hamlet, he had not been raised by her, and he had a sister who was bent on avenging her beloved father.

Now, as I have noted earlier, there is a passage in Euripides' *Orestes* that has no parallel in Aeschylus' or Sophocles' plays. During a brief period when the Furies are not hounding him, Orestes says to Electra, "Had these eyes seen my father, had I asked him / In duty if I ought to slay my mother, / I think he would have prayed me not to plunge / My murdering sword in her that gave me birth; / Since he could not revisit heaven's sweet light, / And I must suffer all these miseries" (Potter, p. 205). This is precisely how *Hamlet* starts. Not only does Hamlet's father revisit heaven's sweet light to reveal that he had been murdered and cuckolded by his brother; but after he obtains Hamlet's pledge to avenge him, he also commands his son very specifically:

> But, howsoever thou pursuest this act,
> Taint not thy mind, nor let thy soul contrive
> Against thy mother aught.   (I, v, 84–86)

Shakespeare, then, either by coincidence or by intent, wrote a play that considers what might have happened if Orestes could have asked his father if he should slay his mother and Agamemnon had beseeched him to spare her.

Both Hamlet and Orestes are obligated to avenge their fathers. Hamlet does not, however, know that his mother colluded in his father's murder; nevertheless, he is incensed by her infidelity, and, as we have seen, he considers her guilty of the murder even if she were ignorant of the deed—an ignorance she specifically avows in the First Quarto version but which is left ambiguous in the later texts. Hamlet is thus saved from the vengeance of the Erinnys, saved from the ravages of remorse for a deed he cannot forget, but is he better off? Instead, he is caught in a bitterness from which he cannot free himself, depressed because of his seething anger toward his formerly beloved mother, and paralyzed into inactivity. He is beset by his need to ward off his matricidal impulses, and his world is emptied by his renunciation of his mother. His torment has to do with self-punishment for the wish and the suppressed intent.

Shakespeare's familiarity with the plays of Euripides would also clarify some other aspects of *Hamlet*. Although it has been suggested that Horatio derives from the shadowy "foster-brother" in Saxo who warns Amleth of the seduction trap, there is no trace of any figure who really resembles him in Saxo or any of the related tales. However, Horatio is almost a double for the faithful Pylades, who accompanied Orestes everywhere, although Pylades actively helped Orestes kill Aegisthus, whereas Horatio is essentially an observer and a person in whom Hamlet can confide. As previously noted, when Hamlet, finally lets himself go and tells Horatio how dearly he holds him, saying, "I will wear him / In my heart's core, ay, in my heart of heart, / As I do thee" (III, ii, 67–69), he stops himself with "Something too much of this" (III, ii, 69). Similarly in Euripides' play, Orestes stops his praise of Pylades with, "But I say no more, lest I embarrass you by praising you so much" (*Orestes*, Arrowsmith, p. 258). In the final scene of *Hamlet* the dying Hamlet tells his friend,

> Horatio, I am dead;
> Thou livest; report me and my cause aright
> To the unsatisfied.   (V, ii, 325–327)

Horatio replies:

> Never believe it;
> I am more an antique Roman than a Dane;
> Here's yet some liquor [poison] left.   (V, ii, 327–328)

These lines are strikingly similar to the exchange between Orestes and Pylades, when Orestes and Electra are on the verge of killing themselves:

> Do thou, Pylades, stand umpire to our
> bloody feat, and, when we both are dead, lay out
> our bodies decently.   (*Orestes*, Coleridge, p. 144)

To this Pylades responds:

> Stay a moment, there is first one point I
> have to blame thee for, if thou thinkest I care
> to live when thou are dead.
>   (*Orestes*, Coleridge, p. 144)

Hamlet, as we have noted, is concerned that his father's ghost may have been an illusion or a hallucination. "The spirit that I have seen / May be the devil; and the devil hath power / To assume a pleasing shape" (II, ii, 574–576). He therefore seeks more certain grounds for taking vengeance. Orestes, before killing his mother, argues with Electra, "Surely it was a fiend in the likeness of the god that ordered this" (*Electra*, Coleridge, p. 96).

Hamlet expresses his feelings of revulsion toward his mother very much as did Orestes. Orestes tells his grandfather Tyndareus, "Your daughter—I blush with shame to call that woman my mother—in a mock marriage, in the private rites of lust, / took a lover in her bed" (*Orestes*, Arrowsmith, p. 225). Hamlet, in turn, expresses a similar loathing about acknowledging his mother, telling her, "You are the queen, your husband's brother's wife; / And—would it were not so!—you are my mother" (III, iv, 15–16); and he, too, condemns her sexual behavior: "to live / In the rank sweat of an enseamed bed, / Stew'd in corruption, honeying and making love / Over the nasty sty" (III, iv, 92–94).[14]

Hamlet's reason for not killing Claudius when he comes upon him praying—"And now I'll do't; and so he goes to heaven" (III, iii, 74), followed by "Oh, this is hire and salary, not revenge. / He took my father grossly, full of bread, / With all his crimes broad blown, as flush as May" (III, iii, 79–82), echoes the ghost's bitter complaint that he was

> Cut off even in the blossoms of my sin,
> Unhousel'd, disappointed, unaneled;
> No reckoning made, but sent to my account
> With all my imperfections on my head;
> Oh, horrible! oh, horrible!, most horrible!
>
> (I, v, 76–80)

The same reason is also used as a motivation for vengeance in Euripides. Electra incites Orestes by telling him, "Dishonoured lies his grave; naught as yet hath it received of drink outpoured or myrtle-spray, but bare of ornament his tomb is left. Yea, and 'tis said that noble hero who is wedded to my mother, in his drunken fits, doth leap upon the grave, and pelt with stones my father's monument" (*Electra*, Coleridge, p. 76).[15] We may note in passing that here Aegisthus is accused of being a drunkard, a vice for which Hamlet condemns Claudius.

Euripides' Orestes, like Hamlet, feels a need and even a desire to kill his mother, coupled with a revulsion against the act. He even says, "I loathe and yet I love the enterprise" (*Electra*, Coleridge, p. 96). He feels intensely that he had been disgraced by his mother's infidelity to his father. For Amleth, in contrast punishing his mother was quite secondary to taking vengeance against his uncle. Thus, Hamlet is in many ways closer to Orestes than to Amleth.

I shall not here consider other relationships between Hamlet and Orestes that are concerned with the sagas and myths rather than the plays. However, I shall return to some of them when discussing the mythological background of *Hamlet*.

If the similarities between *Hamlet* and Euripides' *Electra* and *Orestes* are fortuitous, the coincidences are rather amazing for plays with such closely related themes. If, however, they indicate that Shakespeare was familiar with Euripides' plays, we have reason to believe that Shakespeare purposefully altered the Amleth saga into a play that weighed what would have happened to Orestes if his father had bidden him to spare his mother, and thereby created one of the most subtle and tortured of all tragic heroes.

Nero

Hamlet, Orestes, and Oedipus are all related to Nero; as we know from Hamlet's allusion to him, Shakespeare had him in mind as he wrote the play. Nero, according to Suetonius in his *Lives of the Twelve Emperors*, not only behaved incestuously with his mother Agrippina but also took a mistress who closely resembled her; eventually, he had Agrippina murdered. His behavior became increasingly bizarre, uncontrolled, and mad. Shakespeare accentuates Hamlet's relation to Nero by having

Hamlet refer to him at the moment when he is about to confront his mother in her closet. Struggling to control his matricidal impulsions and his jealousy over her sexual life with Claudius, he admonishes himself:

> O heart, lose not thy nature; let not ever
> The soul of Nero enter this firm bosom;
> Let me be cruel, not unnatural;
> I will speak daggers to her, but use none;

(III, ii, 376–379)

Nero also was jealous of his mother's relationship to a Claudius, for, as I have noted earlier, the Emperor Claudius was his stepfather and great uncle. Nero had less reason than Hamlet to be jealous, for Agrippina reputedly poisoned her husband-uncle to enable her son, Nero, to become emperor, whereas Gertrude kept Hamlet from the throne by her marriage. Further, according to Tacitus, Agrippina sought to commit incest with Nero.

Claudius properly fits into the story for another reason. Born into the royal family when heirs to the throne were being murdered in rapid succession, he managed to survive because he was considered feeble-minded as well as physically deformed; the name Claudius, or lame one, was appropriate. Despite his reputation, he displayed a brilliant intellect at times, and he eventually let it be known that he had only feigned stupidity in order to survive. Having the villain in the play named after an emperor whose wife poisoned him and who had feigned mental incompetence not only helps underline the cyclic recurrence of a theme, but also contrasts Gertrude, whose marriage to Claudius helped deprive Hamlet of the crown, to Agrippina who killed her second husband to make her son emperor. The comparison parallels the one already made between Ophelia and the English princess of the Amleth saga.

The Spanish Tragedy

One other play rather clearly contributed to the dramatic quality of *Hamlet*—to its stage technique rather than to the characters and plot. It has often been suggested and even assumed that Kyd, because of his fondness for ghost scenes, was the author of the *Ur-Hamlet* and thereby influenced Shakespeare's play. Without resorting to such conjecture, we can be certain that Kyd directly influenced the composition of *Hamlet* through his *The Spanish Tragedy*.

The importance of the ghost in *The Spanish Tragedy* to *Hamlet* has been overemphasized. Other plays of the period, following the practice of Seneca, contained ghost scenes. The ghost in *The Spanish Tragedy* is not a character who enters into the play, as does the ghost in *Hamlet*; instead, together with the "Spirit of Revenge," he forms something of a chorus that comments on what is about to take place in the play. Kyd's fascinating use of the play-within-the-play is far more important, a masterful *tour de force* that could well arouse the envy of any dramatist. Hieronymo, to avenge his son's murder, writes a play and induces the murderers to enact it together with his son's fiancée, Bellimperia, and himself. In acting the revenge play-within-the-revenge-play, Hieronymo actually stabs one villain while Bellimperia kills the other and then herself. The audience in the play congratulates Hieronymo on the brilliance of the acting, not realizing that the three actors are actually dead.

Hieronymo's Mad Again is the subtitle of *The Spanish Tragedy*. Distraught over his son's cruel murder, Hieronymo is insane at times, perfectly lucid at others; at still other times, he may dissemble madness to throw his enemies off guard. His intellect remains unimpaired throughout, but he is overwhelmed by grief and rage. Here, as in *Hamlet*, the uncertainty whether the major character is or is not mad becomes a major element in the play.

Saga and Myth in *Hamlet*

The Fool of the Folk Plays

Finally, we must consider another figure with whom Shakespeare was acquainted and with whom Hamlet has a relationship: the Fool of the sword dance, morris dance, and mummer's play—folk performances that were extremely common in Elizabethan England and have even survived into this century. Hamlet refers to them just as the court is about to witness the "dumb-show" prelude to the play-within-the-play. He comments that if his mother has not forgotten his father in the two months since his death, "Then there's hope a great man's memory may outlive his life half a year; but, by'r lady, he must build churches then; or else shall he suffer not thinking on, with the hobby-horse, whose epitaph is, 'For, O! for, O! the hobby-horse is forgot'" (III, ii, 123–127). It is possible that the "dumb-show" may have originated as an elaboration of a folk play or folk dance. The hobbyhorse is a basic character in these ritual performances, along with the Man-Woman, the Fool, and the Captain or King. A common plot in these performances is that the Captain woos "the Woman" and is slain by the eldest son in a fight over her. The Fool may be substituted for the Captain, or the two characters may be fused. The various dances and folk plays, all of ritual origin, have become so syncretized that extant versions are difficult, if not impossible, to analyze and comprehend clearly.[16] The "dumb-show" is about the killing of a king by his nephew for possession of the queen—as, in a sense, is *Hamlet*.

The ritual folk dances and plays are clearly related to fertility rites, to the midwinter rituals for assuring the return of spring and to other related rituals which we shall consider when we contemplate some of the mythologies that form a penumbra about these three tragic heroes, Oedipus, Orestes, and Hamlet, who refuse to remain buried.

Shakespeare's Synthesis

Shakespeare, as we have seen, did not construct *Hamlet* simply on the foundation of an earlier *Ur-Hamlet* or simply from Saxo's story of an early Danish hero; rather, the creativity of his genius recognized the fundamental similarities between Orestes, Nero, Lucius Junius Brutus, and Amleth. He selected and modified episodes from the stories of each and fused them into a cohesive and carefully balanced play; and created a new genus of hero who intrigues and stirs us more deeply than do his predecessors. To provide balance to the play and to consider some essentials about human relationships, Shakespeare created Ophelia, a young woman, if not a heroine, who cannot be found in any of these tales, although the sources for her conception can be found in them.

Although we may conjecture, we cannot know why Shakespeare was attracted to, if not preoccupied with, the legends of Lucius Junius Brutus and Amleth for so many years. However, through the scrutiny of these sources and the uses he made of them, we attain not only a greater appreciation of the creative process,[17] but also some clear understanding of Shakespeare's intentions. The selection and the alteration of the sources have been noted, and I shall here only make a few comments about them, and leave further elaboration to the reader.

Into the Amleth saga, Shakespeare brought the story of Tarquinius Superbus and Tullia to add infidelity, secret poisoning, and a very hasty remarriage to the crime of fratricide and the coveting of a brother's wife. However, Gertrude is not reshaped into the form of the cruel, fratricidal, and patricidal Tullia, or even into the mold of the vengeful Clytemnestra, but is left very much like the rather nebulous Gerutha of the saga. Still, we can appreciate Shakespeare's ambivalence about how guilty he wishes to make her. In the First Quarto version, Gertrude, like Gerutha, swears she knew nothing of her husband's murder, but the matter of infidelity is not mentioned; in later versions her avowal of ignorance of the murder was purposefully eliminated. It seems as if Shakespeare had come to feel that it was sufficient and, perhaps, most important that Hamlet consider his mother to be guilty of murder because of her infidelity. To emphasize the point, in the play-within-the-play, Shakespeare used Hermatruda's pledge to remain faithful to Amleth and not remarry after his death.

Hamlet differs from Amleth in being burdened by strong matricidal impulses. Like Euripides' Orestes (to a greater degree than the Orestes of Aeschylus and Sophocles), Hamlet is infuriated with his mother and feels degraded because of her. However, Orestes was impelled to matricide largely by external forces, whereas Hamlet is deterred by his father's order to spare his mother. As I have already emphasized, I believe Shakespeare took the suggestion to forbid Hamlet from committing matricide from Euripides, and thereby wrote a play concerned with a man's struggle to control such impulsions in the face of his bitterness toward his mother. The complex and contradictory impulsions toward matricide and incest— so common among schizophrenic youths—summoned up for Shakespeare the memory of Nero to serve as a deterrent to Hamlet.

Hamlet does not become a great hero like Amleth or even a head of state like Brutus; nor does he find some sort of resolution to his conflicts later in life, as did Orestes. His life ends when he gains his vengeance—essentially at the point where the first part of the Amleth saga leaves off—as part of a general slaughter that suggests the burning of the Great Hall with its occupants.

By making the girl who seduces Amleth in the wood also the daughter of the courtier who suggests spying on Amleth in his mother's bedroom and is then slain by Amleth, Shakespeare constructs a countertheme with a master stroke that consolidates the play. The sources are, as we have noted, actually more complex. The king of England also sent spies into a bedchamber—into Amleth's when he arrived in England. His daughter loved Amleth, and he was killed by Amleth. The princess, like Ophelia, was caught between her loyalty to and love for her father and her allegiance to her beloved who killed her father. The difference in Ophelia's situation—and in her reaction to Hamlet's rejection and slaying of her father—indicates Shakespeare's wish to accentuate Hamlet's disillusionment with women and to place Ophelia in a dilemma that is akin to Hamlet's and leads to her madness and suicide. Then, Lucretia's suicide and funeral in the Brutus legend appear to have suggested using Ophelia's suicide and funeral as a type of denouement.

We have found a predecessor for Horatio in Pylades, but none for Laertes. Laertes has precursors in the Norse sagas—in the son who avenges a father killed by his sister's suitor or husband—and Shakespeare may have come across these stories in Saxo when reading the Amleth saga.

I do not wish to consider here in detail how greatly Hamlet's character differs from those of his predecessors. He, like the young Amleth, uses wordplays to deceive; he relies on intellect rather than feats of arms, and he values integrity, as did Brutus. He neither feigns imbecility, as they did, nor is he definitively mad, as was Orestes. He does feign madness and it remains uncertain when he crosses the indefinite boundary between sanity and madness. He is capable of action, yet his few bold deeds are carried out impetuously rather than resolutely. He does not pursue his vengeance in accordance with a yearlong plan, as did Amleth; nor does he act with resolve when the opportunity arises, as did Lucius Junius Brutus.

Hamlet is, in many ways, closest to Orestes. Like Orestes, he accepts the fate of being cast in the role of his father's avenger only reluctantly, and he too must come to grips with his feelings for a mother who has betrayed his father. Hamlet, however, does not act against his mother but seeks to change her back into the mother he had once loved and admired—but he cannot undo what has happened. Shakespeare clearly seeks to emphasize his internal conflict rather than the external blocks to gaining vengeance.

Hamlet is so very meaningful to us because he is not like Fortinbras, Laertes, or even Amleth. When we review the myths and sagas Shakespeare knew and utilized, it becomes apparent that from the same sources he could have created a play that focused upon a hero who sought vengeance and could act decisively to gain that end, or one who saved his country from a corrupt ruler; and so forth. The sources do not tell us why Shakespeare selected what he did and altered it as he did, but through noting and examining the selections with Shakespeare's alterations of them we have found many clues to what he sought to convey.[18]

XII

THE NORSE SAGAS

WE HAVE considered the tales and myths that were available to Shakespeare and which, we have reason to believe, entered into the creation of *Hamlet*. Even though they are all accounts of "carnal, bloody, and unnatural acts" (V, ii, 368), they were written during relatively high periods of civilization. I shall now turn to the more ancient myths and rituals that underlie them and which reflect, in more direct form, some of man's most basic impulsions, desires, and fears. It is possible to trace so many interrelated myths and rites that, as happened when Frazer in *The Golden Bough* sought to clarify the worship of Diana of the Wood, we might end with twelve volumes and still leave the topic uncompleted. I shall, however, confine myself to matters that have particular pertinence to the origins or meaning of Hamlet.

I shall first consider the Nordic sagas and rituals that enter into the Amleth saga and provide it with meaning beyond that of a romantic tale of adventure. I first wish to relate Amleth to a real person, the great Viking hero Anlaf Curan.[1] Next, I shall consider Amleth's relationship to mythological figures who were connected to rituals carried out to assure the fertility of the land and the return of spring in the Norse countries. Then, by viewing the Amleth saga (and, to a lesser degree, *Hamlet*) against the rituals and their connections to royal succession, I shall relate Hamlet to the "Mock King" and the "King of Fools," who was sacrificed in place of the king to assure the fertility of the priestess queen and, thereby, the fertility of the land.

References to Hamlet in the Norse myths and sagas prior to Saxo are sparse. The first reference usually cited is a fragment of a verse by the tenth century Icelandic Viking poet Sem Snaebjörn. " 'Tis said that far out, off yonder ness, the Nine Maids of the Island Mill stir amain the host-cruel skerry quern —they who in ages past ground Hamlet's meal" (Gollancz).[2]

It will be recalled from Saxo that when Amleth was passing sandhills along the coast, his companions bade him look at the meal. He replied that it had been ground small by the tempests of the storm. The incident indicates that Snaebjörn's reference was incorporated into Saxo's saga, or that a "kenning" was turned into a riddle; thus the "Ur-Amleth" was a figure associated with riddling remarks that seemed stupid but masked shrewdness.

Anlaf Curan and Amleth

There appears to be, however, a slightly earlier and more significant allusion to Amleth. Gollancz noted that following the battle of Ath-Cliath, which took place near Dublin in the year 904, Queen Gormflaith, who lost her husband, the famed Niall Glundubh, wrote a lament which included these lines:

> Ill for me the compliment of the two foreigners,
> Who slew Niall and Cearbhall,
> Cearbhall was slain by Ulf, a mighty deed;
> Niall Glundubh by Amhlaide.[3]

Amhlaide, Gollancz tells us, was the Irish form of Amlödi or Hamlet. According to several authorities, Niall was slain by the leader of the Norse forces, Sitric, and the name Amhlaide does not occur elsewhere in connection with Sitric. It very likely

refers, however, to Sitric's son Anlaf Curan, one of the greatest
Norse heroes, about whom many legends arose. The second part
of Saxo's Amleth may have had its origins in the exploits of
Anlaf Curan. The connection is made through the Anglo-Dan-
ish tale of Dan Havelok or Havelok Cuheran, a variant of the
Amleth story. Havelok Cuheran is considered to be another
name for Anlaf Curan.*

The story of Havelok, in brief, goes as follows. After King
Arthur's death, England was divided between Adelbrecht, a
Dane, and his British brother-in-law, Edelsi. When Adelbrecht
and his wife died they left their daughter, Argentille, in the care
of her uncle, Edelsi. In order to gain her inheritance, Edelsi
married Argentille to a scullion named Cuheran. He then made
Cuheran his fool. Argentille saw a flame coming from her husband's mouth as he slept, and she took it for a sign of greatness.[5]
After Argentille insisted that Cuheran investigate his origins,
they learned that he was really Dan Havelok (Lord Havelok, in
English), the son of the king of Denmark who had been slain by
Arthur. The Danish queen had fled by sea, but she and all of the
occupants of the ship were slain by pirates except for Dan Havelok and the ship's captain's wife, who then became his foster
mother. After learning of his origins, Dan Havelok and Argentille went to Denmark, where Havelok ousted the usurper and
became king. They then returned to England. There Havelok
fought a drawn battle with Edelsi, but Argentille taught Havelok the trick of fixing the dead to stakes to make them appear
ready to attack. Edelsi's men lost their courage at the apparent
size of Havelok's remaining force and surrendered.

The relationship to the Amleth story is apparent. The hero is
the heir to a Danish throne who goes to Britain, where he
marries the princess; he returns to Denmark to defeat the ruler,
and then goes back to England where he defeats the king in a
battle by propping up his slain soldiers. The major difference is
that here the princess sides with her husband against a wicked
uncle rather than against her father, as in the Amleth saga.

The story of Dan Havelok contains the essential features of
the mythical childhood of the hero as described by Rank.[6] He
loses his real parents but is rescued from the water and raised

by foster parents as their own child. Eventually, his royal parentage is discovered. It is of interest that Havelok, while still Cuheran, was made a fool, supposedly to provide amusement to the court, much as Lucius Junius Brutus and Amleth did. We shall see that being made the spouse of the princess and a fool may have particular significance.

Little, if anything, is known about Anlaf Curan's childhood other than that he supposedly was Sitric's son. The story of Havelok Cuheran fills the gap in a way that is both proper for a hero and also relates him to Amleth. The history (or legendary history) of the adult Anlaf, like the story of Dan Havelok, bears a definite resemblance to the adventures of Amleth in England and Scotland. When Anlaf was driven from his father's kingdom of Northumbria by his stepuncle Athelston, king of England, he took refuge with the king of Scotland and married his daughter. Later, he became king of York and half of England. Then, although already married to a princess, he also married Gormflaith, not she who had lamented Niall's death, but the sister of the king of Leinster, the beautiful but evil Kormlöo of the Niall saga. Like Amleth's Hermatruda, who married Wiglek, Gormflaith married Anlaf's vanquisher at the battle of Tara that ended the power of the Norsemen in Ireland.

Two Frequent Themes in Norse Sagas

Now that we have examined Amleth's—and thereby, Hamlet's—relationship to a real person, the Norse hero Anlaf Curan, I shall turn in the opposite direction and consider his roots in ritual and in related tales concerned with succession to the crown in matrilineal societies.

The Norse sagas contain many tales closely related to Saxo's Amleth saga. For example, in the *Hrolfsaga Kraka*, Frodi murdered his brother Halfdan, married Halfdan's wife and dispossessed their sons Helgi and Hroar, who were subsequently hidden on an island by Halfdan's loyal herdsman. Eventually the two sons attended a feast at the palace in disguise, during which Helgi acted insanely; then, with their sister's help, they nailed up the doors and killed Frodi and their mother.[7] The relationship to the Orestes myth is apparent.

FRATRICIDE REVENGED

Two themes that repeatedly appear in these tales demand our attention because they are found in *Hamlet* as the theme and countertheme, or plot and counterplot. The first theme concerns the alternation of two brothers as king. One brother may go into exile for a period of three or nine years while the other rules; but frequently, the younger brother kills the older, often with the connivance of the queen; and then he is killed, usually by the avenging son of the older brother, and again frequently with the help of the queen. The ceding of the rule of Jutland by Horvendile to Feng for three years and his subsequent murder by Feng, who, in turn, was killed by Amleth, is an example of this theme, as is the story of Halfdan and Frodi. There are many variants of the theme in which a king is killed by his brother, nephew, or son, with or without the help of his wife. Thus, for example, we find in the Ynglinga saga that King Vanlandi was killed by his son Visburr with the aid of Queen Drifa; later, when Visburr was unfaithful to his wife, she sent their two sons to burn him in his palace.

THE HERO WHO SLAYS THE KING AND WINS THE PRINCESS

The second theme is that of the prince who leaves his native land and wins a princess and becomes a king by overcoming her father. The young hero may rescue the princess from being wed to an ogre or giant, and in so doing, he slays not only the ogre but also the king who had betrothed his daughter to the ogre; or he may simply slay the king to win the princess who marries him even though he has killed her father. The father is avenged when the hero is slain by the king's son, the hero's wife's brother. The story of how Amleth won the English princess by guile and later became king by slaying her father follows this pattern; and Hamlet's slaying of Polonius, whose death is avenged by Laertes, is a modified version of it.

The tale of Helgi Hundingsbane in the *Elder Edda* resembles *Hamlet* in that it includes both the vengeance of the bride's brother and the death of the bride from a broken heart. In the story, Sigrun appealed to Helgi Hundingsbane to rescue her from being married to Hodbrodd, to whom she had been betrothed. In rescuing Sigrun, Helgi killed her father and brother. Sigrun married Helgi despite these slayings, but when her brother, Dag, later slew Helgi, she died of a broken heart.[8]

In some stories, the bride helps her suitor or spouse kill her father, as Tullia did in the Brutus legend. In others, the bride avenges her father, as did the daughter of King Frosti of Finland, who killed her husband, Agni, the Yngling king.

The Ritual Origins of the Tales

The reasons for these repetitive tales of horrendous parricidal and regicidal acts have been apparent at least since Zinzow's pioneering study and have been sharpened and elaborated by subsequent scholars. The tales are intimately connected to rites that promoted or secured the fertility of the earth and to related rituals that assured the continuing sequence of nature—particularly that the lengthening winter night of the northlands would begin to abate before the dragon of darkness and cold completely engulfed the world.

The ritual derivations of the Norse myths may be more apparent than those of their Greek counterparts, for many are but partly freed from such origins. Because concerns over the return of spring were felt more intensely in these northern countries than around the Mediterranean;[9] and also because the impact of Christianity came rather precipitately to the Norse countries other than Iceland, the myths still remained in a relatively naive form when recorded by Saemund, Snorri, Saxo, and others.

I cannot present the nature of the basic rites succinctly or with certainty, both because much remains obscure and because

I am not an authority on such matters. However, it is the general concepts that are important to this discussion. The queen as the priestess representative of the Earth Mother was the central figure, and the king was responsible for her continuing fertility. The king was to blame for drought and famine: for example, Donaldi, a Yngling king, was sacrificed after lesser measures failed to relieve a prolonged drought. To assure the earth's vigorous fertility, the king was replaced at regular intervals—after three years in some sagas, but more often after nine.[10] He may have simply exchanged places with his brother, yielding his wife to his brother until he returned after the proper interlude.[11]

In the early days a king could sometimes prolong his reign by sacrificing a son in his stead, and thereby regain his power and potency. Thus, Aun, a Yngling king, sacrificed his nine sons at nine-year intervals and then died of old age when his people refused to let him kill his only remaining son. Later, a mock king who was a member of the royal family, or a substitute selected in some other way,[12] was ritually wedded to the queen and even procreated with her, later to be sacrificed in place of the king.

When the queen died or when she was replaced by her daughter for some other reason, the daughter's husband became king. As we have seen, he typically won the princess by defeating the old king in a contest or by slaying him in combat.[13] Eventually, a time came when the ritual slaying of the king or his substitute was replaced by rituals in which the killing was acted and then by rituals in which the sacrifice was symbolized in a covert form. Gradually, the rituals and their derivative myths that concerned the fertility of the land and concomitantly with the royal succession became intertwined and syncretized with other associated rituals: in some of these that reflected the division of the solar year into two six-month years, the Winter King and the Summer King fought for the queen, as the earth priestess; in other fertility rites, a prince or bridegroom awakened the May Queen from her sleep, and copulated with her in the field.[14] Spring was sometimes represented as an avenging prince, who, after waiting in the dark beneath the snow or beside the hearth where he was scorned as a stupid boy, matured and overthrew the Winter King by burning him in the palace. Such practices have continued into the present in the form of folk drama or folk dance, often with an underlying seriousness that derives from the farmer's uneasiness when fertility rites are omitted.

These myths, whether concerned with the theme of brother killing brother or with that of the prince who kills the king to gain the princess, are concerned with matrilineal succession to the kingship: The man married to the queen is king. The queen's daughter is the significant person in the succession. If the king's son wishes to be king, he must win a princess elsewhere or, perhaps, win a queen from her king. The source of the royal power is made clear in the case of Amleth's second wife, Hermatruda. Saxo says of her, "Indeed she was a queen, but that her sex gainsaid it, might be deemed king; nay (and this is yet truer) whomsoever she thought worthy of her bed was at once a king, and she yielded her kingdom with herself" (¶ 102). Various myths convey the conflicts and confusions that arose as patrilineal succession gradually replaced the matrilineal.

The Helgi Lays of the *Elder Edda*

Throughout the Norse myths, we find variants of a story in which a betrothed hero is replaced by another, often his brother, before the marriage. These tales suggest that the hero represents a substitute priest-king who is the sacrificial victim. Phillpotts suggested that the various "Helgi" legends had such origins.[15] "Helgi," a name that keeps recurring in the *Elder Edda*, particularly for a slain brother, means "holy," and Phillpotts believes that it designated a member of the royal family who enacted the part of the goddess's bridegroom at an annual festival and was then sacrificed.[16] The name "Attis" was used in a similar manner for the son of Cybele, the Magna Mater, to symbolize the short-lived Mesopotamian spring. The various Helgis are thus related to the "Bitter Fool," the King of Fools, and, I would suggest, to Amleth, the Fool.

Phillpotts has given us excellent reasons to believe that the

Helgi lays were early religious dramas that replaced or accompanied the ancient Year Drama ritual. She suggests that these grim dramatic rites of magical importance were differentiated into two distinct types of performance. One, the folk drama, continued to have the primary ritual purpose of assuring a good harvest; the other, the commemorative and historical drama, ballad, or saga, emphasized the stories of heroes and became essentially literary. The folk plays became highly stereotyped as sword dances, mummering plays, St. George pageants, and maypole dances that contain clear residues of fertility rites. The literary productions became increasingly sophisticated, as the characters and their stories became the center of interest. In these the ritual connotations faded into the background, although their residues remained perhaps even when unrecognized by the writers. I believe that such ritual and mythic residues often not only influenced the plot and structure of a play, but also carried with them the strength and emotional repercussions of the myth.

From Fertility Rites to *Hamlet*

We are now ready to return to *Hamlet* and examine more fully its relationship to ritual and myth. In taking his story from the mythologically based legends of Amleth and Brutus, Shakespeare also incorporated into his play fundamental issues and conflicts that, like Amlödi's quern—Hamlet's mill—continue to grind away tempestuously and passionately in the unconscious processes of Everyman.

Although Saxo's saga narrates a story of a great hero and may well have provided the proper mythical childhood and youth for Anlaf Curan, its ritual origins remain apparent. Let us note once again that Amleth was the son of Horvendile and Gerutha. Horvendile gained renown by slaying King Koll, or Collerus, of Norway. These are not casual names, or names that have import because of historic deeds; rather, they elevate Amleth toward

the status of demigod. Horvendile was a Teutonic or Norse god
representative of spring and sometimes dawn.[17] Koll or Collerus
simply meant "cold" or, perhaps, "the hooded one," a god of
winter. Furthermore, Saxo had them battle in a "spring-green
spot" or a sequestered "spring-tide wood." Horvendile then
married Gerutha, whose name, many have pointed out, derives
from "Groa" of the *Edda* and "Gaia" of Greek mythology, the
Earth Mother.[18] Thus, the names themselves lend the Amleth
saga a mythic setting that anthropomorphizes the cycle of seasons. In mythic terms, Horvendile gains Gerutha after slaying
the winter god; he, in turn, is slain by his brother and co-ruler,
Feng, who then possessed Gerutha. After an interlude, he will
be avenged by his son; that is, the new spring god will regain
Earth, the eternal bride and mother. Amleth, then, would at one
level seem to represent the resurrection of the ever-returning
Spring, secretly nurtured by mother Earth; he is first scorned
and unrecognized in the court of the Winter King, until the king
begins to fear that he is sheltering his supplanter and seeks to
eradicate him. Thus, mother-son incest forms an inherent part
of the cycle; and *Hamlet* contains residues of the young hero
representative of Spring marrying the queen representative of
his mother, Earth.

The young hero, the avenger of a father who symbolized
spring or summer, should represent renascent spring, but this
interpretation of the symbolic position of Amleth cannot be
altogether correct. Amleth, and even more so Hamlet, is too
closely associated with death; there is nothing springlike in his
garb, and the tenor of his speech is equally somber. Still, Attis,
who arose in a different climate, represented Spring, fated to die
before blooming fully. I have noted in the discussion of *Hamlet*
in Part One that Hamlet is a young prince whose hopes for the
future, whose faith in the world, and whose promise of bringing
fruition to Ophelia as the Rose of May are blasted by the corruption of the court and disillusionment in his mother; thus, he
becomes an embassy of death. He is, in some respects, an Attis-
like figure.

Amleth as a Mock King

What of the several trials or tests that are set for Amleth? I believe that I perceive in them a familiar theme beneath the elaborations and variations of the story. Why is he sent to copulate in the woods? Why is he spied upon in his mother's bedroom? Why is he sent abroad? What is the duel with Feng and the peculiar exchange of swords about? Let us pause and listen again. As I ponder the story and let my powers of fantasy range after absorbing many related tales, I realize that Amleth is not just the avenging son who represents spring. There is much in him of the royal relative who serves as a substitute for the king and is sacrificed in his place. He is a mock king dressed in royal regalia; he wears the crown for a day, or for the duration of a festival, and is then sacrificed in place of the king. As the mock king, he may even sleep with the priestess-queen to provide her with a young and vigorously fertile mate, but he is put to death shortly thereafter. He is the king's son who is killed to permit the king to live for another year—or another nine years. He may be sent abroad to be slain to avoid polluting the land, and he may, like the pharmakos, carry the impurities of the city with him. He may be the youth who is sent abroad as an annual payment to a conqueror and who is used there as the sacrificial person, as Athenian youths were sent to Crete to be sacrificed to the Minotaur. He may be expected to lose his life in a ritual battle with a king who thus proves himself sufficiently powerful and fertile.

It seems likely that Saxo's Amleth is a composite of such figures and that the saga contains a condensation of various myths of the ritual use of a mock king who dies in the king's stead. He is related to the various Helgis of the *Eddas*, who, as Phillpotts suggested, are heroes representative of the priest-king who dies in place of the actual king. He is, after all, Amleth, the Fool.

Saga and Myth in *Hamlet*

The Return of the Scapegoat, or the Triumph of the Fool

In some places the person selected for ritual sacrifice was mentally or physically defective. The story, then, would contain residues of a peculiar sort of hero—the fool who turns out to be wise, or the youth marked for sacrifice who manages to gain the throne.[19] It is the unexpected triumph of the underdog by the use of his wits, the person that the king will use turning the tables—a theme that holds great appeal for those who feel used or neglected. The theme is related to the stories of the prince who manages to gain the princess by performing the seemingly impossible tasks set by her father. We learn from Saxo that the princess was sometimes permitted to pick the one who would be her mate in the spring ritual or the person who would defend her.[20] She might wish he could remain and become her spouse and king, rather than be sacrificed. Such hopes contain the seeds of romantic tales.

In mythic terms, Amleth's first test was not merely to determine whether he was too mentally defective to "know" a woman; rather, he was sent to carry out the ritual of fertilizing the fields by copulating with the Spring Maiden. Knowing that he would be sacrificed afterward, he feigned being too stupid to carry out the act. The second test, in which he was left with the queen in her bedchamber, reflects the mating of the mock king with the queen in place of the king, after which he would be sacrificed. Amleth again escaped the danger by killing the spy. In the third trial, the exile to England, he was to serve as a ritual sacrifice for the English or as a scapegoat; this time, he managed to substitute his companions for himself. The fourth trial was his return for a ritual feast connected with his death in a duel with the king. Instead, he managed to burn the winter palace, and in the duel in which he was supposed to fight with a wooden sword, he exchanged swords so that Feng had to fight with the useless weapon. These episodes, which are placed together into a story of vengeance for the murder of a father, fit together not logically but rather mythopoeically, as residues of related ways in which the mock hero, the poor "fall guy," is supposed to be killed ritually but manages to escape. Something of these qualities may have been handed down to Hamlet—the hero who is not precisely a hero in the conventional sense but a hero who outwits those in power.

In the second half of the saga, Amleth became a more romantic hero. He was the prince who won his princess and slew her father, but also was the supplanter who married the queen-earth-priestess in the form of Hermatruda—a condensation of two forms of succession in matrilineal societies that was related to maintaining the fertility of the land.

But what of Shakespeare's *Hamlet*? Was it influenced by any such considerations? Hamlet is a very different figure from Amleth. The play is much farther removed from the rituals than is the saga: Hamlet may compare his father to Hyperion, but it is only a figure of speech, and Gertrude is all too mortal.

The Amleth saga told of a mythic figure and, as I have noted, recounted the deeds of a hero, but it did not tell us about a person confronted by a dilemma or caught in conflicts. Shakespeare was not only concerned with essential human dilemmas, but he embodied them in specific characters with very human attributes. Still, in Hamlet, as in *Macbeth* and *King Lear*, Shakespeare was creating a new mythology, what Wheelwright, in *The Burning Fountain*, termed "consummatory myth," which attempts to recapture the lost innocence of the original mythopoeic attitude in order to convey some fundamental ideas about human existence. Shakespeare did not, like Corneille and Racine, alter dramatic versions of Greek mythology to his purposes; he found suitable themes and settings in ancient Anglo-Saxon lore.

How much did the poet sense that the Amleth saga and the story of Orestes both dealt with the annual renewal of the seasons, the combat between winter and summer for the Queen of May? With the theme of resurrection? It may seem remote, but as Janet Spens maintained, Shakespeare appears to have been influenced markedly by folk drama: "He learned to mix his literary matter with the old folk drama, which had the vitality of countless generations in them, and their roots in the far-off mysterious kinship between man and the dumb earth with which his dust mingles in death."[21] Spens suggested that *Twelfth Night, A Midsummer Night's Dream, All's Well That Ends Well,* and *As You Like It* were connected with the customs and myths surrounding different folk festivals. We know of no Hamlet folk tales or plays extant in Elizabethan England, but folk plays about the battle for the May Queen and about the Fool who kills or is killed by the king were ubiquitous.

Although *Hamlet* is far removed from Saxo's *Amleth,* the two major ways in which an old king could be supplanted entered into the structure of Shakespeare's plot. The first half of the play, as I have argued earlier, is built around the slaying of a king by his brother to gain possession of the queen, and the obligation of the king's son to avenge him. The second half uses the theme of the prince who kills a king to gain his daughter and succeed to the throne, but transposed around Ophelia as the Rose of May, the May Queen, and her father. Here, too, we find the brother of the princess—Laertes—avenging his father's death.

Insofar as Shakespeare was interested in the seasonal metaphor, he was seeking to convey disillusion with the aberrations of nature—human nature—that could lead to sterility and tragedy. He was primarily interested in people and their interrelationships, but particularly in the effects of intrafamilial relationships upon their lives. In writing a classic play based on myth, Shakespeare, like his Greek predecessors, emphasized the moral implications of unnatural behavior, which here means unnatural relationships between family members. The mythological tales related to the Year Drama were particularly meaningful sources of dramatic tragedy precisely because the seasonal succession had been anthropomorphized in terms of intrafamilial conflicts, murders, and incestuous relationships; further, these tales reflected the tragic ritual succession of kings to insure the fertility of the land. When the ritual meaning was lost or faded into insignificance, there remained tales and dramas of starkest tragedy that reflected the penalties for living out fratricide, filicide, patricide, incestuous passions, and other infractions of the most fundamental societal taboos.

XIII

ORESTES, OEDIPUS, AND HAMLET

THE TIME has now come to leave the chill northlands and reverse the flow of Western civilization to return to the days when Greece was young in order to reexamine Hamlet's relationships to Oedipus and Orestes. Here we must consider the extremely involved complex of myths that traced the horrendous deeds of generations of royal families back to their supernatural forebears, as well as the refined versions with which the great Greek dramatists provided moral guidance and emotional catharsis for their fellow citizens. As discussed in the Introduction, Freud found the reasons for Hamlet's procrastination in his resemblance to Sophocles' Oedipus. Hamlet, he suggested, could not kill Claudius because he unconsciously identified with Claudius, who had done what Hamlet, like all small boys, had wished as a child to do—namely, kill his father and marry his mother. In contrast, Frederic Wertham, among others, emphasized Hamlet's more apparent resemblance to Orestes. He found the source of Hamlet's inactivity in his preoccupation with matricidal impulses rather than with his obligation to avenge his father by slaying his uncle. We have also seen how Hamlet sought to master the hostility engendered by his mother's infidelity and regain her as a mother by having her re-

173

nounce her relationship, particularly her sexual relationship, with Claudius.

The myths and plays about Orestes and Oedipus have held a particular fascination because they concern two forbidden deeds, matricide and maternal incest, toward which men are drawn and from which they are repelled. Insofar as these myths and stories reflect desires, they also reflect fears. When a boy comes to terms with his father's position and prerogatives with the mother, he does not necessarily wish simply to be rid of the father and possess the mother himself; in fact, when confronted by his mother's attachment to her husband, he can become embittered and even infuriated with his mother, as Wertham emphasized. Such wishes, impulsions, and hostilities are not—or, at least, need not be—instinctual; that is to say, innate responses to specific stimuli that result from the structure of the human nervous system. Far more likely, they are potential consequences of the human condition. Man, born of woman and usually closely attached to the mother during the early years, develops fantasies about her and resents disruptions of the mutuality that exists between his mother and himself, whether due to intrusions by his father, another man, a sibling, or by his mother's withdrawal of her interest in him. Hostile feelings toward parents, on the one hand, and excessive attachments, on the other, are properly kept in check by cultural directives and by proper balance in the family structure, as well as by the fear of the father that has been emphasized in the psychoanalytic literature.

Oedipus and Orestes, the mythical figures, who have served as paradigms for the "complexes" under discussion, did not grow up in a customary manner but rather in unusual ways that could well push them to develop extreme feelings toward their parents; after examining the ways in which they were raised and their specific situations, we will come to realize that Hamlet's predicament is somewhat akin to those of both Oedipus and Orestes and, consequently, that he is vulnerable to the feared impulses of both.

Let us start our comparison of Hamlet with his Greek precursors by noting some similarities between Oedipus and Orestes that also distinguish them from Hamlet. Both Oedipus and Orestes were rejected in early childhood by their mothers because of the dangers they posed to the mother's spouse or paramour. Neither was reared by his own parents, and neither had any reason because of his childhood experiences to feel any emotional attachment to his mother. Each returned to his native land when he became a young man, there to live out his fate. One killed his father, the other his mother. Both survived their shattering experiences with their parents and achieved a new equilibrium as an exile.

We may also note the thematic similarity between these two myths and the two patterns we have been following in the Norse sagas. Orestes' father was killed and supplanted in his marriage and on his throne by his brother—here a supposed half-brother. Oedipus was a prince who went abroad and won a queen and a crown by killing the king (though he won the king's wife rather than his daughter). As in the Norse countries, both themes have ritual origins in the fertility rites that influenced the succession to the kingship.

Moral Issues in the Orestes Plays

Orestes was obligated to avenge his father, Agamemnon, by slaying Aegisthus. The murder of Agamemnon by his cousin Aegisthus, who was erroneously raised as his half-brother, is very similar to the slaying of Horvendile by Feng. In contrast, however, Clytemnestra not only openly helped Aegisthus dispose of her husband but also shared his fear of Orestes; she wished to be rid of her son, and hoped he would be killed.[1] Unlike Hamlet, Orestes had no reason to love his mother and, indeed, had good reason to fear her. After all, these events were part of the myths of the House of Tantalus in which filicide was a recurrent theme; indeed, Orestes' plight was the final penalty for Tantalus' sacrifice of his son Pelops, whom he fed to the Olympians.

In the later versions of the myth and the plays based upon them, the ritual origins of the tale were forgotten. Thus, Clytemnestra was portrayed as a queen who was unfaithful to her husband while he was at war in a distant land and helped kill him on his return rather than again receive him into her bed.

Although Orestes had no qualms about killing Aegisthus, he had difficulty in overcoming his reluctance to slay Clytemnestra, even though she had participated in his father's murder and wished to have Orestes killed. A mother—and especially a queen, who still evoked the awe traceable to her origins as priestess and Earth Mother—was sacred and had the protection of the chthonic deities. Orestes could carry out his dread act only because Apollo ordered him to do so through his Delphic Oracle.[2] Orestes knew that he would be pursued by the Furies —the chthonic Errinys, who would force him to remember and not let him rest.

The various dramatic tragedies about Orestes were not concerned with ancient rites, any more than *Hamlet* is with the Year Ritual and the succession of seasons, but rather with human dilemmas and moral issues. However, the issues are not simple, for the deeds enacted on the stage are but part of an involved skein the Fates had woven. Was Clytemnestra a wanton woman who murdered her husband in order to marry her lover, or was she an avenger whose uxoricide was justified? What happens when a mother is torn between her love for a child and her loyalty to her husband? Agamemnon had taken their daughter Iphigenia from her mother, on the pretext that the girl was to be married to Achilles, and had then sacrificed her to the gods. And for what reason? To gain a favorable wind to permit the thousand becalmed Greek ships to set sail for Troy to regain Clytemnestra's wanton, favored sister for Agamemnon's brother Menelaus. Clytemnestra was also angered because Agamemnon had brought the seeress Cassandra, Priam's daughter, back from Troy with him. Further, she had older and more penetrating grounds to hate her husband. The sacrifice of Iphigenia was not the first time he had killed a child of her's. He, too, was a descendant of Tantalus. Although the Greek dramatists do not mention it, wishing to keep their plays stark and focused, the myths inform us that when Agamemnon had gained Clytemnestra by killing her first husband, Tantalus II, he had also slain her child by that marriage.

Aegisthus, too, though badly treated by the playwrights, had ample justification for killing Agamemnon as well as a valid claim to the throne of Mycenae. His father, Thyestes, had been the alternating king of Mycenae with Agamemnon's father, Atreus. When Thyestes gained the favor of their queen, Aerope, his brother Atreus fed Thyestes a stew of Thyestes' children. Thyestes was then told by the Delphic Oracle that if he had a son by his daughter Pelopia, the son would avenge him. Aegisthus, the son, was thus conceived to be an avenger, and as a young child he had killed Atreus at his father's behest. Aegisthus and Clytemnestra had many reasons for forming an alliance to kill Agamemnon.[3] Nevertheless, Orestes was bound to avenge his father. The laws of vengeance did not consider the justice or injustice of a murder. Should a son's vengeance of his father include slaying his mother? The power of vengeance leads from one tragedy to another, and here reaches the impasse where a son must kill his mother—and then be driven mad because of what he has done.

Hamlet's situation, though similar to that of Orestes, also differs from it in significant ways. Clytemnestra had openly lived with Aegisthus as her paramour and had then shared in carrying out Agamemnon's murder. She had rejected Orestes and sought his death. Electra, who had loved her father and hated her mother, urged Orestes to kill his mother. Hamlet, in contrast, only feels that Gertrude may have plotted to kill his father, or that her infidelity constitutes a betrayal of his father that is equivalent to murdering him. Hamlet was raised by a mother who doted on him; he suffers from murderous impulses not because she has rejected him overtly but because he feels disillusioned by her sensuous attachment to his uncle, which he experiences as a betrayal of his father and himself. He does not have a sister, as Orestes did, to mobilize the hostile side of his ambivalence toward his mother; instead, his superego, which keeps his matricidal impulses in check, is reinforced by his father's commandment not to harm his mother. Every man may have unconscious residues of childhood wishes that his mother abandon his father and even help him kill his father, but not that she take up with another man. He may carry greater or lesser resentments toward his mother for separating from him, but such feelings do not mount to the overwhelming preoccupations that threaten sanity except when fanned by circumstances such as those in which Orestes and Hamlet find themselves. Still, the despair of disillusion in one's mother, and the subsequent fear of the wish to demolish her have at least touched the lives of many.

The plays about Orestes and Electra were based on myths in which the trespasses of each generation led to those of the next, until the curse led to Orestes' ultimate sin. No series of myths can better illustrate Aeschylus' adage, "The father's sin upon the child / Descends, and sin is silent death" (*The Eumenides*, Morshead, p. 303). The Greek dramatists used these myths to consider the ethical implications of fundamental human conflicts. For example, a father who sacrifices his daughter to the gods arouses the vengeance of his wife. Greek civilization had reached a stage when human sacrifice could no longer be countenanced. But the queen no longer had the immunity of the earth goddess, and if she murdered her husband, she too would be subjected to vengeance—even if her own son had to be the avenger. Yet, a son who killed his mother, whatever the reason, would be pushed into insanity by the deed.

The Greek playwrights went beyond these simple and conflicting moralities to find a resolution, holding before their audiences the more general and abstract ethical principles that were essential for a harmonious society. Aeschylus used his plays to convey a social philosophy that emphasized not only the importance of a legal code and trial by jury to civilized society but also the need for people to internalize the code and live by it. He patriotically praised Athens and its patron goddess for replacing a code of vengeance with one of justice and reason. A good society must not only protect the individual but also require the subjugation of individual desire to the collective weal. Thus, Aeschylus has Athena proclaim:

Orestes, Oedipus, and Hamlet

> I bid ye bow
> In awe to this command, *Let no man live*
> *Uncurbed by law nor curbed by tyranny.*
>> (*The Eumenides*, Morshead, p. 295)

Euripides' Orestes also emphasizes the need to curb the endless cycle of retribution. Tyndareus, Clytemnestra's father, admonishes Orestes and Menelaus, "Where, I want to know, can this chain of murder end? Can it ever end, in fact, since the last to kill is doomed to stand under permanent sentence of death by revenge? No, our ancestors handled these matters well by banning their murderers from public sight, forbidding them to meet or speak to anyone . . . they purged their guilt by banishment, not death. And by so doing, they stopped that endless vicious cycle of murder and revenge" (*Orestes*, Arrowsmith, pp. 222–223).

Shakespeare also stood at a point in civilization when vengeance ceased to impress him as an essential component of heroism. Hamlet had other goals in life and could curse the fate that obligated him to avenge his father. Yet, while Shakespeare could deplore acts of vengeance and deride wars fought to aggrandize the leaders, he seems to have been unable to free himself from the feeling that such thoughts were indications of weakness and that the direct and unthinking Fortinbras might be the model for real heroes.

In their transformation into tragedies, myths continued to fulfill the function of reinforcing the cultural "superego." While the Orestes plays derived from a cycle of myths that recurrently told of the consequences of filicidal acts, they supported the rights of the father as against those of the mother. Indeed, the matrilineal descent of the crown, which heightened the power of the mother and her husband's and son's dependency upon her, increased rivalries between fathers and sons and between brothers because of their insecure positions. In any case, the plays emphasized the importance of the integrity of the family to society. Mothers and fathers had to respect each other's rights and were due equal loyalty from their children. The family achieved a new balance. *Hamlet*, a play that moved the theater to an interest in an introspective hero with new values, also had its hero's dilemma arise from his mother's infidelity and disloyalty to his father; and, as in the Orestes plays, familial imbalance is the source of tragedy.

Hamlet and Oedipus

The Oedipus myth holds its fascination because it tells of a man who lived out, albeit unknowingly, the young boy's fantasy of killing his father and marrying his mother. Mother-son incest is stringently tabooed in all societies, not only because it undermines family life but also because the strong ties between mother and son must be loosened to permit the son to achieve a masculine identity and, indeed, to enable him to become a discrete and reasonably self-sufficient individual. Mother-son incest, or even the continuation of a covert incestuous tie into the son's adulthood, jeopardizes his individuation, integrity, and sanity.[4] Although psychoanalytic theory considers oedipal fantasies to be a universal occurrence in early childhood, there is a great difference between a childhood fantasy and its actualization in adult life. Incest is prevented not just by a taboo but by a suitable family structure. Indeed, the need to evoke the taboo usually indicates seriously flawed family transactions.[5] The myth places the occurrence in an abnormal family setting that enables the son to realize such dreams—indeed, that leads him to do so despite his flight from home to avoid marrying his mother.

THE BACKGROUND OF THE OEDIPUS MYTH

Myths, like dreams, can be interpreted at various levels, and differing interpretations need not be mutually exclusive. I believe that the early Theban myths as a group convey attempts to deny the need for a mother,[6] thus undermining matriarchal power; consequently and concomitantly, they present various confusions of sexuality as reflected in incest, homosexuality, change of sex, and male parturition. The later Theban myths that follow those about Oedipus are concerned with sibling rivalries, blood loyalties, and the need to replace talion law by a legal code, much as in the myths of the House of Tantalus. Whatever else the Oedipus myth may have implied or encompassed, it underlines the penalties for infanticide, patricide, and mother-son incest.

Oedipus' father, Laius, who was exiled from Thebes in boy-hood, found refuge at the court of Pelops and Hippodameia. However, instead of winning a princess to become a king in a foreign land, as princes in matrilineal societies commonly did, he fell in love with Pelops' favorite son, Chrysippus—the off-spring of Pelops and a nymph. When Laius eventually returned to Thebes, he abducted Chrysippus. Laius' marriage to Jocasta long remained childless because Laius shunned Jocasta's bed, justifying his behavior by interpreting an oracle from Delphi as a warning that he would be killed by his son. Hera, the protectress of marriage, was offended by Laius' homosexual relationship that kept him from having children, and she sent the Sphinx to lay siege to Thebes. Eventually, Jocasta, like Lot's daughters, enticed Laius into sexual relations by getting him intoxicated. When a son was born, Laius became so apprehensive that Jocasta agreed to commit infanticide. They placed a pin through his heels and gave him to a shepherd to expose on a mountain. The shepherd disobeyed, however, and gave the infant to a Corinthian shepherd who brought the baby to his childless king and queen, Polybus and Merope. The child was named Oedipus because of his swollen feet.[7]

In his youth, Oedipus heard rumors that he was not really the king's son. When his foster parents did not respond to his questions about his ancestry, he consulted the Delphic Oracle, which, instead of clarifying his problem, prophesied that he would kill his father and marry his mother. Fleeing his fate, Oedipus did not return to Corinth but set out for Thebes. At the parting of the ways, where three roads met, he encountered a charioteer and his companions who ordered him to get out of the road and cede the right of way. Oedipus refused, and in the ensuing fight he unknowingly fulfilled the first part of the prophecy, for the charioteer was Laius. Then, approaching Thebes, Oedipus encountered the Sphinx, a monster with a woman's head, a lion's body, eagle's wings, and a serpent's tail. The Sphinx throttled and then devoured anyone seeking to enter Thebes who could not solve its riddle. The riddle, which has been handed down in slightly varying versions, was: "What, that has but one voice, goes on four feet in the morning, two feet at noon, and three at night?" When Oedipus correctly answered, "Man, who crawls as an infant, stands on his two legs as a youth, and uses a staff when old," the Sphinx leaped from the mountain and was shattered on the rocks below. When Oedipus entered the city, the Thebans hailed him as their deliverer and king. Accordingly, he was married to the recently widowed Jocasta, unaware that she was his mother.

After Oedipus had ruled for many years, Thebes was afflicted by a plague. The Delphic Oracle pronounced that it would last until the slayer of Laius was exiled. In Sophocles' version a rapid denouement followed. The blind seer Tiresias was taunted by Oedipus into telling him that Oedipus had killed Laius, but Oedipus refused to believe it. Then, just after he received the news that King Polybus had died and that he had been elected king of Corinth, he learned that he was not Polybus' son but a foundling. Pursuing the truth despite Jocasta's efforts to stop him, he discovered that he was the son of Laius and Jocasta and that they had given him to a shepherd to expose. Jocasta hanged herself; Oedipus blinded himself with a pin from her garment and then set off into exile, accompanied by his faithful daughter, Antigone. The tragedy continued to plague his children: son killed son in a war of succession; and Antigone was entombed alive for holding funeral rites for her brother against Creon's orders.[8]

AN INTERPRETATION OF THE OEDIPUS MYTH

The myth contains elements of its ritual origin. We may surmise that Laius was leaving Thebes when he met Oedipus because his seven-year reign had ended, or because the queen needed a more potent spouse than her homosexual husband to assure the fertility of her land. Oedipus then won the crown by winning a contest—that is, by solving the riddle—and by killing the old king.

The fight where three roads meet may symbolize the father's barring the son's way to the mother's pubic triangle, or the area where her legs and trunk meet; the three roads may also stand for that juncture in adolescence when a youth must leave his parents to find his own identity and his own wife but when Oedipus erroneously returns to his parents. The Sphinx, I believe, represents the overpossessive, controlling mother, whom the son fears will strangle his initiative and devour him rather than permit him to live his own life. She is related to the so-called schizophrenogenic mother, who expects her son to live out the life closed to her because she is a woman and who cannot distinguish her own feelings and needs from those of her child. All boys must overcome the temptation to remain attached to their mothers, and each boy must gain the strength to take care of a woman rather than remain dependent upon one. Oedipus, who was not raised by his parents, did not stand in awe of his father and symbolically refused to yield to him when en route back to his mother; nor was he frightened by the engulfing qualities of a mother, as symbolized by the Sphinx. Indeed, he alone could solve the famous riddle, I presume, because he knew from his experience that a man could get along on his own without a mothering woman: he could crawl when abandoned as a babe, stand on his own feet as a self-exiled young man, and would rely on a cane when old and enfeebled. His independence from women—or from the need for a mother—shattered the Sphinx.[9] As he was not raised by his mother, he was not blocked emotionally from sleeping with her. Although the matrilineal succession in Thebes may have ended with Oedipus, we might say that it died with the Sphinx.[10]

SOPHOCLES' USE OF THE OEDIPUS MYTH

Sophocles appears to have utilized the myth to warn against the sin of hubris and to convey the fragility of greatness to those who might be envious of the mighty. *Oedipus Rex*, as we know it,[11] closes with the Chorus chanting:

behold, this is Oedipus, who knew the
famed riddle, and was a man most mighty; on whose
fortunes what citizen did not gaze with envy?
Behold into what a stormy sea of dread trouble
he hath come! Therefore, while our eyes wait
to see the destined final day, we must call
no one happy who is of mortal race, until
he hath crossed life's border, free of pain.

(*Oedipus the King*, Jebb, pp. 416–417)

Hubris has the connotation of placing oneself above one's father
—and Oedipus, by vanquishing his father and replacing him
with Jocasta, committed the ultimate in the way of hubris. The
play, as the myth, while reinforcing the taboo by recounting the
woes that befell Oedipus, also helps the spectator manage his
guilt and conflicts by letting him know that he is not alone in
having such fantasies. As Jocasta tells Oedipus to reassure him
that his fears that he would marry Merope were groundless:

As to your mother's marriage bed—don't fear it.
Before this, in dreams too, as well as oracles,
many a man has lain with his own mother.
But he to whom such things are nothing bears
his life most easily.

(*Oedipus the King*, Grene, 980–984)

A CRITIQUE OF FREUD'S INTERPRETATION

Now, although the Oedipus myth was taken by Freud as
symbolic of a universal aspect of male development—the young
boy's instinctual wish to kill his father and possess his mother
—when we consider more closely, we find that the myth may
have been wiser. In the myth the jealousy started with the father
rather than the son. Laius did not want to have a son because
he feared his son would eventually kill him.

Does the cycle of patricidal and filicidal wishes and fears start
with the father's wish to be rid of his son or with the son's
desires to be rid of his father? Do the father's filicidal fantasies
arise from his jealousy of his son as a rival who preempts much

of his wife's attention and affection? Does his wife's attention to his son provoke in the father a reemergence of an old sibling rivalry? Or does the father fear his son because he projects onto the child the feelings he had toward his own father when he was a small boy? If he had wished to kill his father, he now fears that his son will seek to kill him. These questions may not be answerable; but the boy's fear that his father will kill or castrate him unless he renounces his desire to possess his mother is not simply a projection of his own aggressive impulses toward his father. It is essential to the harmony of the family and to society that the cycle be broken, so that a son can trust and love his father, seek to become like him, and later be able to cherish his own son rather than fear him.[12] The woman, who is both wife and mother, is the focus of the rivalry, and the stability of the family, as well as that of her husband and child, rests greatly upon her capacities to relate well to both and not to neglect either. The father, in turn, must feel secure enough not to fear displacement by his child. Basically, the young child responds and reacts to his parents' feelings. When a boy can identify with his father, he is less likely to be deterred from achievement because of guilt that he may surpass his father, for he can feel that his achievements are extensions of his father's. The potential for patricidal and filicidal feelings, incestuous longings, or bitter hatred between siblings is present in every family. Some such tendencies are inevitable, but whether they flourish or are overcome depends largely upon the circumstances.

The Oedipus myth presents circumstances that opened the way for abnormal relationships. Laius was homosexual. He feared his son would kill him, perhaps as a projection of his childhood wish to kill his father. Because he avoided sexual relations with his wife, he would readily fear being displaced in her affections. He sought to kill his son, and Jocasta, instead of protecting her baby, agreed to commit infanticide. Then by merely abandoning him, she left open the possibility that Oedipus would return as a stranger to whom she might be attracted. Oedipus sinned unwittingly, but as Sophocles has the chorus say of Jocasta after she has killed herself, "ills wrought not unwittingly, but of purpose. And those griefs smart most which are seen to be of our own choice" (Jebb, p. 409). The myths tell of circumstances that enabled a son to kill his father and marry his mother but not of conditions which would foster a boy's oedipal attachment to his mother, or which confronted Hamlet.

Recapitulation

Hamlet, in contrast to both Orestes and Oedipus, was not only raised by his mother, but also greatly cherished by her. Intense oedipal attachments arise when a mother has difficulty in fostering a child's separation from her or, at times, when after a close relationship the child is prematurely displaced, leaving him insecure and fixated in attempts to regain the care and security he needed as a small child. We cannot know from the play whether Hamlet has remained inordinately attached to his mother. As I noted in Part One, he has been able to leave home to study abroad, but if he is a thirty-year-old bachelor rather than a youth at the start of the play, we might assume that an oedipal fixation has prevented him from marrying.

We do know that Hamlet is embittered and even obsessed by his mother's remarriage and her sexual life with Claudius. However, the upsurge or recrudescence of such feelings toward his mother, as well as his animosity and contempt for his stepfather, rests on his acceptance of his own parents' relationship, including his father's sexual prerogatives as a husband. Gertrude's former admiration of his father encouraged Hamlet to identify strongly with his father in order to become a man his mother would admire and to gain the love of a woman like his mother when he grew up. The direction he thus obtained helped him achieve a firm identity. Then, in his late adolescence or early adult life, when his mother remarries hastily—and, even more, when Hamlet learns that she was unfaithful to his father—he loses his self-image based on his relationship with his parents, and his stability is undermined. He has erred in believing that his mother confined her sexual life to his father. His mother has deceived him in praising his father. Apparently, identifying with his father was not the way to gain a woman like his mother. His mother is more interested in sexuality than she was in his father or in him. Marriage does not provide security but can even lead to the husband's murder. Finally, women are perfidious; mothers and wives cannot be trusted; and, therefore, life itself seems treacherous.

I have examined the myths and plays about Orestes and Oedipus and compared them to the myths about Amleth and to Shakespeare's *Hamlet,* in order to clarify the nature of the fundamental problems of human existence that they consider. Hamlet's great appeal has endured throughout the more than 350 years of his existence and across so many cultures because he incorporates so much of what is most intriguing about both Orestes and Oedipus. I have, however, also examined the family configurations of all three tragic figures because of their implications to psychoanalytic theory and, insofar as analytic theory can be applied to *Hamlet,* to our appreciation of the play. Freud took a myth and play in which a man killed his father and married his mother, even though he had no conscious or unconscious reason to hate his real father until he encountered him, and no reason because of childhood attachments to love his real mother. Freud emphasized an instinctual, inborn pattern of an almost mystical nature; despite later modifications, this emphasis has had a serious and, I believe, unfortunate influence upon the theoretical and practical development of psychoanalysis.

XIV

MYTHOLOGY AND THE STUDY OF HUMAN BEHAVIOR

I N RELATING a psychoanalytic or psychodynamic understanding of *Hamlet*—and, specifically, of Hamlet and Ophelia—to mythology, we have entered upon the importance of the study of cyclic, recurrent phenomena to the scientific study of human behavior. We may usefully ponder whether there have not been serious shortcomings in scientific thinking that have impaired our efforts to understand human affairs. There is reason to heed the voices of those who argue that science has brought knowledge but little wisdom. Disenchantment with the products of science (though often with amazing disregard for the benefits people have gained from it) has engendered a resurgence of interest in the mystic and the mythic.

Although the *mystic* concerns the supernatural, I believe that, in essence, it largely seeks intuitive knowledge derived from preconscious and unconscious mental processes, rather than from reason; but the mystic may also fall back on efforts to control nature by ritual and by magic, that is to resort to childhood types of thinking—in which nature is anthropomorphized, a person's thoughts are believed to influence others—and other such preconceptual cognitive processes to which people tend to regress when reason fails. The *mythic* seeks to derive insights and directives for living from cyclic phenomena that recur from season to season, life to life, generation to generation, and even from civilization to civilization. These phenomena recur because they are inherent in the human condition: the cycle of life from birth to death, the dependency of all infants on a mothering person, the rivalries between fathers and sons, the jealousies between siblings, the incompleteness of each sex, the displacement of each generation by the next, and other such timeless circumstances that are symbolized in the myths of Oedipus, Orestes, Amleth, Persephone, Antigone, Cybele, and many others. These tales are always old yet always new, as new times, customs, and listeners give them new meanings.

Mythic thinking involves a different use of man's cognitive abilities than usually practiced in science. The pure scientist is thought to deal with hard data and with the sequence by which physical events necessarily lead to others. But this is not the only scientific way of thinking, and the recent attempt to model the behavioral and social sciences after the physical sciences has been detrimental to efforts to understand human lives and to attain wisdom to guide ourselves and others. In the pursuit of the behavioral sciences too little attention has been paid to the scientific study of cyclic, recurrent phenomena, which has its precursors in the mythic. One is apt to overlook how much our ability to predict outcomes—a major function of science—depends on the study of cyclic recurrences. In human affairs, the recurrences are less clear-cut than in astronomy or botany, and the differences in the phenomena when they recur often obfuscate the essential similarities. No human experiences are ever identical; but then neither are any natural phenomena. We could never learn from experience or develop a scientific approach unless we abstracted the critical attributes of experiences in order to make predictions based on their essential similarities while minimizing or disregarding the differences. In human affairs the critical attributes are more difficult to extract or abstract, but the principle remains the same.

History, including the history of the single individual with an emotional disorder, develops from a humanistic pursuit to become a humanistic science when the sequence of events is abstracted and compared with other sequences to increase predictability. The general approach provided by Giambattista Vico in his *New Science* has unfortunately been greatly neglected. Only since Freud have the recurrent themes in human lives that follow upon the structural similarities of all human beings have been a topic of scientific investigation. As I have noted earlier, Freud's discovery of the Oedipus complex was of momentous significance, not so much because of the correctness of his conceptualization, but rather because it initiated the comparison of various phases of childhood in different persons to study how the manner in which the child lived through the phase affected his subsequent life. Among the most significant contributions of both Freud and Piaget are their documentations of the universality of the phases of the child's psychic development. As dynamic psychiatry is concerned with unconscious forces and the irrational—seeking to bring order to these disordered areas—as well as with the cycle of human life, it also seeks to replace the mystical with the rational and to understand the lessons that can be found in myth. Jung devotedly pursued these matters in his later life, but unfortunately often became entangled in the mystical rather than in studying myths to elucidate the constants that exist in human lives because of the similarities in the structure and existential conditions of all persons. When the recurrent cyclic phenomena and the sequences within such cycles in human affairs are examined scientifically, and the reasons for the sequences sought, they can not only provide new insights into human behavior but also increase the wisdom needed to direct human affairs.

When we recognize that lives of men have many common aspects from generation to generation as well as from individual to individual, and we then move beyond observation to seek basic reasons for the repetitive phenomena, we realize that not all basic institutions, customs, taboos, and other restraints imposed by societies upon their members are arbitrary. We live in an era when, increasingly, ethics are considered relative and any guiding ethos is distrusted. Parental wisdom and guidance as well as the lessons learned from history are discounted as unsuited to the rapidly changing ways of living. To some, there seem to be no clear reasons but only the weight of custom or prejudice as to why children should be raised in families, why young adolescents should not be sexually promiscuous, or why incest should not be practiced. It may be time to listen to myths again and to recognize that from their tales of days when heroes gave way to their sexual and aggressive impulsions toward family members which led to tragedies that continued to unfold from generation to generation, we may recognize that everywhere the human condition requires man to live under certain basic constraints. Perhaps, those who have been insisting that man can only realize his full potentialities by freeing himself from the confines of convention may appreciate that although repression of instinctual drives may cause neuroses, the lack of social delimitation and internalized controls brings chaos—inner chaos and interpersonal confusion that bar meaningful relationships.

The interdependency and love that make a life worthwhile even if filled with troubles or hardships require trust; trustworthiness demands acceptance of responsibility; and responsbiility involves delimitation. We return to what our ancestors learned at the awful price paid for giving way to unbridled desire and hostile impulse, and to what they seem to have conveyed through myth after myth—that through delimitation alone can we achieve freedom and security. The human condition requires the constraint of social systems that superficial commentators often attribute to arbitrary tradition. It is even possible that through the scientific study of man that focuses on the repetitive and recurrent from person to person rather than through seeking to examine him as if he were an inanimate object—or an asymbolic animal that does not rely on tradition, culture, or conscious decision—we may gain some of the stable guides we need to lead us into the future.

We have wandered far from the pages of *Hamlet* to examine the mythology in which it had its distant origins, but which silently and almost mysteriously influenced both its content and form. These ancient but timeless tales help us grasp the play's power and its appeal across centuries and cultures. The classic drama relates to myth and carries myth's functions of holding up basic universal human conflicts for us to experience by empathy; Shakespeare's *Hamlet* is the epitome of this order of drama. It incorporates and holds in apposition some of the most salient, ever recurring problems that beset, perplex, and unsettle man. Here Shakespeare considers with us the sweep of the consequences of a breach in the basic morality of the family that "hath the primal eldest curse upon't" (III, iii, 37), and leads the hero and heroine into disillusion, revulsion, loss of faith in others and in life; and then, to madness and self-destruction.

PART THREE

Hamlet's Implications for Psychoanalytic Psychology

✧◈◈✧

XV

HAMLET'S MOURNING AND MELANCHOLIA RECONSIDERED

T HROUGH exploring the depths and ambiguities of *Hamlet*, I have found neither the philosopher's stone nor the secret wellsprings of the human dilemma, but I have deepened my appreciation of the play and sharpened my acuity as a psychoanalyst. In this final section, I shall consider the significance of *Hamlet* to psychoanalytic psychology. As with the search for the play's roots in mythology, its repercussions can reverberate through the entire field of psychoanalytic theory, and I shall seek to limit the discussion to areas of special salience. Here, I shall be concerned primarily with how *Hamlet* can contribute to our understanding of human behavior, rather than with the structure and understanding of the play itself. This shift in focus will require some reexamination of material considered in Part One.

When we first meet Hamlet, the king and queen are admonishing him to cast his "nighted colour," off and not with "vailed lids / Seek for thy noble father in the dust. / Thou know'st 'tis common; all that lives must die, / Passing through nature to eternity" (I, ii, 70–73). When Hamlet allows that it is "common," his mother asks him, "If it be, / Why seems it so particular with thee?" (I, ii, 74–75). Here, in this exchange, are two matters that require our consideration. One concerns the inevitability of death and the sequence of generations—that Nature's "common theme / Is death of fathers" (I, ii, 103–104)— a topic we have already examined in our study of the pertinent mythology. The other is the queen's query, "Why seems it so particular with thee?" The query not only places the question that must be answered if we are to understand Hamlet but also encompasses the essence of dynamic psychiatry: that the moment of a situation to a person—whether it is traumatic or helpful, and how seriously it affects him—can be understood only in terms of that person's own past experiences and current circumstances.

It is the purpose of psychoanalytic and psychodynamic psychology to find the constants that occur from life to life and to provide the psychiatrist with guidelines for orientating himself amid the concatenation of events in a patient's life. However, just how any circumstances, whether an inevitable consequence of the human situation or not, affect an individual depends upon his or her specific life history. Hamlet's mood in the first act of the play can be explained in part by the psychological processes commonly encountered in persons who are in mourning, but why he is affected so profoundly requires an understanding of Hamlet as an individual confronted by a particular set of circumstances.

Freud's Differentiation of Mourning and Melancholia

Ernest Jones utilized Freud's footnote about Hamlet's Oedipus complex to explain Hamlet's delay in avenging his father. However, in his essay "Mourning and Melancholia," Freud made another comment about Hamlet that leads to a more pertinent analysis of Hamlet's difficulties. In discussing the melancholic's self-accusations, he wrote "that if anyone holds and expresses to others an opinion of himself such as this (an opinion which Hamlet held both of himself and of everyone else) ['Use every man after his desert, and who shall scape whipping?'] he is ill, whether he is speaking the truth or whether he is being more or less unfair to himself."[1] Indeed, the play is an excellent exposition of much of Freud's thesis in the essay, which continues to stand as a landmark in the study of melancholia and as one of his most cogent insights into psychopathology. Let us consider once again why Hamlet is "ill" in the sense of suffering from melancholia, that is, of being in the grip of a depressive mood that pervades his orientation to life, his relationship to others, and his capacity to act. In the process, we shall also see why he swings into episodes of rather rash activity, during which he becomes paranoidally aggressive.

As Freud pointed out in his essay, the symptoms of mourning and of melancholia are very similar, but we do not regard mourning "as a morbid condition and hand the mourner over to medical treatment."[2] We properly anticipate that the pain of mourning will gradually diminish as the "hypercathexis" of the lost loved person is worked through, and the interest, attention, and energy consumed in attempting to retain the attachment are reinvested in the living. Hamlet's mother and stepfather are perplexed and disturbed because Hamlet seems unable to complete the work of mourning, regain his equilibrium, and resume his former interests. As Freud explained, mourning can become intense and prolonged when, because of his ambivalence toward the person who died, the mourner punishes himself for the death wishes he has had, perhaps unconsciously believing that such wishes had magically killed the person he mourns. As I have noted in the Introduction, not only may Hamlet have had such wishes during his early childhood, but as an adult he may also have hoped soon to succeed to his father's throne.

Hamlet's melancholic mood does not, however, derive from his childhood hostile wishes toward his father. Psychoanalysts are interested in childhood traumas and fixations, as well as in developmental deficiencies and distortions, primarily because they interfere with a person's capacities to cope with current problems, including the inability to form satisfactory relationships with others. As we learn from Hamlet's first soliloquy, he is no longer primarily mourning the loss of his father, but rather the loss of his mother through her callous, hasty remarriage. The severely depressed person typically feels himself to be worthless and accuses himself of various moral deficiencies. Hamlet derogates himself repeatedly and also feels that his fellowmen have few redeeming features. Freud insightfully noted that, "If one listens patiently to the many and various self-accusations of the melancholic, one cannot in the end avoid the impression that often the most violent of them are hardly at all applicable to the patient himself, but that with insignificant modifications they do fit someone else, some person whom the patient loves, has loved or ought to love."[3]

The Reasons for Hamlet's Self-Castigation

The psychodynamics of the process by which a depressed person accuses, blames, and punishes himself rather than the external target of his bitterness is complicated and can be understood in several different ways. It involves both identification with, and some degree of dependency upon, a significant person; consequently, that person's betrayal, desertion, or perfidy causes a grave loss of self-esteem. The self-depreciation is also a defensive maneuver, but a defense not primarily of the self but of the person whose worth has been essential to one's own integrity and self-esteem. The blame is introjected; that is, taken onto, or into, the self. In its simplest form, the mechanism is one in which a person seeks to say, "She is not to blame for deserting me, no one could love someone as worthless and culpable as I am." Hamlet may also be trying to tell himself that he had no right to expect his mother to behave in a proper, ethical manner for he was only naïve and idealistic to expect better of her for realistically, the human race, including himself, is a sorry lot. However, as much as Hamlet needs to preserve a positive image of his mother, he is unable to contain his disillusionment and anger through introjection. The mental mechanisms that originally caused him to become depressed do not suffice.

Narcissistic Injury in Childhood

The psychoanalytic explanation of profound depressions posits a childhood narcissistic injury that becomes reactivated and exacerbated in adult life by a circumstance that precipitates the depressed state. The initial narcissistic injury postulated is the experience of desertion or rejection by the mothering person during infancy—the "oral phase" of development—a period before the child has clearly differentiated from the mother and is particularly vulnerable to her absence. In the past few decades, evidence has accumulated that the prolonged withdrawal of the mother during the second half of infancy or early childhood will, unless an adequate substitute has been properly provided, lead the child into serious difficulties of a depressive nature. Vulnerability to depressive psychoses—that is, to profound and incapacitating depressions—may be limited to persons who experienced such deprivations in early childhood and, who, perhaps, also have a predisposition to depressive states because of something in their biological makeup. However, the capacity to suffer fairly severe depressive reactions is widespread, if not common to everyone: but then, it may be inherent in the way people grow up, an unavoidable aspect of the human condition—that they will suffer some narcissistic injury in childhood.

We know nothing of Hamlet's early childhood.[4] The only indication that Shakespeare affords us of what Hamlet's early relationship with his mother may have been like comes when Claudius explains to Laertes that he did not take more stringent measures against Hamlet after he slew Polonius because "The queen his mother / Lives almost by his looks" (IV, vii, 11–12). However, we may assume that, like all persons, male and female, he had experienced a narcissistic blow in childhood when he had realized that he was not the sole person important to his mother or even the person to whom she was most attached. As the child's primary narcissism diminishes—an egocentric state in which the child is aware only of a world that seems to center on him and on the satisfaction of his needs—the child becomes aware of the importance of others, particularly his father and siblings, to his mother. The child then experiences frustration and a sense of a diminution of his importance to his mother, as well as a feeling of insecurity because his mother will not always be available to him. The sense of loss is augmented by the actual and necessary frustration of the child by the mother, as she gradually withdraws her total care and total acceptance to lead the child to utilize his or her own capabilities and to assume increasing responsibility for himself. Frederic Wertham, as I have noted in the Introduction, designated as the "Orestes complex" the resentment toward the mother that ensues and which can, at times, reach matricidal proportions. Wertham believed that herein could be found the key to Hamlet's indisposition.

THE OEDIPAL RESOLUTION AS A DEFENSE

When they appreciate that their mothers have other interests, most children develop defenses against the loss of security and self-esteem. The first efforts occur while the child's understanding of his circumscribed world is still very limited. The boy decides that he will marry his mother to retain her to look after him and love him. The girl may find another basic "love object" in her father.[5] It is moot whether such wishes are primarily erotic expressions of the child's "infantile sexuality," as Freud taught, or rather natural security operations. This early fantasy properly fades as the child recognizes his parents' priority with one another, the differences in generations and their prerogatives, the claims of siblings for the parents, and other such "reality factors"; as well as because of the dynamic that Freud emphasized: the child's fears of the father, caused by the child's projection of his own wishes to be rid of the father. These factors are often augmented by the child's awareness of the father's real jealousy because of his wife's devotion to the child.

At this juncture, the child does not develop a mental mechanism of defense against experiencing anxiety, but rather a defensive pattern to protect the self against reexperiencing the insecurity and loss of self-esteem that could evoke untenable feelings of anxiety or depression.

Although it is not the only possibility, the typical defensive pattern a boy develops is that described by Freud as the boy's way of resolving the oedipal situation. The boy recognizes his mother's attachment to his father and consciously or unconsciously begins to identify with this man who could gain and hold the mother the boy loves and needs. He accedes to his father's prerogatives not only to assuage his fears of his father but also to retain his parents' affection and protection. He finds his place as a member of a family and identifies with his family. In the process, he learns to postpone the gratification of his erotic feelings in a mutual relationship with a woman until he grows up; but he gains integrity and strength from finding the directive to become a man like his father and from the belief that he too will develop into a man who is desirable to a woman like his mother. In repressing his own sensual desires, he tends to repress any knowledge of his mother's sensuality and what it has to do with her relationship to his father. The defensive pattern permits him to achieve a new emotional equilibrium and also to develop cognitively by overcoming his childhood "preoedipal" or, in Piaget's terms, his "preoperational" egocentricity. If his defensive pattern is undercut or overthrown at some later time, he will be vulnerable to reexperiencing a profound loss of self-esteem and to becoming depressed. The defensive pattern and the boy's self-esteem, as I have already emphasized, rest to a great extent upon his belief that his mother loves the man with whom he has identified or, at least, esteems him, but also upon the continuation of his feeling that his mother is an admirable person whose love is worth having.

Hamlet's melancholic mood, emotional instability, and inability to move decisively to avenge his father need not be attributed either to an unusually strong attachment to his mother (that is, to an intense oedipal fixation) or to his childhood resentment that his mother frustrated his wishes for her total and all-encompassing care. Hamlet's difficulties could have arisen from the events that occurred just prior to the onset of the play. These were enough to undermine his defensive pattern and leave him prey to a reopening of the narcissistic wound he had suffered in childhood—an injury that may or may not have been unusually severe.

The situation that is "so particular" to Hamlet is, of course, not his father's death. At the time the queen asks the question, his mother's hasty remarriage not only disgusted him, but it undermined his self-esteem by showing him that his mother neither held him second to his father in her affections nor even respected or loved his father sufficiently to mourn for him before remarrying. He is more than unhappy; he feels embittered and depressed. Still, this is a situation from which we might expect him to regain his equilibrium and go on with his life as heir apparent—perhaps rather less idealistic and somewhat more cynical about women—a sadder but more worldly, if not wiser, man.[6]

HAMLET'S DEFENSES UNDERMINED

The revelations by his father's ghost, however, do not simply shake the foundations of his integration but totally undermine them. His uncle murdered his father to possess his wife and crown; his mother was unfaithful to his father and may have connived in his murder. If these revelations are true, his mother has shown herself completely untrustworthy, for she has been pretending to love and admire his father while cuckolding him with his father's brother. Clearly, she was governed by sensuality rather than fidelity. Now his security operation, his defensive patterning collapses. His identification with his father, including his acceptance of his father's moral teachings, do not assure him the love of his mother or the ability to win the love of a woman like his mother. Indeed, even if he gained a wife like his mother, it would not bring security but would only leave him vulnerable to another narcissistic blow, when she betrayed him with another man. If his own mother helped murder his father to gratify her sexual desires, then no woman can be trusted, and marriage is a dangerous undertaking rather than a source of gratification and security. Further, if a man cannot trust his brother with his life, wife, and crown, upon whom can he rely? In any case, Hamlet has good reason once again to feel that he is very secondary in his mother's affections; she has deserted him at this special moment when he had expected to succeed to many of his father's prerogatives.

Hamlet has suffered a narcissistic blow and loss of self-esteem that leave him depressed. However, the mechanism of introjection, in which he blames and punishes himself in order to displace his hostility away from his mother and protect his image of her, cannot work. His suffering and self-torment achieve the gain of making his mother suffer and also mar the joys of her newly wedded state, but it can neither regain her from her husband nor remake her into the mother he once loved. There are good reasons why Hamlet feels the world to be barren and dark; why he finds his fellowman no longer worthy of his concern; why he could no longer trust sufficiently to love Ophelia, and why he believes there should be no more marriages. He can hate his uncle, but killing him in vengeance cannot lessen the blow he has suffered, reestablish his self-esteem that rested on his identification with his father, or redeem his mother. Feeling embittered, enraged, and betrayed, he becomes volatile and dangerous.

Hamlet's rage, directed at his mother, cannot be contained by the mechanisms that led him to be depressed. Though tempted to commit suicide and withdraw from the worthless world, he is not of a disposition so melancholy that he will, or can, give up so easily. There is the slim hope that he may regain some faith in the world by rehabilitating his mother. For this he must mobilize her feelings of guilt and shame. The task presents difficulties—not the usual difficulties confronting a hero, those that involve overcoming a foe or a monster, but the problems of surmounting his position as a child in relation to his mother and of containing the violence of his feelings. He utilizes the words of the Player Queen to awaken his mother's guilt over her remarriage; then, he admonishes himself not to let his matricidal fury overwhelm him when he directly confronts his mother in the closet scene. His self-control is so tenuous by the time he enters his mother's room that she fears he may murder her; her screams lead to Hamlet's impetuous slaying of Polonius. To control his mounting fury, Hamlet then requires the intervention of his father's ghost—or his hallucination of him—for him to maintain adequate control as he became increasingly incensed over his mother's sexual behavior with Claudius. The intrapsychic task of reversing childhood and parental roles demands that Hamlet set aside the usual superego injunctions of honoring a mother and following the moral tenets she teaches or imposes upon her child. Shakespeare, as I have noted, seems to have been very much aware of the unusual and difficult position in which Hamlet finds himself. He has Hamlet deplore "these pursy times" in which "Virtue itself of vice must pardon beg" (III, iv, 153–154), and tell his mother that when she is "desirous to be blest, / I'll blessing beg of you" (III, iv, 171–172).

Hamlet's Loss of Ego Controls

In overcoming some parental constraints in order to become his mother's conscience, Hamlet, at times, loses his ego control. In Freud's terms, because his ego has overcome his supergo, he loses self-control and becomes somewhat manic. However, to understand the dynamics in such "structural" terms, we must appreciate that his "ego" by now has encompassed superego standards taken over from his father.[7] He is experiencing a conflict between the standards he has internalized from his parents and his observations of what his mother is and does. One may dispute the idea that he is hallucinating when he sees and hears his father's ghost, but he then displays the grotesque behavior with which Act IV starts—the dragging of Polonius' corpse around the palace, the fox-and-hounds chase with Rosencrantz and Guildenstern, the dangerous insults to Claudius. Then, as happens when depressed persons feel a resurgence of self-esteem, the aggressive impulses that had been suppressed are now released.[8] There is a flare-up of projective defenses that replace the introjective, and paranoid behavior not uncommonly becomes part of the manic picture. Impulsiveness supersedes inhibition. It is in a state such as this that Hamlet paranoidally sends his former close friends Rosencrantz and Guildenstern to their deaths.

Whether or not Hamlet's direct release of his feelings by telling his mother what he thinks of her behavior might have resolved his emotional difficulties and relieved his depression remains problematic. In the First Quarto version of the play, as in the Amleth saga, the queen becomes Hamlet's ally, giving Hamlet reason to believe that his effort to rescue his mother has succeeded. However, in the play we now have, the consequences of the slaying of Polonius augment both the external and internal problems that beset Hamlet, increase his weariness with the world, and lead to his death.

Now, having considered most, though not all, of the reasons why the death of his father seems "so particular" to Hamlet and leads to his depressed condition, I wish to turn to the importance to psychoanalysis of the fact that "all that live must die" and that the common theme of nature "is death of fathers." Then, we can examine more fully the nature of Hamlet's dilemma and how our understanding of it can contribute to psychodynamic theory.

XVI

LIFE OR DEATH?

MAN, like all living organisms, goes through a life cycle that inevitably ends in death. What is unique for man is that he alone is confronted by death. From early childhood, he is aware that sooner or later he will be separated from his mother and other significant persons either by their deaths or his own; this concern over isolation from those he needs causes him anxiety. He also experiences an uncanny feeling about being dead and the state of nonexistence. Virtually all religions have sought to cope with the problem of death. The ways in which religions seek to reassure their adherents differ widely, but as we have noted in examining rituals and myths in Part Two, commonly they provide belief in a rebirth or resurrection through analogy with the annual renewal of plant life.

Aware that he will ultimately die, man seeks to achieve some sense of completion which has a great deal to do with human motivations—and he usually seeks some continuity with those who follow after, particularly through offspring. Parents' rivalries with their children are countered by their identifications with them. As family and society become fragmented, an emphasis upon individual survival and gratification tends to supplant concerns for the continuity of the group and for one's children, with a consequent decline in ethical values.

Because he is confronted by death and because of his ability to choose between alternative courses into the future, man has the ability to decide whether he will live or die and, like Hamlet, to weigh the benefits and burdens of life in making the decision. He cannot, however, place in the balance the benefits or ills of that "undiscover'd country from whose bourn / No traveller returns" (III, i, 79–80). Religions usually seek to spare people the awesome decision by interdicting suicide, sometimes by threatening greater woes after death than can be suffered in life or, as in Hinduism, by making suicide a barrier to the ultimate surcease from the troubles of the world that all sufferers so greatly desire.

Freud on Death

Freud's approaches to the problem of death and death anxiety, which greatly influenced the development and practice of psychoanalysis, have been rather puzzling. He considered anxiety about death to be a displacement from a more basic castration anxiety, and he sought to relieve anxiety concerning death and dying by analyzing its origins in castration fears arising from oedipal hostility toward the father. It is an interesting though rather strange way to cope with a key existential problem and was possible for Freud only because of his belief in the instinctually directed central position of the Oedipus complex in human development. Unless taken in a purely metaphorical sense, Freud's position is difficult to defend and requires some very circuitous reasoning when applied to women.

Freud also sought to account for a person's weariness with life and desire for death—as well as for much human aggression— by postulating a death instinct, and a conflict between Eros and Thanatos, the life instinct and the death instinct. One might consider that as Freud grew older, and particularly as he contemplated the holocaust of World War I, he almost took as a model Hamlet's conflict between his love of life and his suicidal ruminations and self-destructive acts. Yet, we need not posit a death instinct to understand why Hamlet is so much possessed by death throughout the play.

Persons often prefer to die rather than lose those who make life meaningful for them or even prefer death to surrendering the customs and value systems upon which they depend. Rather than have one's family or even one's culture annihilated, persons often choose to die in their defense. Death seems frightening to the young, but as people age and those with whom they had significant relationships die, and as times and customs change, the aging lose their attachments to life. Death may not be sought or even welcomed, but it may come to seem more friend than foe.

Why Hamlet and Ophelia Make Friends with Death

Neither Hamlet nor Ophelia had to wait for age to snow white hairs upon them to lose their investment in life. Hamlet lost his father by death and loses his mother through disillusionment; her infamous behavior together with Claudius' lead Hamlet to feel alienated from life. Currently, we can observe how the betrayal of a country's ideals by leaders who conduct brutal and senseless wars and make deception a virtue has led countless youths to care little about life and to seek to escape their existence through drugs. When the ever-present choice between life and death swings to the side of death, we usually find that it is because the person feels that those he seeks to love and cherish are not worth loving, or that he is embittered because they have turned from him. The decision to commit suicide, even when it seems at first to be a response to the prime existential question of the value of life, is almost always found to be a response to the question of the value of a significant person or persons.

Ophelia, for whom the worth of life depends so greatly upon her attachments to others, does not weigh the problem intellectually, nor can she express her hostility toward the man who kills her father but whom she loves. She can only act on feelings that have become completely confused by what occurred; and deprived of hope, she finds death. Hamlet has tighter and more numerous bonds to life; prior to his father's murder, he found the earth a "goodly frame," the air a "most excellent canopy," the sky a "majestical roof fretted with golden fire," and man "What a piece of work. . . . how noble in reason! how infinite in faculty! in form and moving, how express and admirable! in action, how like an angel! in apprehension, how like a god! the beauty of the world! the paragon of animals!" (II, ii, 290–299). Thus, he does not relinquish his hold on life so readily. Clearly he was not always such a somber and embittered person. Even at the end of the play, he does not actively seek to end his life; instead as we noted in Chapter VII, he is prepared to accept what comes, well aware that death, "If it be now, 'tis not to come; if it be not to come, it will be now; if it be not now, yet it will come; the readiness is all" (V, ii, 208–210). This is Hamlet's answer for himself and for those countless persons who have listened to him.

In his essay "Mourning and Melancholia" which has so much pertinence to the understanding of *Hamlet*, Freud found no need to relate an individual's loss of interest in life, and preoccupation with or fear of death to either castration anxiety or to a death instinct. He understood the critical narcissistic blow that undermines self-esteem essentially to derive from disillusionment with and animosities toward "some person whom the patient loves, has loved, or ought to love."[1] So it appears to have been with Hamlet and Ophelia.

XVII

THE OEDIPAL
TRANSITION:
AN EXISTENTIAL
INTERPRETATION

MAN'S AWARENESS of the inevitability of his death
has formed a central issue in existentialist philosophy and psychiatry. The biological structure of man also defines many other
aspects of the human condition. The study and understanding of
human behavior have often been impeded because certain sequences of behavior are considered as instinctual when they are,
rather, necessary or highly likely consequences of the human
condition. Thus, even though Hamlet's melancholic state and
emotional instability are related to how he resolved his childhood
attachment to his mother, his predicament cannot be understood
on the basis of an instinctual, inborn Oedipus complex, according to which a son seeks to possess his mother and kill his father.

It is not a quibble to argue that the child's initial symbiotic,
narcissistic attachment to his mother, his primitive egocentric
understanding of his relationship with her, and also his ways of
coming to terms with the narcissistic injury he suffers as he

gradually becomes aware of the actual situation are all part of the human condition rather than instinctual. The change is essential to release psychoanalysis from its rigid focus on instinctual patterns, on drives as the only sources of basic motivation, and on inborn sources of fixation, a focus that has led to the promulgation of unnecessarily complex and confusing theories, as well as to therapeutic misunderstandings.

The oedipal transition concerns more than the boy's repression of his erotized attachment to his mother and his identification with his father in order to be rid of his projected fear that his father will kill or castrate him. In essence, it has to do with the child's movement out of a mother-centered world to find his or her place as a boy or girl member of a family unit. The child must learn the prerogatives, limitations, and roles of parents and children and of males and females. The child properly, though reluctantly, progressively rescinds the need for special closeness to the mother and for her specific care to gain increasing initiative and the security of belonging to a family that provides shelter within and against the remainder of society.

Familial Determinants

The outcome of the oedipal phase of development is not determined by an instinctual pattern, nor primarily by innate tendencies toward fixations that affect instinctual determinants, but rather by many factors in the child's family. The oedipal transition cannot be understood through scrutiny of the mother-child relationship alone or even of the relationships between both parents and the child. Minimally, a triangular relationship exists between the parents and child that affects each of them, and usually other children will be present in the arena or later enter into it; relationships with members of the extended family —whether in actuality or internalized within the parents—are also always significant. The family is the epitome of a small group in which the actions of any member affect every other member. Reciprocally interrelating roles must be found for all members, or the personalities of one or more members will be disturbed or even distorted. The failure to focus upon the family setting in which the child's personality develops and which profoundly influences his intrapsychic life has seriously limited psychoanalytic theory and its application to therapy.

I cannot and shall not attempt to discuss or even enumerate the multiplicity of factors that influence the oedipal transition. The basic setting is usually established by the interaction of the personalities and backgrounds of the couple who marry. The birth of the first child transforms a marriage into a family and the spouses into parents; their marital partnership is changed by the need to make emotional room for a third person. The baby, the product of their union, can form a strong bond between the parents, providing a common source of interest and shared identification, but a child is also a divisive influence—in different proportions in each marriage, a unifying and separating force. For both the child and the parents, a great deal depends on how the parents relate to one another and how they incorporate the child into their relationship.

Commonly, and perhaps inevitably, a father feels displaced by the baby in his relationship with his wife. The intensity and duration of such feelings depend not so much upon the baby's needs as upon the father's needs for his wife's attention, the extent to which his wife relies on her child rather than her husband as her primary source of gratification, the capacities of the parents to feel secure in their relationship despite the baby's demands, and other such factors. A father's jealousy of his child can give a son—or even a daughter—reason to fear that his father wishes to be rid of him, and a jealous father who intrudes prematurely into the mother-child relationship can augment the child's jealous wishes to be rid of his father. However, when the father desires the child, gains pleasure from it, and is a source of pleasure and security to the child, patricidal impulses are likely to be short-lived, if they appear at all.

A boy may, of course, repress his desires for his mother simply out of fear and then identify with his father, who seems to have power over his mother, but in so doing, the boy internalizes a punitive and frightening figure. His defensive pattern against reexperiencing the narcissistic blow of losing his priority with his mother leads in such cases to the internalization of aggressive or sadistic characteristics. The boy's development is more likely to be felicitous if he gives up his rivalry with his father and seeks to identify with him, both because his father provides him with a sense of security and pleasure and because his father is a person his mother cherishes and admires. As I have already emphasized, a boy's self-esteem usually stems from his identification with a father his mother admires. He is not motivated to identify with a man his mother derogates or despises or who makes his mother's life miserable. When a son identifies with his father instead of remaining his rival, he can feel that his achievements are extensions of those of his father, and he is not inhibited lest he surpass him.

Obviously, there are still other ways in which a boy can cope with the oedipal situation and seek to defend against the anxieties and depressive feelings it can arouse. When, as happened to Orestes, the mother rejects her son and wishes to be rid of him, the child's resentment can be directed primarily toward his mother. Hostile feelings can spill over and lead to misogynistic tendencies. As he grows up, the child may then also seek to give other boys the affection he had wished to receive from his mother, and thereby develop homosexual tendencies. If the boy feels engulfed and overwhelmed by a possessive mother and has a weak or absent father who does not intervene, he may grow up seeking a father figure he can internalize and gain strength from; and thus have another type of homosexual development. These various developmental patterns do not devolve from innate factors—such as the greater or lesser strength of male or female components in the bisexual tendencies in all persons that Freud hypothesized, but are alternative ways of coping with the various intrafamilial forces impinging upon the child.

The manner in which the child resolves his oedipal conflict, then, depends not only upon how each parent relates to the child but also upon how the parents relate to each other and upon what sort of persons the parents are. The child properly needs two parents: a parent of the opposite sex, whose love he seeks; and a parent of the same sex, with whom he identifies in order to gain a person like the parent of the opposite sex. However, neither parent can fill the appropriate function if he or she is denigrated and undercut by the spouse or is a source of turmoil and anxiety for the spouse and the child.

Hamlet, as we have seen, is distraught because his mother's betrayal of his father strikes at the heart of his self-esteem and his emotional attachment to her. In brief, Hamlet becomes unstable not primarily because of the way his mother—or his father—related to him, but because of the way in which his parents related to each other. Such important and even obvious developmental dynamics not only have had little, if any, place in psychoanalytic theory but until recently could not even be perceived—or if perceived, acknowledged—because of theoretical preconceptions.

Sibling Relationships

Although Hamlet's emotional instability and his preoccupation with death follow from his mother's infidelity to his father, the intrafamilial conflict that sets the stage for the play, so to speak, is the consequence of sibling rivalry, that "primal eldest curse . . . / A brother's murder" (III, iii, 37–38). Cain was jealous of Abel because God favored him, but brothers in subsequent generations have fought out of rivalry for parents' attentions. Across the ages older children have been jealous of the attention preempted by younger siblings, and younger children have envied the prerogatives of the older.

The decrease in the attention a mother gives a firstborn when a second baby arrives is almost unavoidable, and the older child experiences the change as a narcissistic injury. Despite the relative neglect of sibling rivalry in Freud's writings, conflict and rivalry between siblings are major determinants of character formation and malformation and are almost as omnipresent as oedipal conflicts. Here, too, the mother is usually the focus of the rivalry, particularly in very young children, but the father's favor can also be central. Jacob cheated Esau to obtain his father's blessing, and Jacob's preference for Joseph incited Joseph's brethren to seek his death. In *Hamlet*—or, more precisely, prior to the start of *Hamlet*—Claudius murdered his older brother to gain his queen and his crown; as I have suggested in the Introduction, the envy that led to the fratricide probably had its origins in the brothers' rivalry for their mother as well as in Claudius' envy of his older brother's prerogatives in affairs of state.

The rivalry between children in a family is also a consequence of the human condition. Because feelings of displacement or neglect stimulate aggression, including the physiological processes that accompany it, they can have much to do with the development of hostile characteristics in a person. However, it is obvious that the parents' behavior toward the children and with each other can greatly influence how the children in a family relate to one another. Staying with the stories in Genesis, we note that Abraham sent Ishmael into the desert to placate Isaac's mother, Sarah. Similarly, Rebecca planned the way in which her favorite son, Jacob, would steal his father's blessing from Isaac's favorite, Esau. (The ensuing conflict between the symbolic descendents of Jacob and those of Ishmael and Esau who intermarried, continues into the present.) Jacob bestowed the cloak of many colors on Joseph because he was the long-awaited firstborn of Rachel, the wife whom he loved far more than Leah, whom he had been tricked into marrying.

A parent's favoritism of one child over another, preference for a child of one sex over the other, or unfavorable identification of a child with a disliked spouse, and other such matters can heighten the rivalry between siblings to a bitter and lasting animosity. On the other hand, the natural rivalry between siblings fades—or, at least, is repressed and may be replaced by reaction formation—when the parents seek to balance the attention they give and the affection they show to their children. Further, jealousy can be lessened when older children can identify with the parents' caretaking attitudes toward younger children because such behavior by a parent is appreciated by the spouse or because the children perceived such caretaking activities to be a source of pleasure to the parent. When the family forms a true entity in which each member considers the well-being of the others as part of his own welfare, and gives the family's weal some priority over his own wishes and even his needs, then the rivalries between children are modified and identifications with one another as members of the same family gain in importance.

Ophelia and the Female "Oedipal" Transition

In *Hamlet* we find that Shakespeare makes the rivalry between two brothers—Claudius and Hamlet's father—the motivating force in the development of the play's major theme; but he made Laertes' attachment to Ophelia together with the bond between Ophelia and Polonius, a major aspect of the countertheme. The crisis in Ophelia's life, which develops over her emergence from her family to find fulfillment in marriage, illustrates a major way in which female development differs from that of the male.

Laertes' protective attitude toward his sister contains elements of jealousy of her love for Hamlet as well as a desire to protect the family reputation. Brother-sister love commonly includes sexualized overtones that can accentuate resentment of a lover as an intruder into the familial relationships. Although various commentators have considered Laertes' display of grief at Ophelia's funeral to be hyperbolized, there is ample indication that Laertes loves his sister deeply; furthermore her death, which comes before he has had time to absorb, mourn, and avenge the death of his father, leaves him entirely without a family. Laertes and Hamlet, potentially related through their common love for Ophelia, are at swordspoint over her and are eventually united in death because of their love for her.

Shakespeare prepares the ground for Ophelia's predicament and for the hostility between Hamlet and Laertes in Act I, scene iii when Laertes warns his sister not to trust Hamlet and

The Oedipal Transition: An Existential Interpretation

Polonius forbids his daughter to "slander any moment's leisure" with him (133). The play thus turns to the difficulties fathers often have in permitting their daughters to find a new love in a suitor. The entire countertheme of *Hamlet* involves the potential animosities between the father and brother of a girl and her lover or suitor; it also concerns the girl's difficulties in making the essential transition from daughter to wife and mother. Because of its importance to the power of the play, I wish to consider briefly why a young woman often finds the transition from dependency upon a parent to a primary attachment to a suitor or lover more difficult than does a young man.

Late in life, Freud came to realize that a girl's oedipal transition could not be understood in the same terms as a boy's. He recognized that a girl first forms her "oedipal" attachment to her father at the time when the boy resolves his intense attachment to his mother.[1] At the same time, Freud also appreciated that the girl does not repress or rescind her attachment to her father until she approaches puberty and that the attachment may always remain strong. Perhaps no subject confused Freud so much as feminine psychology and female development. Though I do not agree with the reasons he gives for the girl's shift to find a love object in her father[2] and why the attachment endures, his observations are crucial to understanding the female developmental process.

It is inevitable and essential for all children to experience progressive frustration, first, of their symbiotic ties to their mothers and, second, of their intense primary attachment to their mothers, in order to establish clear boundaries between the self and others and to move toward individuation. The prepubertal girl, in contrast to the boy, can retain her primary identification with her mother as a female and also find a new basic "love object" within the family in her father. She does not yet need to shift her energies and attachments beyond the family. She will experience her mother as a rival and may wish to be rid of her—but she also carries over an identification with her mother. If relationships between her parents are good, she will repress her hostility and seek to become a woman like her mother.

Fathers commonly gain considerable narcissistic gratification from their daughters' obvious adulation of them. Since the father often continues to show overt affection for his daughter, she can continue to fantasy that she is more desirable to him than her mother is. Sexualized fantasies about the father and daydreams of replacing the mother often remain more or less conscious; at least, they are not so severely repressed as a boy's fantasies about his mother. Unlike the child's initial attachment to the mother, the father-daughter bond is not primary and need not be frustrated so early in order to foster the child's individuation. Repression of the attachment usually comes as the girl approaches puberty, when her changing physique and the increasing sexualization of her fantasies lead both the father and the daughter to place emotional distance between them. However, because of the late and relatively mild degree of repression, the attachment is difficult to overcome. Still, the adolescent girl cannot achieve an identity as a woman capable of sexual fulfillment and of having a family of her own unless she can shift her investment to a man outside her family. To a greater or lesser degree, the adolescent girl will be caught between her loyalty and attachment to her father and her desires for a man who loves her. The father's attitude can be critical, for if he seductively tries to hold his daughter to him and belittles every youth who is interested in her, she may be unable to detach herself; or if he makes it obvious that he prefers the daughter to his wife and needs her more, her fantasies of eventually supplanting her mother may persevere.

Traditionally, the girl's move away from her family into marriage is made under the father's aegis. The father, however reluctantly, gives his daughter away as a bride. In ordering his daughter to stay away from Hamlet, Polonius can expect obedience, but in so doing he heightens Ophelia's inner conflict and augments Hamlet's hostility toward him. The situation reflects the various myths discussed in Part Two and the many tales of contests and mortal conflicts between a father and his daughter's suitor in which the girl's ambivalence is expressed; in some tales she helps the suitor kill the father, whereas in others she either helps her father or helps her brother avenge her father by killing her suitor.

Developmental Tasks in *Hamlet*

Viewing the timeless appeal of *Hamlet* from a somewhat different perspective than in either Part One or Part Two, we can now see that Shakespeare in this play considers critical developmental problems of both the young man and young woman. He places Hamlet, who is on the verge of entering manhood,[3] in a situation that blocks the transition by re-igniting his oedipal problems. His father's death permits a recrudescence of his attachment to his mother and his fantasy of succeeding his father in her affections, but he is again frustrated and disillusioned with his mother and suffers a severe narcissistic blow when she marries his uncle. Once again, he is caught up in hostile feelings toward a father figure. Then, because the father is a stepfather, the play opens the way for a father and son to live out their filicidal and patricidal fantasies while still permitting the hero to identify with his own father. In this way, the play can consider and emphasize the importance of the mother in fostering the son's identification with his father; it also shows how a mother's infidelity can shatter her son's self-esteem and his faith in the worth of intimate relationships. In the process, the son can express his childhood disillusionment with his mother when he learns of the importance of sexuality to her.

Then, by creating a countertheme in which Hamlet, as a hero, comes between Ophelia and her father, Shakespeare encompasses the girl's critical developmental step into womanhood, when she must free herself from her attachment to her father in order to invest her life in a lover and husband. Ophelia is first blocked by her father's insistence that Hamlet is only seeking to seduce her and his instructions that she rebuff his suits of love;

then, when her father decides he has erred and encourages her hopes, Hamlet, because of his mother's perfidy, becomes incapable of pursuing his suit, rejects her, and then kills her father. Torn by grief and the obligation to turn against Hamlet, Ophelia finds release in death. With her death, for which he feels responsible, life becomes even more meaningless to Hamlet. Hamlet's and Ophelia's blighted hopes—the hopes of youth and for youth—and their chill deaths follow upon the transgressions of the prior generation, and with them the audience's hopes for fruition and continuity perish.

XVIII

PSYCHOANALYSIS
AND THE FAMILY

PSYCHOANALYTIC THEORY cannot continue virtually to ignore the family setting in which the child grows up, and psychoanalytic theorists should not consider that those who seek to examine the influence of the interpersonal environment are diluting psychoanalysis. Those interested in the intrafamilial influences are apt to be dubbed "environmentalists" and called superficial, in contrast to the "depth" of those who confine their attention to intrapsychic problems. This connection of environmental with superficial and intrapsychic with depth is naïve. Hamlet and Ophelia are both caught up in untenable and, perhaps, insoluble intrapsychic conflicts, but these conflicts derive primarily from their conflicted and hopeless relationships with the significant persons in their lives, and not essentially from faulty instinctual drives or from developmental fixations due to innate proclivities.

A person who develops a neurosis or a psychosis suffers from intrapsychic conflict, and the nature of the conflict can be stated in different ways. The focus can be placed upon conflict between the id, ego, and superego; between opposing unconscious motivations; between conflicted introjects of parental figures, and so forth. All of these bear some relationship to the intrafamilial environment in which the person grew up and which continues to influence current significant relationships. The person who suffers from inner conflicts may have been vulnerable because of some "constitutional" tendency to react to troubling situations with anxiety, depression, or rage, or because of a low threshold to external and internal stimuli, but by now it has become apparent that the more usual and significant factors involve shortcomings, conflicts, and distorting influences in the family environment, the matrix in which the child's personality develops.

We do not know if Hamlet—or, let us say, if Shakespeare intended us to believe that Hamlet—has some hereditary tendency toward depression or exaggerated cyclic mood swings; or if he is vulnerable to depressed moods because Gertrude was absent or inattentive to him for a period when he was a toddler. We do know that Hamlet's intrapsychic turmoil, like that of real life "Hamlets" (such as the matricide whom Wertham studied), relates directly to the behavior of his mother and how her infidelity to his father undermined his self-esteem and constituted an unbearable narcissistic injury to him. Similarly, Ophelia may have been vulnerable to losing her wits because of some biochemical imbalance in her brain or because, for all we know, her mother died when she was born and her father indulged her unduly. What we do know is that her hopes are shattered and the foundations of her life blasted when Hamlet inadvertently kills her father and that she is intrapsychically torn because of her opposing and irreconcilable feelings toward Hamlet.

Family Relationships in Psychoanalytic Practice

In practice rather than in theory, psychoanalysis deals primarily with the patient's relationships to the significant figures in his life—usually, how difficulties in relating to others derive from intrafamilial relationships. When an analysis does not consider such matters but remains focused primarily on vicissitudes of drives and on intrapsychic structures, without reference to actual relationships, the therapy is usually sterile and ineffectual.

In practice, psychoanalysis is concerned with how the superego causes undue repression which means largely what sort of parental teachings and behavior have been internalized; with rejecting, oversolicitous, or incorporating mothers, considerations which properly require attention to the mother's relationships with her husband and the patient's siblings; with the internalization of irreconcilable parents or with a parent who has become an "internal saboteur";[1] with faulty gender identities due to faulty gender attributions by parents and confused identifications with parents, as well as many other such matters. Indeed, the psychoanalyst's use of himself as a "blank screen" onto which the patient transfers earlier significant relationships —a practice that is central to psychoanalysis—is to a very large extent a means of reexamining the patient's relationships with parental figures. Unfortunately, the examination has often been skewed by the theory that the patient's internalized views and feelings about his parents have been distorted primarily by his oedipal fantasies and bear little relationship to what the parents were really like. Reexamination of Freud's case reports—such as the "Dora," "Wolfman," and "Schreber" cases—in light of what is known about these patients' parents shows how far afield such concepts can take us. Similarly, the attempt to understand Hamlet in terms of his inevitable, instinctually determined childhood fantasies of wishing to kill his father and sleep with his mother, rather than in the light of what actually transpired in his family and what sort of a mother he has, have obscured more than they have enlightened.[2]

In recent years a number of psychoanalysts, in their search for the causes of psychiatric disorders, have focused attention upon the importance of the family setting in which the patient grew up. Much human unhappiness and intrapsychic conflict relate to parental and societal inabilities to provide a stable and secure family setting in which to raise children. We have also noted that *Hamlet, Macbeth, King Lear, Oedipus Rex,* the *Oresteia,* and other plays that derive from myth continue to carry out the ritual function of seeking to keep nature in its course and, specifically, of keeping human nature within the bounds required for societal existence. Although such plays are concerned with the fates of states and of persons whose lives determine the weal of many, we have seen that they, too, hold before us the woes that ensue from infractions of the basic rules governing intrafamilial relationships. They recount tales of filicide, patricide, uxoricide, fratricide, incestuous passions, rivalries between brothers for wives and power, conflicts between fathers and suitors, which often transmit tragedy from generation to generation until the line comes to an end.[3]

Psychoanalytic Psychology, Ethics, and the Family

When psychoanalytic psychology seeks guidelines to lessen intrapsychic conflict and to improve interpersonal relationships, it is also concerned with ethics. The fact that both psychodynamic psychology and classic tragedies focus on deficiencies in the family leads to the suggestion that if we wish to find a solid foundation for ethics, we might do well to cease looking to the supernatural or to philosophic abstractions and come down to the very tangible and meaningful arena of family life.

It is, after all, in the family that ethical principles have concrete meaning. Here, self-interest is not very different from the wish to help and please others—others whom one loves or seeks to love even when one hates them, and whose lack of affection breeds despair and anger. The well-being of spouses are vitally, though no longer irretrievably, linked. Here, in the family, children learn to place the welfare of the collectivity above their own because the security provided by the family is of paramount importance to them. Even more than what they teach, what parents do provides children with their earliest directives for relating to others; and the parents' ways, and their teachings of what behavior is prescribed, permitted, or proscribed become internalized as ego ideal and superego. The children's suffering can be a punishment to parents; and disgrace of parents brings shame to their children. Parents are carried beyond interest solely in the present of their own lives into concern about the future in which their children will live.

In general, a child will feel secure and will trust others if his parents have placed his needs on the same level with their own and with those of his brothers and sisters. He will rebel and seek to hurt if he is neglected or disillusioned, and he is apt to become devious and dishonest if he can only gain his needs—whether for material things or affection—through circumvention. The child emulates who the parents are rather than what they pretend to be. The ethical principles a child learns in the family do not depend so much upon precepts as upon the parents' characters, the nature of the home they provide, and how much of themselves they can give to those who need them and depend on them.

Not only are the ethics of individuals involved but also the continuity of the society's ethos. If the emotional needs of a child are not met within his family of origin, when the child becomes an adult he requires more from a marital relationship than a spouse can give, and then he is often unable to give to a spouse and children because of the pressure of his need to receive. The family then offers less to its children, and when these children become parents, they are willing to sacrifice less for their families. When the security and contentment that derive from close interpersonal relationships fail, people turn to narcissistic pleasures and hedonistic pursuits. Marriage declines, divorce increases, responsibilities of parenthood are avoided, and children feel less secure. The family that everywhere forms the matrix of society, becomes weakened and no longer serves adequately as the carrier of the essential cultural tradition. When a large proportion of the population places immediate pleasure and personal gain above the common weal and the laws and customs that insure it, the society totters. Those who cannot, when necessary, subjugate impulse and immediate gratification to more lasting objectives—with due consideration for the rights of others and the rules of the social system—are termed sociopathic, deficient in superego controls. The superego, with its moral guidance, derives from internalization of parental directives and enables the person to see beyond immediate needs and desires to long-range objectives and to gain pleasure from the esteem he elicits from others. Ethical principles, even though often presented in terms of man's relationship with his gods, primarily involve man's relationship with his fellowman.[4]

The family is the basic social unit in all societies. It is within the family of origin that the child learns to value or devalue the institutions of the family, marriage, and parenthood; the reliability or arbitrariness of authority; the worth of collaboration; the roles of parent and child, father and mother, husband and wife, male and female; and so forth. Here, in the family the foundations are laid for how a person relates to social systems and evaluates the worth of social institutions in general.

Psychoanalysis has sought to relieve patients of their neuroses by making the unconscious conscious—or, in terms of Freud's later structural theory, by replacing id impulsion by ego direction ("where id was, there shall ego be"). Freud, in a sense, relied upon a person's ability to guide his own life wisely, if freed from unconscious motivations and unknown conflicts. Psychoanalysis, however, in seeking to guide people into more harmonious and satisfying lives, has found that release from repressive forces does not necessarily liberate but, indeed, can lead to intrapsychic chaos, personal bewilderment, and societal disruption, unless a person has the emotional stability and intellectual knowledge to guide himself wisely.

I have previously discussed the significance of mythology and the scientific use of recurrent, cyclic phenomena in human events. When we seek basic reasons why such similar tales and events recur from life to life, generation to generation, and culture to culture, we realize that not all customs and taboos that societies impose upon their members are arbitrary. The human condition requires that each child grow up in a society and assimilate its cultural mores and instrumentalities in order to become a person and survive, a need which sets certain imperatives for and limitations on human behavior everywhere. We have seen that in *Hamlet*, as in other such plays that derive from myth and consider essential problems of the human condition, tragedy originates in infractions of cardinal rules of family life. Increasingly, psychodynamic psychiatry has come to recognize a similar origin for the private tragedies we term psychoses. In seeking to diminish the incidence of mental disorders, it becomes necessary to recognize that when science is applied to human affairs, values cannot be excluded, and that ethical issues related to family life have pertinence to mental health and its transmission to subsequent generations.

NOTES

INTRODUCTION

1. See J. Kott, "Der Hamlet der Jahrhundermitte," in *Hamlet Heute: Essays und Analysen*.

2. The origin of the drama from ritual and myth in ancient times—from the Dionysian ritual in Greece and the ritual succession of Osires by Horus in Egypt—continues today. The first three plays written by Indigenes of Papua / New Guinea were produced at the First Niugini Arts Festival in Port Moresby in 1971; all three were dramatizations of myths.

3. S. Coleridge, *Coleridge's Writings on Shakespeare*, ed. T. Hawkes, p. 158.

4. Ernest Jones, *Hamlet and Oedipus*, p. 88.

5. See O. Rank, *Das Inzest Motiv in Dichtung und Sage*.

6. See F. Wertham, "The Matricidal Impulse," *Journal of Criminal Psychopathology* 2 (1941): 455–464.

7. See G. Murray, "Hamlet and Orestes," in *The Classical Traditions in Poetry*.

8. Cited by Ernest Jones in *Hamlet and Oedipus*, p. 61.

9. See Wertham, "The Matricidal Impulse."

10. For example, Freud failed to mention the impending separation of the parents in the "little Hans" case or to include the impact of the seriously disturbed parental relationship in his study of the "Dora" case.

11. Thus, to note a few examples. Hamlet returns to Elsinore for his father's funeral, and Laertes for his father's; they meet at Ophelia's funeral. Hamlet is incited to vengeance by his father's ghost, Laertes by the "ghost" of Ophelia. In the first half, Laertes and the envoys to Norway depart and Hamlet remains, and in the second half, Hamlet and the envoys to England depart and Laertes remains. Gertrude and Claudius upbraid Hamlet for his unmanly behavior; later, Hamlet upbraids his mother for her unseemly behavior. Rosencrantz and Guildenstern are first brought to save Hamlet; then they are sent away to accompany Hamlet to his death. Other such reversals will become apparent as we follow the course of the play.

Mark Rose makes some interesting comments in *Shakespearean Design* (pp. 124–125) about the structure in each scene in *Hamlet*.

12. Erik Erikson, *Identity, Youth and Crisis*, p. 240.

13. See H. Furness, *A New Variorum Edition of Shakespeare*, vol. I, footnotes to p. 175.

14. See Chapter XI.

15. See C. Spurgeon, *Shakespeare's Imagery and What It Tells Us.*

16. I do not wish to interpolate at this juncture a partial defense of Knight's position, choosing instead to reserve it for Part Two. There are reasons to take Hamlet as a symbol of winter or death. He is related to the mock king who was sacrificed in place of the real king to insure the fertility of the priestess-queen; and to the scapegoat. Gilbert Murray also comments on Orestes', and thereby Hamlet's, relationship to a god of winter. However, Hamlet also relates to a mythic figure who carries the promise and hope of life through the dark winter. See Chapter XII.

17. See C. Spurgeon, *Shakespeare's Imagery;* K. Muir, "Ego and Reality," *Études Anglaises* 17 (1964); and M. Charney, *Style in Hamlet.*

18. Charney, *Style in Hamlet,* p. 6.

19. Spurgeon, *Shakespeare's Imagery,* p. 318.

20. Ibid.

21. See H. Levin, *The Question of Hamlet.*

22. It is interesting that Hamnet Sadler, after whom Shakespeare's son was named, is referred to as "Hamlet" in Shakespeare's will.

I / INSANITY IN SHAKESPEARE'S PLAYS

1. That is, that emotional disturbances are usually the result of a confluence of factors rather than of a single, specific cause.

2. D. Wilson, *What Happens in* Hamlet.

3. See Saxo Grammaticus, *The First Nine Books of the Danish History of Saxo Grammaticus,* trans. O. Elton.

4. I. Ray, "Shakespeare's Delineations of Insanity," in *Contributions to Mental Pathology.*

5. A. Brigham, "Shakespeare's Illustrations of Insanity," *American Journal of Insanity* 1 (1844): 27–49.

6. See R. Ravich, "A Psychoanalytic Study of Shakespeare's Early Plays," *Psycho-analytic Quarterly* 33 (1964): 388–410.

7. Quoted in *The Age of Shakespeare,* ed. B. Ford, vol. 2, p. 97.

8. See H. Grimm "Hamlet," *Preussiche Jahrbucher* 35, pt. 4 (1875): 385.

II / THE SEARCH FOR THE CAUSE OF HAMLET'S MADNESS

1. Although "jealousy" in Elizabethan times meant suspicion, it had at least the connotation of "suspicion of rivalry," which eventually led to the word's current meaning.

III / HAMLET AT THE START OF THE PLAY

1. The phrase "dearest foe in heaven" is echoed two lines later when Hamlet says, "My father,—methinks I see my father" (I, ii, 183), providing a rather clumsy opening for Horatio to inform Hamlet of the ghost. Hamlet could very well be unconsciously designating his father as his "dearest foe"—the person he considered a rival for his mother and yet a person he loved.

2. It is customary to talk of a good *pre*oedipal and a bad *post*oedipal father—but it is the postoedipal father with whom the boy identifies and the preoedipal father whom he envies and wishes to be rid of.

3. See Part II, page 134.

4. The First Quarto version of the play (as will be discussed in Part Two) follows the

Amleth saga and has Gertrude assure her son in the closet scene, "I swear by heaven I never knew of this most horrid murder," but her disavowal says nothing about infidelity.

5. Some commentators consider this to set two restrictions, but I read "taint not thy mind" as also referring to feelings and acts against his mother. Today we might be more likely to say, "Taint not thy soul nor let thy mind contrive."

6. As I shall develop later when we look at Hamlet's precursors, Shakespeare may well have intended to write a play which develops an alternative suggested by a passage in Euripides' *Orestes*. During a moment of lucidity when the Furies are not pursuing him, Orestes conjectures, "Had these eyes seen my father, had I asked him / In duty if I ought slay my mother, / I think he would have prayed me not to plunge / My murdering sword in her that gave me birth; / Since he could not revisit heaven's sweet light, / And I must suffer all these miseries" (*Orestes*, Potter, p. 205). This is, after all, precisely how Shakespeare starts his play, with Hamlet's father returning from purgatory to revisit heaven's sweet light to order his son not to slay his mother despite her misdeeds. In Part Two I shall counter the belief held by Gilbert Murray and others that Shakespeare could not have been familiar with Euripides' play.

7. During the onset of both manic and schizophrenic psychoses, patients sometimes believe they are putting on an act to deceive others, particularly to deceive imagined persecutors, and they try to convince the psychiatrist—and sometimes do—that they can control their behavior.

IV / HAMLET'S PRECARIOUS EMOTIONAL BALANCE

1. In his *Heart of Hamlet*, Bernard Grebanier is somehow able to assert that Hamlet neither is insane nor feigns insanity at any time during the play.

2. Hamlet's praise of this speech may seem misplaced, and many readers would tend to agree with Polonius, who is bored by it. However, Shakespeare was consistent in having a university student, Hamlet, admire a classic play. Shakespeare took as a model and improved a passage from Marlowe's *Dido, Queen of Carthage*, that may well have been written by Nash after Marlowe's death. It is far from a "modest" speech. However, the questionable artistic merit of the speech should not let us neglect its importance both in furthering the movement of *Hamlet*, and also in setting a mood by inveighing against that strumpet, Fortune.

3. S. Freud, "Mourning and Melancholia," in *The Standard Edition of the Complete Psychological Works of Sigmund Freud*, ed. J. Strachey, vol. 14, pp. 246–247.

4. Consciousness or inmost thought.

V / CONFRONTATIONS

1. To whom he has been married precisely as long as Hamlet's father and mother.

2. I do not wish to imply a diagnosis of "manic-depressive psychosis"; rather, with the turn to action after prolonged inhibition and repression, I believe Hamlet undergoes a swing to overactivity and insufficient inhibitions.

3. A fairly common reason why schizophrenic men withdraw and become asocial is the fear of the conflicting impulses toward matricide and incest. The patient may feel a need for paralyzingly rigid control to prevent him from committing one or the other forbidden act. He has not differentiated himself properly from a seductive, symbiotic mother, and he is tempted to reunite with her in the sexual act—or free himself the only way he can, by getting rid of his mother, who is so overly possessive. Although we may conjecture that such factors enter into Hamlet's distraught state, he is here enraged by

his mother's betrayal of his father and himself. As will be considered below, there are both hypomanic and paranoid components to his behavior as he casts off "superego restraints."

4. The essence of the hero in myth—the archetypal hero, we might say—since Freud focused on Oedipus and since Rank elaborated the theme in *The Myth of the Birth of the Hero*, has been that of the man who can live out the oedipal fantasy of killing his father and marrying his mother.

VI / THEME AND COUNTERTHEME

1. Psychodynamically, he can feel elated because he has triumphed over parental, superego figures. He has, as we have seen, extrojected his mother as a superego figure and chastised her, and he has killed the spying Polonius, whose edicts Ophelia has internalized and obeyed. However, his manic behavior here primarily concerns his feelings or, at least, his ambivalence about killing Polonius.

2. I was pleased to note that Kurt Eissler, in his *Discourse on Hamlet and Hamlet*, emphasizes the same reasons for Ophelia's madness: "Ophelia's disorder is a masterfully drawn psychosis. . . . With her father's murder by Hamlet, reality takes a turn that was too painful to be borne by the ego, and Hamlet became inacceptable as a love object. Where she loves is precisely where she ought to hate; where she hates is where she would wish to love . . . the *relevant* issue in Ophelia's disturbance is not that her father has died, but rather that the man whom she loves has killed him" (p. 137).

3. Though Gertrude's "closet" was probably not her bedchamber but her private sitting room, in the Amleth saga the scene occurred in the room in which she slept. In one version of the story, Feng's spy was hidden in her bed straw; in another, under her bed cover.

4. Death by water—the drowning may symbolize the psychotic Ophelia's wish to regress even further and return to the womb.

VII / THE FINAL ACT—DEATH

1. Whereas Ophelia has drowned, Hamlet now reappears in the graveyard, unexpectedly returned from a sea voyage that was to have taken him to his death. It is a brief resurrection, related to the rebirth of the hero as a child from water as found in many myths of the hero—and as happened to one of Amleth's precursors, Dan Havelok (see Part Two).

2. The dramatic here takes precedence over the reasonable. Hamlet is considered mad, and is being watched because he is dangerous, yet he is asked to fence for amusement. The episode, a variant on dueling to preserve honor, comes after the encounter in the cemetery. Basically, Laertes and Hamlet are still fighting over Ophelia, jealous of each other even though she is dead.

VIII / HAMLET AS HERO

1. He was at least as old as Hamlet and probably older, for his father was slain on the day Hamlet was born. Thirty was scarcely "young" in Elizabethan times. Just why Shakespeare carefully specified that Hamlet was thirty is a problem on which I can shed no light, except to note that Shakespeare was thirty or thirty-one when his son Hamnet died. In his Preface to the *New Variorum Edition*, Furness calls attention to "the two series of times" in the play. One is "suggestive and illusory, and the other visible and

explicitly indicated." Shakespeare, he notes, deals with the dramatic element of time by conveying two opposite ideas of its flight—swiftness and slowness—thus "by one series of allusions we receive the impression that the action of the drama is driving ahead in storm, while by another series we are insensibly beguiled into the belief that it extends over days and months" (pp. xiv–xv). Such dramatic usage of time can help to explain Hamlet's maturation from a student to a man of thirty, even though the action of the play takes place within a span of months.

X / THE FUNCTIONS OF MYTH

1. Myth is considered by various authorities to originate from ritual; its origins lie in what is said along with, or to explain, the ritual acts that antedate myth. From my studies of myths associated with Cargo cults in New Guinea, this explanation seems overinclusive. Various myths have evolved in *conjunction* with Cargo ritual to explain the basic equality of the Indigenes with Europeans, and how it happened that the ancestor spirits bestowed the Cargo—that is, the material goods, particularly manufactured articles and canned goods—on the Europeans rather than the Indigenes. To some extent, the myths then directed the form a ritual might take. See P. Lawrence, *Road Belong Cargo*; K.O.L. Burridge, *Mambu: A Melanesian Millennium*; and R.W. Lidz, T. Lidz, and B.G. Burton-Bradley, "Cargo Cultism: A Psychological Study of Melanesian Millenarianism," *Journal of Nervous and Mental Disease* 15 (1973): 370–388.

2. See T. Lidz, "August Strindberg: A Study of the Relationship Between his Creativity and Schizophrenia," *International Journal of Psycho-Analysis*.

XI / SHAKESPEARE'S SOURCES

1. The first production of Shakespeare's *Hamlet* is usually placed between 1598 and 1601 on rather slim evidence. In his *Palladis Tamis, Wit's Treasury*, published in 1598, Francis Meres praised Shakespeare and listed a dozen of his plays without including *Hamlet*, as he probably would have done had the play been performed by that date. The first clear reference to Shakespeare's *Hamlet* is a marginal note in Gabrial Harvey's copy of Chaucer. He wrote the year 1598 on the title page, but this probably refers to the year he acquired the volume, and the note about *Hamlet* could have been written any time prior to the early weeks of 1601.

There is, however, good evidence that Shakespeare wrote a version of *Hamlet* earlier than the play known to us through the Second Quarto and the Folio editions. The First Quarto, published in 1603, is either a pirated version based on memory or shorthand or, as seems far more likely, a version used by a troupe on tour, not only abbreviated to suit the limited patience of the provincial audience but also modified to enable members of a small touring company to play two or more roles. (See A. B. Weiner's, Introduction to *Hamlet, The First Quarto*.) However, it is an abridgement not of the Second Quarto version but rather of an earlier version. In the closet scene, as in the Saxo tale, the queen swears to Hamlet that she never knew that his father had been murdered and promises to help him gain vengeance; subsequently, Horatio reports Hamlet's escape at sea, as well as Rosencrantz' and Guildenstern's fate, to Gertrude, now Hamlet's ally. In the Second Quarto, Shakespeare leaves the question of Gertrude's collusion in the murder ambiguous. Although the lines in the First Quarto are in many places identical with the more complete versions, in other places the poetry lacks the majesty and maturity of the

Notes

Second Quarto and Folio versions. The length of the Second Quarto version—almost 4,000 lines, far too long for an ordinary production—would seem to indicate that Shakespeare remained preoccupied with the play and continued to emend it.

2. I do not know if there is reason to believe that Shakespeare is more likely to have read the French than the Latin. The versions are so similar that the question is significant only because, if Shakespeare read the original Saxo, he may well have read other sagas in the volume, some of which are mythologically related to *Hamlet*, and these may have influenced the conceptualization of Ophelia and the structure of the play. I shall not refer to the English translation of Belleforest, which was first published in 1608. It was probably published because of the interest created by the play, and it was altered to be more like Shakespeare's *Hamlet* than was the French version.

The differences in the Saxo and Belleforest versions have been carefully noted by G. Bullough in his *Narrative and Dramatic Sources of Shakespeare*, vol. 7.

3. Since "eaten" and "eating" were pronounced identically in Elizabethan times, the wordplay is even more subtle than is apparent to the contemporary reader (Marie Borroff, personal communication).

4. See J. Schick, *Corpus Hamleticum: Hamlet in Sage und Dichtung, Kunst und Musik.*

5. Perhaps suggested by a report sent in 1588 by Daniel Rogers, who represented Queen Elizabeth at the accession of Christian IV of Denmark. Rogers sent the report by messenger, who, he hoped "might pass safely, for the seas are very full of pirates, and few or none from home adventure by the long seas to England." It seems almost certain that Shakespeare was familiar with the report, for it tells of the magnificence of the Castle at Elsinore, where Rogers was lodged, and also mentions George *Rosencrantz*, Master of the Palace, as well as Peter *Guildenstern*, Marshal of Denmark. See G. Bullough, *Narrative and Dramatic Sources of Shakespeare*, vol. 7, p. 184.

6. According to these histories or legends of the early years of Rome, Servius Tullius had been a slave brought up in the home of the first Tarquin king, Tarquinius Priscus. When he was still a boy, it was noted that his head blazed with fire as he slept. The queen, Tanaquil, regarded the sign as an omen of his future greatness and insisted that he be educated as if he were their own child. Later married to the king's daughter, he succeeded to the throne when Tarquinius was assassinated, in keeping with the type of matrilineal succession in which the queen's daughter's husband becomes king. The miraculous flame, taken as an omen of high birth and future greatness, relates Tullius mythologically to Dan Havelok, one of the legendary variants of Amleth, whose royal wife saw him breathe fire while he slept. (See Chapter XII for further discussion of Dan Havelok.)

7. It is not clear whether Hamlet originally meant "doltish" or gained this meaning from the behavior of legendary Amleth figures. A. Zinzow offers another derivation of the name. He says that "Amleth" and "Amlodi" can be traced in the Norse languages from *amr, ambr,* or *ambl,* which has to do with working assiduously without getting anywhere. Zinzow argued that the term related Amleth to the endless work of the waves pounding the rocks to sand, or to the fire god who, like Loki, hardened his newly cut wood in the hearth. This etymology supposedly connected Amleth to the unborn spring hiding beneath the snow or waiting in the dirt to blossom. Because Amleth is a "Cinderella" figure working at menial tasks that achieve little and gain no recognition, the association with stupidity arose. I can only refer the reader to Zinzow, as I cannot judge his etymological argument. See his *Die Hamletsage an und mit verwandten Sagen erläutert.*

8. I shall therefore hazard that if it concerned a snake in the palace, the response would have warned Tarquinius that Brutus, whom he had raised in his palace, would overthrow him—an interpretation made through analogy to Clytemnestra's dream that she had given birth to a snake, which, as she recognized just before being murdered, referred to Orestes. If it concerned a plague, I would assume that the reply referred to Tarquinius' unholy, incestuous marriage to his brother's wife by analogy to the oracle that

let Oedipus know that the plague that beset Thebes was due to his murder of his wife's husband, and so forth.

9. As the son of Tarquinia, Brutus was the grandson of Tarquinius Priscus; he therefore had some claim to the throne—actually the same claim as Amleth had to the throne of Denmark as Gerutha's son and Rorick's grandson. Matrilineal succession, however, would pass to a daughter's husband but not to a daughter's son—though Gerutha had no daughter.

10. These few pages of Roman history would seem to enter into Shakespeare's creations in addition to *Hamlet* and *The Rape of Lucrece*. In Lucius Tarquinius' wife, Tullia, the ambitious virago who pushes her husband into murdering the king and ends by supervising the murder herself, we would seem to have something of a model for Lady Macbeth; to a lesser degree, Lucius Tarquinius may have been a forerunner of Macbeth, who piles crime upon crime to preserve his crown. Considering Tullia as a daughter rather than as a wife, some sense of Goneril and Regan is conveyed by this woman who betrayed and killed her old father in her impatience to gain power. Finally, Lucius Junius Brutus, whose statue stood before the Roman Senate, served as a model of a defender of Rome against tyranny for Marcus Brutus, who killed his father, Julius Caesar, to restore the republic. Lucius Junius, like Hamlet and Marcus Brutus, was an intellectual and may constitute something of a link between Shakespeare's two notably intellectual heroes, Hamlet and Marcus Brutus.

Such, we may think, are the ways of genius—the use of fragments to contribute to the conceptualization of masterpieces.

11. G. Murray, "Hamlet and Orestes," in *The Classical Traditions in Poetry*, p. 238.

12. F. Anderson, "The Insanity of the Hero: An Intrinsic Detail of the Orestes Vendetta, in *American Philosophical Association Transactions*, 58 (1927): 431.

13. Aegisthus was the offspring of Agamemnon's uncle, Thyestes, and Thyestes' daughter, Pelopia, whom he had raped just before she married Agamemnon's father, Atreus. Atreus had believed Aegisthus was his son.

14. At least one translator appears to have been influenced by the similarity, rendering Orestes' words to Tyndareus as "Thy daughter, for I dare not call her mother, / Forsook her royal bed for a rank sty / Of secret and adulterous lust." See Euripides, *Orestes*, trans. R. Potter, in *The Plays of Euripides in English*, ed. E. Rhys, p. 212.

15. The lack of proper funeral rites is even more critical in Aeschylus' version, in which the Chorus says that Agamemnon's corpse was mangled to lay his ghost.

16. See D. Kennedy, *England's Dances: Folk-Dancing To-day and Yesterday*; and V. Alford, *Introduction to English Folklore*.

17. In a manner somewhat akin to Albert Rothenberg's studies of author's revisions in order to study the creative process in general and the creative processes of various novelists, playwrights, and poets in particular. See his "The Iceman Changeth: Toward an Empirical Approach to Creativity," *Journal of the American Psychoanalytic Association* 17 (1969): 549–604; "The Process of Janusian Thinking in Creativity," *Archives of General Psychiatry* 24 (1971): 195–205; and "Poetic Process and Psychotherapy," *Psychiatry* 35 (1972): 238–254.

18. Bullough considered some of the topical reasons for the composition of a Hamlet play between 1587 and 1599. Among these, the pressure on James VI of Scotland to avenge the murder of his father, Lord Darnley, which was probably carried out with the connivance of his mother, Mary Queen of Scots, and Bothwell, has particular pertinence, as does James' marriage to Princess Anne of Denmark in 1589. See G. Bullough, *Narrative and Dramatic Sources of Shakespeare*, vol. 7, pp. 18–19, 40–44.

Notes

1. In so doing, I shall rely heavily on I. Gollancz's *Hamlet in Iceland* and recapitulate some of his material primarily because Gollancz's book is now difficult to obtain.

2. The verse apparently defies precise translation. Oliver Elton provides a different but even less understandable English rendition. See Saxo Grammaticus, *The First Nine Books of the Danish History of Saxo Grammaticus*, trans. O. Elton, p. 402. The original is recorded in Snori's Sturleison's *Prose Edda*. "Hamlet's meal" seems to be an Icelandic "kenning" for sand; and "skerry quern" may be a "kenning" referring to the milling sea. A "kenning" is a poetic metaphor whose meaning is obscure unless its specific origin, usually in mythology, is known to the listener. "Kennings" bear a relationship to the Norse fascination with riddles, which held magical connotations, and to their use in verbal combats, or "flytings."

3. From *Annals of Ireland by the Four Masters*, ed. O'Donovan, cited by Gollancz, *Hamlet in Iceland*, p. li.

4. See Gollancz, *Hamlet in Iceland*, p. xl; he cites Ganiar's "Havelok the Dane," a thirteenth-century English poem.

5. There is a similarity between Argentille's marriage to a scullion and the marriage of Euripides' Electra to a peasant.

6. See O. Rank, *The Myth of the Birth of the Hero*.

7. A similar story that must be a later elaboration of the same legend is found in Saxo, *Danish History of Saxo Grammaticus*, pp. 216–218. Frode and Harald were co-rulers of the Danes, and took turns at sea roving. Harald so surpassed his older brother that the jealous Frode had him slain secretly. His efforts to kill Harald's sons, Harald and Halfdan, were thwarted by guardians who made it appear that they had been eaten by wolves, showing Frode the remains of a bondswoman's children they had killed for the purpose. The boys were hidden in an oak and fed with food provided for the dogs. When the brothers grew up, they attacked Frode but were defeated. They saved their own lives by acting insanely, since Frode considered it shameful to slay madmen. However, they attacked again on the following night, crushed the queen under a mass of stones, and burned the palace, suffocating Frode in a tunnel. The tale suggests a relationship between the sons' madness and lycanthropy.

8. The situation was far more complicated in the case of Helgi Hundingsbane's son and grandson, the famous Rolf, or Hrolf Kraka, which I cite because it illustrates the continuity of intrafamilial evil from generation to generation, much as in the myths of the House of Tantalus that I shall consider in the next chapter. Helgi raped Thora (Saxo, *Danish History of Saxo Grammaticus* ¶ 51–52); she later took vengeance by having him seduce his own daughter, Urse, who then gave birth to Hrolf. When Hrolf was grown, Urse helped him rob her husband, King Athisl, of his treasure and of herself. Once, when Athisl saw Hrolf reclining with his mother at a banquet, he taunted them about "impure intercourse between brother and sister," to which Hrolf replied that it was honorable for a son to embrace a beloved mother. Hrolf later slew Athisl.

9. The difference in the seasons of the hot river cultures of Mesopotamia was also reflected in the mythology. Spring brought only a transient blooming that was followed by a hot, killing summer. The new year with its celebration of the reappearance of crops, came with the autumn rains.

10. In Greek and other Mediterranean countries, the king's tenure was usually for a "long year"—that is, for seven solar years, until the solar and lunar years again coincided.

11. Saxo, for example, relates that when Odin was betrayed by his wife, Frigga, with one of her servants, he, in his shame, went into exile and was replaced by Mit Othin, who reigned for nine years until Odin returned and banished him (*Danish History of Saxo*

Grammaticus, ¶ 25). From Snorri we learn that when Odin once absented himself for so long that his people feared he would never return, his two brothers, Ve and Vili, divided his reign, but both "took to wife his spouse Frigga" until Odin returned and reclaimed his wife.

12. A similar practice existed among the Aztecs (a very different culture and with totally separate origins insofar as is known) who selected the handsomest and bravest prisoner of war a year before his execution in honor of the god Tezcatlipoca. Priests taught him the manners of a ruler, and he received the homage due Tezcatlipoca himself. For a month before his sacrifice, four lovely girls dressed as goddesses attended his every want. His sacrifical procession was marked by great jubilation, during which he was treated with honor. See G. Vaillant, *Aztecs of Mexico: Origin, Rise and Fall of the Aztec Nation.*

13. The prototype is found in one of the oldest tales recounted by Saxo. Gram heard that Groa had been betrothed by her father to a giant. He went to her disguised in an animal skin, representing himself as the brother of her betrothed, but won her by revealing his natural beauty like spring emerging from its winter garb. Learning that Sigtryg, her father, could only be conquered by gold, Gram killed him with a gold-knobbed mace. I would assume that the gold knob represents the sun or sunlight that conquers the winter; the gold hidden in the staves carried by Amleth and Brutus may have some such origin. We may further note that Gram's true worth was, at first, hidden by his animal garb, much as Amleth's was by his dirtiness and imbecility.

14. Frazer (p. 133) reported that in the neighborhood of Briançon on May Day a youth is wrapped in green leaves and feigns sleep. A girl who would like to marry him wakes him, and the pair then lead a dance. Unless they marry within the year, they are barred from the company of other young folk. The youth is called the Bridegroom of the Month of May. See J. Frazer, *The Golden Bough: A Study in Magic and Religion.*

15. B. Phillpotts, *The Elder Edda and Ancient Scandinavian Dramas.*

16. Aside from Helgi Hundingsbane, who has been mentioned, we refer to two others. Helgi Hjorvardsson was betrothed to Svava, but his younger brother Hedin was induced by an evil spirit to swear that he would marry Svava. In remorse, Hedin confessed to Helgi, who said that it did not matter, since he felt he would soon die anyway. Three days later Helgi was killed by Alf, who was avenging his father; on his deathbed, Helgi persuaded Svava to marry Hedin if Hedin would promise to be Helgi's avenger. Another Helgi wooed Aud, but her father, King Ivarr, wed her to Helgi's brother Hraerek. Hraerek then killed Helgi when Ivarr told him that Helgi had already secretly won Aud's favors.

17. According to Gollancz, *Hamlet in Iceland,* p. xxxvii, the name Orvendyl is related etymologically to "dawn" or "morning star" and perhaps to Easter and indirectly to spring. It is of interest that, according to the *Prose Edda,* when Thor was carrying Orwendel from Vatenheim in a basket, Orwendel's toe stuck out and froze. Thor broke it off and flung it at the sky, where it became a star called "Orvandels-ta." When Orvendile was "Christianized" his star was glorified as the "true light, which lighteth every man that cometh into the world" (ibid., pp. 10, 154). Horvendile has also been related to Venus or Sirius; see G. DeSantillana and H. Von Dechend, *Hamlet's Mill: An Essay on Myth and the Frame of Time,* p. 356.

18. In Saxo, who sought to be somewhat historical, Gerutha was the grandchild of Hother, the antagonist of Balder in the almost endless battle for possession of Nanna. Balder was a son of Odin, as Hother may also have been. The battle for Nanna, then, was another instance of brothers—winter and summer—fighting for the earth goddess.

19. H. Frankfort, in *Kingship and the Gods,* tells of a Mesopotanian king, Irra-imitt, who tried to avert a disaster predicted for his house by installing his gardener, Enlil-Gani, as a temporary substitute. When the king died by accident during this period, Enlil-Gani did not relinquish the throne but was installed as king.

20. See the story of Rugnhild's choice of Hadding (Saxo, bk. I, ¶ 31) and more pertinently, Esa's choice of Ole, dressed as a peasant (¶ 253).

21. J. Spens, *An Essay on Shakespeare's Relation to Tradition*, p. 3.

XIII / ORESTES, OEDIPUS, AND HAMLET

1. In the plays by Sophocles, Euripides, and Seneca, though not in Aeschylus's *Agamemnon*.

2. The Delphic Oracle, though Apollonian, had a chthonic origin. The priestess often gave ambiguous messages to the suppliant that enabled him to carry out his id impulsions or his unconscious forbidden desires, rather than reasoned acts.

3. The many ramifications of the tales of Tantalus' descendants need not be reviewed here. They are excellent illustrations of how the various ritual means of insuring fertility and prosperity—the sacrifice of sons, the replacement of the queen's spouse by his brother, and so forth—were turned into myths involving the queen's infidelity, as well as uxoricide, filicide, and incest. Pelopia may well have been the priestess-queen, the daughter of Aerope, whose husband became king. Thyestes and Atreus were both husbands and consorts not only of Aerope but also of Pelopia. Atreus married Pelopia not knowing she was pregnant with Thyestes' child and thus accepted Aegisthus as his own son. Aegisthus, whom Pelopia exposed, was nursed by goats, and his name may mean "goat strength." However, his name may also indicate that he filled the role of the member of the royal family who was substituted for the king, as I have suggested for Amleth; his "goat" name has an implication of scapegoat.

4. In all but one of the handful of cases of mother-son incest I have encountered, the son had become schizophrenic.

5. See S. Fleck et al., "The Intrafamilial Environment of the Schizophrenic Patient: Incestuous and Homosexual Problems," in *Schizophrenia and the Family*, by T. Lidz, S. Fleck, and A. Cornelison.

6. This interpretation matches those that consider the Oedipus myth to reflect the displacement of matrilineal descent by the patrilineal, and, concomitantly, the loss of the queen's power as the priestess representative of the earth mother. Lévi-Strauss, building upon the initial Theban myth of the "sown men," the warriors who sprang out of a dragon's teeth sown in the soil, suggests that the Theban myths as a group, and the Oedipus myth in particular, concern the belief in the autochthonous origins of man. Though I do not find his essay a convincing demonstration of his structural approach to myth, the interpretation also points to an undermining of the importance of mothers.

7. The swollen feet caused by a pin through the heel seems an essential part of the myth (and may well be some residue of a ritual sacrifice), but it is unclear why the pin was placed through an *infant's* feet. The supposition would be that a young boy rather than an infant was put out to die and had to be kept from walking. Here, too, the myth may contain residues of the sacrifice of a son in place of the king, when the king was to be replaced at the end of a "long year" to assure the fertility of the priestess-queen and the soil. The "swollen feet" may be a displacement from the penis, indicating the phallic power of the man who married his mother, but I think it unlikely. Lévi-Strauss contended that the impediments to locomotion implied by the names Laius and Oedipus, had to do with the autochthonous origins of the line.

8. The subsequent fate of Oedipus does not concern us here. According to some versions, he was given refuge by Theseus near Athens. Something awesome or holy clung to Oedipus, and reputedly his shrine was sacred. In *Oedipus at Colonnus*, Sophocles depicted him as an aged blind seer like Tiresias—indeed, as almost indistinguishable from him.

9. This is but one aspect of the denigration of the power of women and motherhood

in Theban myth. The tale of the "sown men," the fierce warriors who arose from the earth when Cadmus planted the dragon's teeth, would seem to reflect a birth from semen —that is, from the male agent without any mother except earth. Semele was impregnated by Zeus, but her son Dionysus was born from Zeus' thigh rather than from her womb, and he had notable bisexual qualities. Pentheus was rent asunder by his mother Agave. Tiresias, the almost timeless seer, was turned into a woman after he had seen two snakes copulating and killed the female—an act that may be symbolic of male homosexuality—but later became a man again. Laius introduced sodomy into Attica. Jocasta rejected her mothering role and exposed Oedipus. Oedipus related to Jocasta as a husband rather than as a son.

I do not wish to enter upon the possible relationship of this series of myths to the rites of Adgistis and Attis, or of Cybele and Attis, or other related Near Eastern religions. In these mother-son incest was either stated in the mythology explicitly or implied; and the priests of the Great Mother castrated themselves. In a sense, all kings who married the priestess-queen representative of the Earth Mother were symbolically committing incest. Lucius Junius Brutus had some such awareness when he kissed the earth after hearing the Delphic Oracle's pronouncement that the son who first kissed his mother would succeed to the rule of Rome.

10. The Sphinx's riddle may also be considered as an oracle. Oracles were commonly given in riddle form, permitting the suppliant to project his unconscious wish into the pronouncement; this may account for the number of forbidden id impulses fostered by the Delphic Oracle. Indeed, the famous picture of Oedipus and the Sphinx on a fifth century B.C. urn in the Vatican Museum depicts the Sphinx as an oracle rather than as a horrifying monster. The oracular riddle would then be a prediction that Oedipus, who had survived on his own as an abandoned infant and who, at the time he encountered the Sphinx, walked alone, would depend on his staff when old and blind in his third exile.

11. Some classicists believe that these lines may not have been written by Sophocles but were added later.

12. The Greek myths of the origins of the Olympians reflect the father's jealous fears of a son and that if a father insists on killing his offspring, he may eventually be overthrown by a son with the aid of his wife. Uranos pushed his children back into Gaia until she groaned with pain, and Gaia eventually helped Kronos castrate his father and liberate his siblings. Kronos hated his children in turn and devoured them until Rhea substituted a stone for Zeus and Gaia hid him on Crete to protect him from Kronos. Zeus, differing from his forebears, was a paterfamilias who protected his offspring and immortalized many of them. Although Hera had probably been an "Earth Mother" like Gaia, when she married Zeus (that is, when she was taken over by the Olympian religion) she became the protectress of marriage and the family.

XV / HAMLET'S MOURNING AND MELANCHOLIA RECONSIDERED

1. S. Freud, (1917), "Mourning and Melancholia," in *The Standard Edition of the Complete Psychological Works of Sigmund Freud*, vol. 14, ed. J. Strachey, pp. 246–247.

2. Ibid., p. 153.

3. Ibid., p. 158.

4. The author is aware that Hamlet—the character in the play—had no childhood but emerged full grown as a youth or young adult from Shakespeare's imagination. (What-

ever origins he has are in the sagas and myths discussed in Part Two.) however, we are here discussing not Hamlet but a theoretical individual who suffers in a situation akin to Hamlet's.

5. See Chapter XVI.

6. An important aspect of the defensive patterning of many persons who suffer depressive and manic-depressive psychoses is the need to be eminently successful; they seek to gain the mother's love by restoring her self-esteem and prestige through their success. The expectation of such reward is fostered by the mother, and the person becomes depressed either when his success is not thus rewarded by his mother or when he cannot achieve sufficient success to allow him to expect such recognition. Such factors might be considered significant in Hamlet's depressed condition, but such conjectures lead us away from the text of the play.

7. See H. Loewald, "Ego and Reality," *International Journal of Psycho-Analysis* 32 (1951): 10.

8. See E. Bibring, "The Mechanism of Depression," in *Affective Disorders*, ed. P. Greenacre.

XVI / LIFE OR DEATH?

1. S. Freud, (1917), "Mourning and Melancholia," in *The Standard Edition of the Complete Psychological Works of Sigmund Freud*, vol. 14., ed. J. Strachey, p. 158.

XVII / THE OEDIPAL TRANSITION: AN EXISTENTIAL INTERPRETATION

1. See S. Freud, *New Introductory Lectures on Psychoanalysis.*

2. Focusing on the girl's resentment toward her mother for not giving her a penis (and her disillusionment in her mother when she realizes that her mother does not have a penis) leads to inconsistencies in psychoanalytic theory. The boy also learns his mother does not have a penis. Why should not the girl believe the father castrated her, as the boy fears he will?

3. Even though Shakespeare sets Hamlet's age at thirty at the time of the last act, Hamlet is usually regarded as being much younger. See the discussion of this paradox in Chapter VIII, n. 1.

XVIII / PSYCHOANALYSIS AND THE FAMILY

1. See W. R. Fairbairn, "Endopsychic Structure Considered in Terms of Object-Relationships," *International Journal of Psycho-Analysis* 25 (1944): 70–93.

2. The need for an even more thorough appreciation of the importance of the family to human development and maldevelopment, to human adaptation and maladaptation, will not be considered here, for though important to psychodynamic and psychoanalytic psychiatry, they are not germane to a study of Hamlet or *Hamlet*. I have elsewhere emphasized that the infant does not develop into a person simply through the unfolding of his potential. Instead, he requires a different kind of nurturance at each stage of his development; the structuring of his personality through the direction and delimitation of the structural organization of his family; the inculcation of social roles and institutions; and enculturation into his culture's adaptive techniques, including a solid foundation in its systems of meanings and reasoning.

3. Both *Hamlet* and the plays about Orestes are concerned with a fundamental change in ethics that accompanies a shift from primary reliance upon a feudal or "trustee"

Notes

family to reliance upon civic or civil law. Hamlet is still caught up in loyalty to family
law and its reliance upon vengeance to protect its members, though he bemoans the
obligation. Aeschylus was more specific in stressing the replacement of the law of
vengeance with a legal code. In brief, for an urban society to function, the feudal family
with its laws of vengeance had to be replaced—a new ethic had to develop. The conflict
was particularly clear in medieval Florence where feudal conflict led to the strife between the Guelfs and Ghibellines, and also between the Neri and Biancchi, and required
the demolition of the intra-urban family fortresses to enable the city to function. The
conflict also appeared in the Greek plays about Antigone. Creon could only restore
peace to Thebes by outlawing further acts of family vengeance. In contrast, in the
middle of the twentieth century, when the power of the state seems to threaten individual freedom and initiative, Anouilh uses the same myth to depict Creon as a fascist
tyrant who sets the state above human values.

4. See T. Lidz, *The Family and Human Adaptation*, Chap. 1, for a more thorough
discussion of these matters.

BIBLIOGRAPHY

Aeschylus. *The Eumenides*, trans. R. Lattimore, in *Complete Greek Tragedies*, ed. D. Grene and R. Lattimore. Chicago: University of Chicago Press, 1959.

Aeschylus. *The Eumenides* and *The Choephori*, trans. D. Morshead, in *Complete Greek Drama*, ed. W. Oates and E. O'Neill, Jr. New York: Random House, 1938.

Alford, V. *Introduction to English Folklore*. London: G. Bell & Sons, 1952.

Anderson, F. "The Insanity of the Hero: An Intrinsic Detail of the Orestes Vendetta," *Transactions of the American Philosophical Association* 58 (1927): 431.

Beatty, A. "The St. George, or Mummers' Plays: A Study in the Etiology of the Drama," *Transactions of the Wisconsin Academy of Sciences, Arts, and Letters.* 15 (1906): part 2.

Bibring, E. "The Mechanism of Depression," in *Affective Disorders*, ed. P. Greenacre. New York: International Universities Press, 1953.

Bradley, A. (1904) "Lecture IV: Hamlet," in *Shakespearean Tragedy*. New York: Meridian Books, 1955.

Brecht, B. (1928) *Dreigroschen Oper* in *Gesammelte Werke*. New York: Adler, 1969.

Bridges, R. *The Testament of Beauty: A Poem in Four Books*. 2d ed. Oxford: Oxford University Press, 1930.

Brigham, A. "Shakespeare's Illustrations of Insanity," *American Journal of Insanity* 1 (1844): 27.

Bright, T. *A Treatise of Melancholie*. London: Thomas Vautrollier, 1586.

Bullough, G. *Narrative and Dramatic Sources of Shakespeare*, vol. 7. New York: Columbia University Press, 1973.

Burridge, K. O. L. *Mambu, A Melanesian Millennium*. London: Methuen, 1960.

Burton, R. *The Anatomy of Melancholy*. Oxford: Iohn Lichfield & Iames Short, 1621.

Charney, M. *Style in Hamlet*. Princeton: Princeton University Press, 1969.

Coleridge, S. (1813) *Coleridge's Writings on Shakespeare*, ed. T. Hawkes. New York: G. P. Putnam's Sons, 1959.

DeSantillana, G. and Von Dechend, H. *Hamlet's Mill: An Essay on Myth and the Frame of Time*. Boston: Gambit, 1969.

Dionysius of Halicarnassus. *Roman Antiquities.* 7 vols. Cambridge: Harvard University Press, Loeb Classical Library, 1937–50.

Eissler, K. *Discourse on* Hamlet *and* Hamlet: *A Psychoanalytic Inquiry*. New York: International Universities Press, 1971.

Eliot, T. S. (1919) "Hamlet and His Problems," in *Selected Essays*. New York: Harcourt, Brace and World, 1950.

Bibliography

Erikson, E. *Identity, Youth and Crisis.* New York: W. W. Norton, 1968.

Euripides. *Electra* and *Orestes,* trans. R. Potter, in *The Plays of Euripides in English,* ed. E. Rhys. London: J. M. Dent & Sons, 1906.

Euripides. *Electra* and *Orestes,* trans. E. P. Coleridge, in *Complete Greek Drama,* ed. W. Oates and E. O'Neill, Jr. New York: Random House, 1938.

Euripides. *Orestes,* trans. W. Arrowsmith, in *The Complete Greek Tragedies,* ed. D. Grene and R. Lattimore. Chicago: University of Chicago Press, 1959.

Fairbairn, W. R. "Endopsychic Structure Considered in Terms of Object–Relationships," *International Journal of Psycho-Analysis* 25 (1944): 70.

Fleck, S., Lidz, T., et al. (1959) "The Intrafamilial Environment of the Schizophrenic Patient: Incestuous and Homosexual Problems," in *Schizophrenia and the Family,* comp. T. Lidz, S. Fleck, and A. Cornelison. New York: International Universities Press, 1965.

Ford, B., ed. *The Age of Shakespeare.* London: Penguin, 1955.

Frankfort, H. *Kingship and the Gods: A Study of Ancient Near Eastern Religion as the Integration of Society and Nature.* Chicago: University of Chicago Press, 1948.

Frazer, J. *The Golden Bough: A Study in Magic and Religion.* New York: Macmillan, 1927.

Freud, S. (1900) "The Interpretation of Dreams," in *The Standard Edition of the Complete Psychological Works of Sigmund Freud,* ed. J. Strachey, vols. 14 and 15. London: Hogarth Press, 1953.

Freud, S. (1901) "The Psychopathology of Everyday Life," in *The Standard Edition of the Complete Psychological Works of Sigmund Freud,* ed. J. Strachey, vol. 6. London: Hogarth Press, 1960.

Freud, S. (1917) "Mourning and Melancholia," in *The Standard Edition of the Complete Psychological Works of Sigmund Freud,* ed. J. Strachey, vol. 14. London: Hogarth Press, 1957.

Freud, S. *New Introductory Lectures on Psychoanalysis.* New York: W. W. Norton, 1933.

Furness, H. (1877) *A New Variorum Edition of Shakespeare.* New York: Dover Publications, 1963.

Gollancz, I. *Hamlet in Iceland.* London: David Nutt, 1898.

Grebanier, B. *The Heart of Hamlet.* New York: Thomas Y. Crowell, 1960.

Grimm, H. "Hamlet," *Preussiche Jahrbucher* 35, pt. 4 (1875): 385.

Herder, J. G. von (1800) *Literatur und Kunst,* in *Sämmtliche Werke.* Stuttgart: J. G. Cotta, 1827–1830.

Heywood, T. *The Iron Age.* London: Nicholas Okes, 1632.

Holland, N. *Psychoanalysis and Shakespeare.* New York: McGraw-Hill, 1966.

Jones, E. "The Oedipus-complex as an Explanation of Hamlet's Mystery," *American Journal of Psychology,* 21 (1910): 72.

Jones, E. "The Problem of Hamlet and the Oedipus–Complex," Introduction to *Hamlet,* by W. Shakespeare. London: Vision Press, 1947.

Jones, E. *Hamlet and Oedipus.* New York: W. W. Norton, 1949.

Jonson, B. *Complete Works,* ed. F. Norris. Port Washington, N.Y.: Kennikat Press, 1928.

Joyce, J. *Ulysses.* Paris: Shakespeare & Co., 1922.

Kaiser, J., ed. *Hamlet Heute: Essays und Analysen.* Frankfurt am Main: Insel Verlag, 1965.

Kennedy, D. *England's Dances: Folk–Dancing To-day and Yesterday.* London: G. Bell & Sons, 1950.

Knight, G. W. (1930) *The Wheel of Fire.* Rev. ed. London: Methuen, 1949.

Kott, J. "Der Hamlet der Jahrhundermitte," in *Hamlet Heute: Essays und Analysen,* ed. J. Kaiser. Frankfurt am Main: Insel Verlag, 1965.

Kyd, T. (c. 1586) *The Spanish Tragedy,* ed. T. Ross. Fountainwell Drama Text, No. 6. University of California Press, 1968.

Lawrence, P. *Road Belong Cargo.* Manchester: Manchester University Press, 1964.

Bibliography

Levin, H. *The Question of Hamlet*. Oxford: Oxford University Press, 1959.

Lévi-Strauss, C. "The Structural Study of Myth," in *Myth: A Symposium*, ed. T. Sebeok. Bloomington: Indiana University Press, 1958.

Lévi-Strauss, C. *The Savage Mind*. Chicago: University of Chicago Press, 1966.

Lidz, R. W., Lidz, T., and Burton-Bradley, B. G. "Cargo Cultism: A Psychosocial Study of Melanesian Millenarianism," *Journal of Nervous and Mental Disease* 157 (1973): 370.

Lidz, T. *The Family and Human Adaptation*. New York: International Universities Press, 1963.

Lidz, T. "August Strindberg: A Study of the Relationship Between His Creativity and Schizophrenia," *International Journal of Psycho-Analysis* 45 (1964): 399.

Lidz, T. "The Family: The Source of Human Resources," in *Human Resources and Economic Welfare: Essays in Honor of Eli Ginzberg*, ed. I. Berg. New York: Columbia University Press, 1972.

Loewald, H. "Ego and Reality," *International Journal of Psycho–Analysis* 32 (1951): 10.

Lucas, F. *Literature and Psychology*. London: Cassell, 1951.

Muir, K. "Imagery and Symbolism in Hamlet," *Études Anglaises*, 17 (1964).

Murray, G. (1914) "Hamlet and Orestes," in *The Classical Traditions in Poetry*. Cambridge, Mass.: Harvard University Press, 1927.

Phillpotts, B. *The Elder Edda and Ancient Scandinavian Drama*. Cambridge: Cambridge University Press, 1920.

Piaget, J. (1936) *The Origins of Intelligence in Children*, trans. M. Cook. New York: W. W. Norton, 1963.

Rank, O. *Das Inzest-Motiv in Dichtung und Sage. Grundzüge einer Psychologie des dichterischen Schaffens*. Leipzig: Deuticke, 1912.

Rank, O. *The Myth of the Birth of the Hero*. New York: Robert Bruner, 1952.

Ravich, R. "A Psychoanalytic Study of Shakespeare's Early Plays," *Psychoanalytic Quarterly* 33 (1964): 388.

Ray, I. (1847) "Shakespeare's Delineations of Insanity," in *Contributions to Mental Pathology*. Boston: Little, Brown, 1873.

Rose, M. *Shakespearean Design*. Cambridge, Massachusetts: Harvard University Press, 1973.

Rothenberg, A. "The Iceman Changeth: Toward an Empirical Approach to Creativity," *Journal of the American Psychoanalytic Association* 17 (1969): 549.

Rothenberg, A. "The Process of Janusian Thinking in Creativity," *Archives of General Psychiatry* 24 (1971): 195.

Rothenberg, A. "Poetic Process and Psychotherapy," *Psychiatry* 35 (1972): 238.

Saxo Grammaticus. *The First Nine Books of the Danish History of Saxo Grammaticus*, trans. O. Elton. London: David Nutt, 1893.

Schick, J. *Corpus Hamleticum: Hamlet in Sage und Dichtung, Kunst und Musik*. Berlin: Verlag von Emil Felber, 1912.

Schlegel, A. W. von. *A Course of Lectures on Dramatic Arts and Literature*, trans. J. Black; rev. A. Morrison. London: Bell & Daldy, 1871.

Shakespeare, W. *A Midsummer Night's Dream*, ed. W. Clemen. New York: New American Library, 1963.

Shakespeare, W. *Macbeth*, ed. C. Lewis. New Haven: Yale University Press, 1949.

Shakespeare, W. *King Henry the Fourth*, ed. T. Brooke and S. Hemingway. New Haven: Yale University Press, 1954.

Shakespeare, W. *The Comedy of Errors*, ed. W. Clark and W. Wright, in *The Complete Works of William Shakespeare*. New York: Grosset & Dunlap, 1911.

Snorri Sturluson. *The Prose Edda*, trans. A. G. Brodeur. New York: American–Scandinavian Foundation, 1916.

Sophocles. *Oedipus the King*, trans. R. Jebb, in *The Complete Greek Drama*, ed. W. Oates and E. O'Neill, Jr. New York: Random House, 1938.

Bibliography

Sophocles. *Oedipus the King*, trans. D. Grene, in *Greek Tragedies*, ed. D. Grene and R. Lattimore, vol. 1. Chicago: University of Chicago Press, 1960.

Spens, J. *An Essay on Shakespeare's Relation to Tradition*. Oxford: Blackwell, 1916.

Spurgeon, C. *Shakespeare's Imagery and What It Tells Us*. Cambridge: Cambridge University Press, 1935.

Tillyard, E. M. W. *Shakespeare's Problem Plays*. Toronto: University of Toronto Press, 1950.

Titus Livius. *The History of Rome by Titus Livius*, trans. G. Baker. London: A. Straham; T. Cadell, Jr.; & W. Davies, 1797.

Vaillant, G. *Aztecs of Mexico: Origin, Rise and Fall of the Aztec Nation*. Sante Fe, New Mexico: Gannon, 1950.

Weigert, E. "The Cult and Mythology of the Magna Mater from the Standpoint of Psychoanalysis," *Psychiatry* 1 (1938): 347.

Weiner, A., ed. *Hamlet, the First Quarto, 1603*. Great Neck, N.Y.: Barron's Educational Series, 1962.

Wertham, F. *Dark Legend: A Study in Murder*. New York: Duell, Sloan and Pearce, 1941.

Wertham, F. "The Matricidal Impulse: Critique of Freud's Interpretation of Hamlet," *Journal of Criminal Psychopathology* 2 (1941): 455.

Wheelwright, P. *Burning Fountain: A Study in the Language of Symbolism*. Bloomington: Indiana University Press, 1968.

Wilson, J. D. *Life in Shakespeare's England*. Cambridge: Cambridge University Press, 1911.

Wilson, J. D. *What Happens in Hamlet*. Cambridge: Cambridge University Press, 1935.

Zinzow, A. *Die Hamletsage an und mit verwandten Sagen erläutert. Ein Beitag zum Verständnis nordisch-deutscher Sagen-dichtung*. Halle: Verlag der Buchhandlung des Maifenhaufes, 1877.

INDEX

Abel (Old Testament), 214
Abraham (Old Testament), 126, 215
Achilles, 17, 64, 74, 176
Acts: I, 47–59; II, 60–66; III, 67–83; IV, 84–96; V, 97–106; motif of, 19–20
Adelbrecht, 161
Adgistis, 239
Adriana (in *The Comedy of Errors*), 37
Adultery, *see* Infidelity
Aegisthus, 74, 147, 149, 151, 175, 176, 177, 235, 238
Aemelia, Abbess (in *The Comedy of Errors*), 37
Aeneas, 64
Aerope, 177, 238
Aeschylus, 145, 146, 156, 178–79, 235, 238, 241
Affection, and intrapsychic conflicts, 13
Agamemnon, 75, 93, 115, 117, 146–47, 175, 177, 235
Agamemnon (by Aeschylus), 238
Agave, 239
Agression: basic socialization through myths of, 120; death instinct and, 207; narcissistic injury and, 213; self-esteem and, 204; sibling rivalry and, 215
Agni, 164
Agrippina, 151, 152
Ajax, 42
Alexander, 99
Alf, 237
Alienation: of Amleth, 147; of Hamlet, 208
All's Well That Ends Well, 172
Ambivalency, in mourning, 49
Amhlaide, 160
Amleth, 115, 133–37, 144, 235, 238; alienation of, 147; Anlaf Curan and, 159, 160–62; as demigod, 167–68; as Fool, 167; Hamlet

compared with, 5, 137–38, 141, 151, 156, 157, 172; Helgi Lays and, 166; as Mock King, 169; symbolism of, 168
Amleth saga: Brutus legend and, 142; closet scene related to, 231, 232; Gertrude related to, 54, 139, 141, 155–56, 230; Hamlet related to, 35, 108, 131, 137–41, 144, 155, 167, 187, 234; Hamlet's wordplays and, 24–25; hero who slays king theme in, 163, 237; Horatio related to, 140, 148; madness theme in, 35, 42, 58, 131; matrilineal succession in, 166; Nordic sagas and, 159, 160–62; Ophelia related to, 141, 152; queen as son's ally in, 78, 205; renewal of seasons cycle in, 171, 189; summary of, 133–37; *Ur-Hamlet* based on, 132
Amlödi, 160, 167, 234
Anatomy of Melancholy (Burton), 41
Ancestors in myth, 122, 124, 126–27
Anderson, F., 146
Anglican Catholicism, 40
Anglo-Saxon lore, 171
Animism, and control of nature, 124–25
Anlaf Curan, 159, 160–62, 167
Anne of Denmark, Princess, 235
Anouilh, J., 241
Anthropomorphization of nature, 6, 124–25, 168, 172, 188
Antic disposition, *see* Madness (in Hamlet)
Antigone, 182, 189, 241
Antihero, Hamlet as, 107
Antipholus of Ephesus (in *The Comedy of Errors*), 36
Anxiety: death, 207; defense against, 201
Apollo, 3, 238
Argentille, 161, 236
Arrowsmith, W., 149, 150, 179

Index

Index

Index

Index

Index

Index